0
333.9516 DiSilvestro, Roger
DiSilvestro

THE REAL ENDANGERED SPECIES is mankind. As we waste away our world, we waste away our odds for survival. "Audubon Perspectives" will motivate many—hopefully enough—to do something about those odds. I'm really pleased to lend my support to the Audubon Television Specials and to this stunning book. Watch the shows, read the book and let's change the odds.

R. E. (TED) TURNER
Chairman of the Board and President
Turner Broadcasting System, Inc.

AS THE HUMAN POPULATION continues to slash a destructive path across the Earth, our planet's ecosystems hang in precarious balance. *Audubon Perspectives: Fight for Survival* not only deals with the destructive nature of our relationship with Earth, but also with the potential liberation that re-establishing a friendship with our Home can bring.

PAUL EHRLICH

BEAUTIFULLY ILLUSTRATED and wonderfully written, this book is essential to our understanding of the planet, its creatures, and where we're all headed in the future.

RICHARD CHAMBERLAIN
Actor

MUCH OUTRAGEOUS human behavior is rooted in an arrogant disregard for all species but our own. We've broken a lot of Nature's little laws, and the big laws are starting to catch up with us. No one can read this volume without understanding why all this must change. Its prose is graceful, its contents are erudite, its photographs are stunning, and its impact is overwhelming. Buy this book. Read it. And give it to your friends.

DENIS HAYES
Chairman and Chief Executive Officer
Earth Day 1990

THIS TIMELY BOOK provides the hope and direction necessary for millions of us individuals worldwide to become part of the solution to the threat of humankind's cumulative assault on the Earth.

RUSSELL PETERSON
Vice Chairman
Better World Society

THIS COMPELLING BOOK reminds us of the on-going relationship between humankind and the flora and fauna with which we share this planet. "Audubon Perspectives" helps us understand our neighbors better and, through such knowledge, allows us to develop a blueprint for the 21st century.

DONALD TRUMP

AUDUBON
PERSPECTIVES

FIGHT *for* SURVIVAL

A COMPANION TO THE AUDUBON TELEVISION SPECIALS

Roger L. DiSilvestro

Executive Editor
Christopher N. Palmer

Principal Photographer
Page Chichester

WILEY

JOHN WILEY & SONS, INC.
New York / Chichester / Brisbane / Toronto / Singapore

If you would like to receive information about the National Audubon Society write
to: National Audubon Society
     Membership Department
     950 Third Avenue
     New York, NY   10022

Library of Congress Cataloging-in-Publication Data

DiSilvestro, Roger L.
    Audubon perspectives: the fight for survival / by Roger L.
DiSilvestro; principal photographer, Page Chichester.
      p.   cm.
    Includes bibliographical references.
    ISBN 0-471-50835-7
    1. Nature conservation.   2. Environmental protection.   3. Man—
Influence on nature.   I. National Audubon Society.   II. Title.
QH75.D57   1990
333.95'16—dc20   89-28873
                                                              CIP

Printed in the United States of America

90 91 10 9 8 7 6 5 4 3 2 1

This book is dedicated to the many devoted people who have striven unselfishly for the protection of wildlife and our environment.

FOREWORD

TWO DECADES AFTER the first Earth Day awakened the world's environmental consciousness, a "green" movement is blossoming around the globe. In eastern Europe and the Soviet Union, environmental quality-of-life issues such as air and water pollution are high on the agenda of the burgeoning reform movement. In many nations in Latin America, Africa, and Asia, leaders gifted with great foresight are calling upon the sustainable development of land, water, and other natural resources as the only commonsense path out of poverty. Environmentalism has become a startling, formidable force within the electoral politics of many western European nations.

In the United States, the anti-environmentalism of the Reagan administration was firmly rejected on a bipartisan basis by Congress and the American people. Out of this turmoil has emerged a renewed commitment to enhancing environmental quality within the United States and to reasserting America's historic leadership role in addressing international environmental issues.

This dramatic resurgence of global environmentalism comes at a time when we, as citizens of the world, need it most. Extremely difficult problems approach us on all fronts. Global warming, ozone depletion, overpopulation, ocean pollution, and the rapid extinction of many plant and animal species are among the most alarming.

Individually and collectively, environmental problems pose an enormous threat to humankind. But throughout the world, concerned citizens—activists—are rising to the challenge. In the best tradition of thinking globally and acting locally, people worldwide are working on countless environmental projects, such as recycling, wetlands protection, waste-dump cleanup, and the protection of endangered species and vanishing habitats. It is in this spirit that the National Audubon Society proudly offers *Audubon Perspectives: Fight for Survival* as part of our organization's wide-ranging efforts to build an ever-larger, informed constituency for environmental protection and resource conservation.

Peter A. A. Berle
President
National Audubon Society

ACKNOWLEDGMENTS

A CRUCIAL PARTICIPANT in the Audubon specials and, therefore, in the production of this book is Ted Turner. He is well known for his many outstanding achievements, but the one Audubon values most is his commitment to environmental quality. Because of his early support, the Audubon Television Specials have become an established part of America's television landscape. Time and time again, Ted Turner has rejected the reactive, the timid, and the limiting in favor of the visionary, the optimistic, and the expansive. He is one of those rare people determined to invent the future. Audubon salutes Ted Turner for supporting conservation goals and for his enduring commitment to building a better environment. Others at the Turner Broadcasting System who deserve special recognition are Sue Barnett, Steve Carter, Jeff Cohen, Alison Fussell, Jeff Grimshaw, Gerry Hogan, Marty Killeen, Bob Levi, Kate McSweeney, Mike Oglesby, Chuck Shultz, Joel Westbrook, and Robin Yates.

Funding for many of the programs upon which chapters in this book were based came from The Stroh Brewery Company. The Stroh Brewery Company was threatened with a boycott of its products by the logging industry in the summer of 1989 when advertisements for the Audubon Television Special, *Ancient Forests: Rage Over Trees*, appeared in the Pacific Northwest. The company had been a strong and much appreciated ally for Audubon television since the beginning but, faced with serious financial difficulties, withdrew funding from all future programs. The logging industry turned its heavy guns on the Turner Broadcasting System, which first aired the program in September 1989. TBS had filled every advertising slot for the show, but the loggers used their economic clout to persuade all the sponsors to withdraw their advertisements. Ted Turner aired the program anyway, without any commercial sponsors, running public service announcements instead. We wish to thank the Turner Broadcasting System and Ted Turner for such staunch support despite tremendous social and economic pressure to cancel the show.

Many of our colleagues at the National Audubon Society have helped greatly in the production of this book. Peter A. A. Berle is president of the National Audubon Society. It is through him and his unwavering trust and energy that programs such as the Audubon Television Specials can flourish. Other Audubon staff who helped by reviewing the manuscript for this book are Dede Armentrout, Hope Babcock, Pat Baldi, Jan Beyea, Dorie Bolze, Mary Joy Breton, Marshal Case, Dave Cline, Susan Drennan, Mike Duever, Dusty Dunstan, Brock Evans, Chuck Frith, David Henderson, Maureen Hinkle, Ron Klataske, Mercedes Lee, Cynthia Lenhart, Rob Lester, Connie Mahan, Pamela Manice, Jack Meeder, Dave Miller, Pete Myers, Ed Pembleton, Jim Pissot, Walt Pomeroy, George Powell, Carse Pustmueller, Liz Raisbeck, Carl Safina, Rob San-George, Chuck Sisco, Tom Shoemaker, Gary Soucie, Fran Spivey-Weber, Sandy Sprunt, Ann Strickland, Ken and Marie Strom, Dan Taylor, Bob Turner, Chris Wille, Brooks Yeager, and Audubon board members Jan Burch, Helen Engle, Bart Rea, and Scott Reed. Audubon staff to whom we also owe a debt of gratitude are Carmine Branagan, Jim Cunningham, Tom Exton, Susan Martin, Carole McNamara, Chuck Warren, and Ann Weisberg.

Critical to the preparation of the manuscript and to the care and gathering of photographs were Delores Simmons and Pia Caro of the Audubon Television Department. In addition to benefiting this book, they have been vital to the department's overall success.

Many people outside Audubon have also been very helpful. Experts who reviewed chapters or helped with comments and material include Durward Allen of Purdue University; Chuck Bavin of the U.S. Fish and Wildlife Service Law Enforcement Division; Ben Beach of the Wilderness Society; Michael Bean of the Environmental Defense Fund; Lester Brown, president of the Worldwatch Institute; Amy Brautigan, deputy chairman of the Trade Specialist Group of the International Union for the Conservation of Nature and Natural Resources; sea turtle biologist Richard Byles of the U.S. Fish and Wildlife Service; Merry Camhi, a Rutgers University sea turtle biologist; Curt Carley, who was instrumental in the success of the red wolf releases; Stephen Fritts, a Fish and Wildlife Service wolf biologist; Steve Hildebrand, U.S. Fish and Wildlife Service; dolphin biologist Steve Leatherwood of Hupps Seaworld; John Morrissey, a shark biologist at the University of Miami; Bob Nelson, the U.S. Forest Service's director of Wildlife and Fisheries; Peter Pritchard of the Florida Audubon Society; James Ross of the Caribbean Conservation Corporation; Steve Schwartz of the Center for Marine Conservation; Jerome S. Smith of the U.S. Fish and Wildlife Service Law Enforcement Division;

Dave Stein of the Earth Island Institute; and Mike Weber of the Center for Marine Conservation.

Special thanks are extended to the following people for the time they generously gave and for the openness they showed during interviews: For the wolf chapter, Tom Arrandale, president of the Mexican Wolf Coalition; Dave Brewster, Saskatchewan's Provincial Deer Biologist; Wayne Runge, Saskatchewan furbearer biologist; Todd Fuller of the Minnesota Department of Natural Resources; Wain Evans, assistant director of the New Mexico Game and Fish Department; Bill Montoya, director of the New Mexico Game and Fish Department; Kent Newton, chairman of the Mexican Wolf Captive Breeding Program; Vicki O'Toole, administrative director of the Wild Canid Survival and Research Center; Warren Parker of the U.S. Fish and Wildlife Service's Endangered Species Office in Asheville, North Carolina; Robert Ream, a wolf biologist at the University of Montana; Peter Siminski, curator of mammals and birds at the Sonora Desert Museum outside Tucson, Arizona; Rolland Smith, Point Defiance Zoo in Tacoma, Washington, who heads the red wolf captive breeding program; John Taylor, manager of the Alligator River National Wildlife Refuge; and John Weaver, a wolf and grizzly biologist with the U.S. Forest Service.

For the shark chapter, Jack Casey, a shark biologist with the National Marine Fisheries Service; shark biologist Grant Gilmore of the Harbor Branch Oceanographic Institute in Fort Pierce, Florida; Samuel "Sonny" Gruber, a shark biologist with the University of Miami; and Gordon Hubbell, veterinarian at the Miami zoo and owner of Jaws International.

For the sea turtle chapter, Llewellyn Ehrhart, a sea turtle biologist at the University of Central Florida; Milford R. Fletcher, the National Park Service's chief of Resources Management in Albuquerque; John Gavitt, head of the Fish and Wildlife Service's covert operations; Ann Haas of the Fish and Wildlife Service law enforcement public affairs office; and Jack Woody, the Fish and Wildlife Service's lead sea turtle biologist.

For the chapter on poaching, Fish and Wildlife Service special agents James Bartee, John Cooper, Terry Grosz, Dave Hall, Scott Pearson, and Joel Scrafford; National Park Service biologist and forensics expert William Cook; Loren Ellison, who received the longest prison term ever handed down in a poaching case and provided Audubon with an invaluable interview during his time in prison; Zack Green, Fish and Wildlife Service wildlife customs inspector; Michael Pelton, a black bear biologist with the University of Tennessee; Roger Powell, a black bear biologist with North Carolina State University; and Montana wildlife law enforcement officer Robert Winfield.

For the chapter on ancient forests, northern spotted owl biologists Harriet Allen and Eric Forsman; George Atiyeh, Oregon's intrepid defender of Opal Creek; Forest Service plantologist Jerry Franklin; lumber mill owner Robert Freres, Jr.; James Montieth, one of Oregon's foremost forest experts; and John B. Dewitt, executive director of Save the Redwoods League, Inc.

For the chapter on the sandhill cranes, Don Clapp, manager of the Mule Shoe National Wildlife Refuge in west Texas, and John VanDerwalker, director of the Platte River Trust.

For the chapter on dolphins, Bob Schoelkopf, director of the Marine Mammal Stranding Center in Brigantine, New Jersey.

Many of the people interviewed made a further contribution by reviewing the manuscript of this book and deserve a resounding thanks for their efforts.

An invaluable partner in completing this book was David Sobel of John Wiley & Sons, Inc., whose erudite editing is much appreciated. Wiley's Peter Clifton, Gwen Jones, Tasi Manicas, Lee Northshield, Margie Schustack, and Veronica Welsh also are greatly appreciated for the expertise they brought to the book project. Deserving special mention are Stephanie Laidman of the Jane Rotrosen Literary Agency, and also Tammy Robinson and Jenny Thorpe of WETA-TV, who work closely with Audubon on production of the Audubon Television Specials.

Also to be recognized for their fine and utterly indispensable work are the following producers of Audubon Television Specials: Phil Burton, Franz Camenzind, Graham Chedd, David Clark, Robert Drew, Larry Engel, Pam Hogan, Hardy Jones, Karen Kelly, James and John Lipscomb, Tom Lucas, Bob Nixon, Wolfgang and Sharon Obst, Leslie Reinherz, Mark Shwartz, Roger Snodgrass, and Julia Whitty.

The narrators of the Audubon Television Specials covered in this book have been generous in donating their time. Their contribution is critical to the success enjoyed by the programs. They are Jane Alexander, Peter Benchley, Richard Chamberlain, Michael Douglas, Paul Newman, Leonard Nimoy, Robert Redford, and Meryl Streep.

And finally, special thanks go to a particularly persevering trio, Gail Shearer, Carolyn Welliver, and Ini Chichester for their generous understanding of the various social strains and familial absences that come with the production of a book of this sort.

Christopher N. Palmer
Roger L. DiSilvestro
Page Chichester

PREFACE

by Christopher N. Palmer,
EXECUTIVE PRODUCER,
AUDUBON TELEVISION SPECIALS

SOME YEARS AGO, the Diak people in Borneo were suffering severely from malaria. Officials from the World Health Organization investigated the problem and came up with what seemed a logical solution. They sprayed DDT generously throughout Diak villages, hoping to kill off the mosquitoes that carried the malaria. At first, the plan seemed to work. The mosquitoes died, and the incidence of malaria dropped off. But then the unexpected happened. Shortly after the DDT was sprayed, the roofs of the Diaks' houses literally started crashing down on them.

A link between DDT and falling roofs was soon found. The pesticide had killed off parasitic wasps that ate thatch-eating caterpillars. With their enemy gone, the caterpillars proliferated and ate into the roofs. But that was just a beginning. In the wake of the DDT operation, the Diaks also suffered a sudden rat infestation. The reason: Insects poisoned by the pesticide were eaten by lizards which in turn were eaten by cats. The DDT in the lizards' tissues poisoned the cats. As the cats died, the rats on which they preyed flourished. The rats overran the decatted area, and sylphatic plague began to spread. As a result of its anti-malarial campaign, the World Health Organization soon found it necessary to parachute live cats into Borneo.

This story shows clearly how human society, even when its intentions are good, can create tremendous problems for itself because of a lack of sound ecological knowledge. Unfortunately, it seems that the greater our technological skills, the worse the problems that we create. As the twentieth century draws to a close, we find we have created environmental problems that threaten all life. For some of these problems, such as ozone depletion and global warming, definite solutions continue to elude us. A better understanding of the environment is thus becoming crucial to human survival.

Ecological problems are becoming increasingly urgent partly as a result of a growing human population. The greater our number, the greater the problems we create. No one needs a crystal ball to see where the future is going. By 2030, the world's 5 billion people will double to 10 billion. With this unimaginable mushrooming of our numbers will come an equally unimaginable growth in the industries that support our global society. In 1900, the world economy was $600 billion. Today, the world economy grows by more than this amount every two years. By

2050, the predicted world economy will be $13 trillion—five times as large as it is today. The huge increases in industrial waste, pollution, and greenhouse gases that would result from such economic growth could prove catastrophic to the Earth and its inhabitants. Unless a clean environment becomes an overriding priority for politicians everywhere, we will never develop the technologies that will allow economic growth while reducing pressures on the natural environment.

In a democracy, political priorities are heavily influenced by voter interests. We can meet our environmental challenges if we demand that our governments place a priority on solving ecological problems. There is an awesome, untapped power in individual action. The conservation movement's goal is to help ensure that environmentally concerned individuals combine their actions and learn to speak with one well-informed voice. We want to avoid polarization and instead forge a general consensus based on the notion that a decent and healthy environment is in the interest of all Americans and indeed of everyone in the world.

In order to win in a democracy you need only 51 percent of the people behind you, not 100 percent. And creating this majority often requires only a small shift in national values. The Earth is endangered, and environmentalists must act as missionaries if the planet is to be saved. The broad diffusion of knowledge about our increasingly complex and interdependent global society is vital if environmentalists are to help guide society in making wise decisions about the use of the Earth.

One of the most important tasks undertaken by the National Audubon Society is this broad diffusion of knowledge. With its television programs and companion books, Audubon reaches out far beyond its membership of 600,000 people, to an audience of millions. With the companion books, we hope to build on the excitement and concern generated by the Audubon Television Specials. The books enlarge on the information contained in the films and tell viewers what they can do to help solve some of our many vital environmental problems. We hope that the programs and books will help give readers and television viewers the knowledge and confidence that they need to take action in behalf of sound conservation.

The television programs and companion books are not the only tie-ins to the Audubon television programs. My department also is developing companion videodisc-based interactive multimedia programs that focus on various ecological subjects. We already are marketing computer software programs—Audubon Wildlife Adventures series—that graphically teach users about such diverse subjects as grizzly bears and whales. All these projects are integrated with our television programs and companion books. Print, software, and video thus all have mutually supportive roles in our environmental education efforts.

The essential message of each Audubon Television Special is that we must live in harmony with our natural ecosystems. If we damage them, we cannot meet basic human needs and enjoy economic growth. Some of the programs are about a particular species, habitat, or ecosystem. Others deal with resources such as groundwater, wild rivers, energy, and soil. Still others are on biotechnology as it is applied to the conservation of species and ecosystems. And all the programs are about individual people who are making a difference.

The Audubon Television Specials are produced under my direction by freelance filmmakers. Audubon does not own a camera, stage, or recording studio. We keep no writers, directors, or cinematographers under long-term contracts. Instead, I assemble these elements on a project-by-project basis. The beginning point of every Audubon Television Special is a brief concept paper that outlines the story. Sometimes the story idea is my own; sometimes it is given to me by others. I never hire a producer who cannot give a good answer to the question, "What is the story?" or who says that the story will become apparent while we are shooting the film. In the brief paragraphs of the concept paper lie the seeds of success or failure for the program.

The producers of the Audubon Specials are the best in the business. They are artists devoted to their craft and dedicated to telling the truth about environmental issues. They understand that good filmmaking involves far more than just the use of film and camera. If the basic concept is not right, the program will fail.

While the Audubon programs are provocative and deal with tough environmental issues for which no easy solution exists, we also do our best to show all sides of every issue. We have tried to bring the same excellent reporting quality to this companion book.

The bulk of the book is composed of eight chapters, each one based on an Audubon Television Special:

Wolves, produced by Franz Camenzind and narrated by Robert Redford, sheds light on the relationship between people and wolves, from the animal's early eradication throughout most of the United States to current efforts to restore it.

Sharks, produced by Stan Waterman and narrated by *Jaws* author Peter Benchley, examines the concerns of marine specialists working to learn more about this misunderstood predator in order to prevent it from becoming depleted.

Sea Turtles: Ancient Nomads, produced by Bob Nixon and Karen Kelly and narrated by Jane Alexander, examines the plight of one of the most exploited animals in the world.

If Dolphins Could Talk, produced by Hardy Jones and Julia Whitty and hosted by Michael Douglas, focuses on dolphins and porpoises and their struggle for survival in seas beset by pollution and laced with deadly fishing nets.

Ancient Forests: Rage Over Trees, produced by James and John Lipscomb and hosted by Paul Newman, looks at the ancient forests of the Pacific Northwest and the battle between the timber industry and conservationists over trees up to 200 feet high, 8 feet thick, and 1,000 years old.

Arctic Refuge: A Vanishing Wilderness?, produced by Wolfgang and Sharon Obst and narrated by Meryl Streep, takes us to an untouched national wildlife refuge in northeast Alaska, site of a heated debate between the oil industry, which wants to drill the refuge for oil, and conservationists, who want the refuge left unspoiled.

Crane River, produced by Wolfgang and Sharon Obst and narrated by Leonard Nimoy, brings into viewers' homes the celebrated annual stopover of half a million sandhill cranes on Nebraska's Platte River, a river besieged by water projects that threaten much of the river's wildlife.

Greed and Wildlife: Poaching in America, produced by Mark Shwartz and narrated by Richard Chamberlain, goes behind the scenes to look at those who kill wildlife illegally for profit or sport and at the law enforcement officers who work to stop them.

The goal of this book is to deepen and enrich the impact of the Audubon Television Specials. To the millions of people who love the television programs, this book will serve as a reminder of the fundamental importance of a healthy planet. For those not yet familiar with the programs, this book will help make up for what has been missed. Videocassettes of the television programs are available from Vestron and WETA-TV. You can call the Audubon Television Department (202/547-9009) for more information. The television staff can tell you how to obtain not only videocassettes but also teacher guides, computer software, and other fine materials to help you learn about and enjoy the environment.

The National Audubon Society offers *Audubon Perspectives: Fight for Survival* with the profound conviction that it says something vital about the world's future and the need for wise stewardship of our planet. It includes reading that is entertaining and informative, reassuring and alarming. As David Suzuki, a biologist and one of Canada's best-known broadcasters, has written, "We cannot avoid confronting the very uncomfortable reality that it is *our* appetites and demands that are a direct contributor to the loss of what we cherish."

Robert Northshield, a distinguished executive at CBS and creator of "Sunday Morning," recently wrote an article in the *New York Times* in which he argued that television nature shows should offer more than just beauty and entertainment. He wrote, "What we need are tough broadcasts that equip us to want to take part in the decision-making necessitated by such modern conceptions as overpopulations, greenhouse effects, ozone diminution, forest depletion, water and air and noise pollution, extinction, and the esthetics of conservation."

I believe that every Audubon Television Special is exactly the type of hard-hitting, fact-filled, compelling programming that Northshield is calling for. This book, and the Audubon Television Specials upon which it is based, show that natural resources, wildlife, habitat, and people—like the Diaks and the parasitic wasps—are not isolated entities, but are dependent upon one another. The book and the specials are two tools that we hope will help society avoid the need for parachuting more live cats.

March 1990

CONTENTS

GREED AND WILDLIFE: POACHING IN AMERICA
Based on the Audubon Television Special
by Mark Shwartz, narrated by Richard Chamberlain

HUMANITY AND NATURE: TOMORROW'S DILEMMA

HUMANITY AND NATURE
THE ANCIENT CONFLICT

PRESUMABLY, long, long ago the human species fit into the scheme of nature just as any other wild creature does, living in balance with naturally occurring food sources. What we have learned, surmised, and deduced about prehistoric human life suggests that this was so.

Prehistoric humans apparently lived in small groups, and the groups probably were built around family relationships. In this, humans were much like other social animals—gorillas, monkeys, wolves, lions, even some dolphin species. They lived by gathering the edible parts of wild plants and by hunting. Like any other species, their success and prosperity must have fluctuated with the seasons and the vagaries of climate. When droughts parched the earth and vegetation withered, or when winters were unusually harsh, the early human bands must have found themselves losing their weaker members to hunger, stress, and disease. Controlled by the natural cycles of ecosystems and food bases, their populations in the long term would have tended to stay in balance with the natural world.

But even in those times long, long ago, humans were differentiating themselves from other animals. They were able to do this because they possessed a uniquely important set of physical characteristics—brains that endowed them with intelligence, hands that allowed them to manipulate objects and give material shape to their intellectual ideas, and an upright posture that freed the hands from tasks of mere transportation. This was a dangerous combination, an evolutionary experiment from which nature may never recover. It allowed even the earliest humans to make complex tools, and among the tools they made were weapons. They were able to combine those weapons—implements of stone, wood, and bone—with their native intelligence and their knack for coordinated group activities to become one of the most formidable creatures on the planet. Working as an armed pack, Stone Age people could reasonably expect to hold at bay the largest cave bear or saber-toothed cat. To provide themselves with meat, they could challenge the largest, most dangerous herbivores—the mammoths, mastodons, and woolly rhinos.

Some evidence suggests that Stone Age humans contributed to, and perhaps even caused, the extinction of the large mammals that flourished through the Ice Ages. Mammoths, giant sloths, giant beavers, woolly rhinos, and the rest seem to disappear from the geological record at various places in the Old and New Worlds at just about the time that humans first appear. Not all experts accept this as proof that human hunters wiped out the big mammals. Climate was most likely a major factor in the extinctions, too. Humans may merely have provided the coup de grace to species already vanishing as a warming trend changed their habitat. But it is interesting that no one seems to doubt that early humans *would* have wiped out the animals they hunted had they been equipped to do so. We all seem to accept readily that all through history, and presumably through prehistory, our species' tendencies for destructiveness were limited only by the technology of the moment.

This destructive potential reached a new high some 10,000 years ago, when technological development experienced a revolutionary convulsion with the invention of agriculture. Agriculture permitted humanity to escape at last all the bonds of nature that until then had held human society in check. It was an invention that shook the world as nothing else would until the day a group of scientists split the atom for purposes of war.

It is difficult to tell exactly when agriculture—the cultivation of plants and the husbandry of livestock—began. The only way to trace its origins is to look at the artifacts buried at the sites of ancient villages. But the evidence is ambiguous. Today's domestic plants and animals are generally easy to distinguish from their wild relatives, but in the earliest days of domestication species raised by humans differed little or not at all from their wild forebears. Seeds found where they were stored 10,000 years ago in earthen jars may be a sign of agriculture, or they may be merely collected stores of seeds from wild plants. The bones of the earliest domestic livestock cannot be reliably distinguished from the bones of wild goats, sheep, and cattle killed by hunters. Despite these difficulties, anthropologists have been able to place the origin of agriculture in the Middle East at no later than 10,000 years ago. From there it radiated into Egypt and Asia.

People who took up agriculture were freed of some of the uncertainties of hunting wild animals and gathering wild plants. They were able to store reserves of food against times of famine. Acre for acre, cultivated land could feed more people more reliably than could untilled earth, so the limits that hunting and gathering had put on human popula-

tions expanded. Familial bands could combine into communities; communities could take the shape of villages, towns, cities. Because the crops that grew on the land could be owned by the people that grew them, the land itself could be owned. Land became property just as an arrowhead was property. It became a basis for prosperity, and it could be handed down through generations.

Agriculture seemed to make nature superfluous. The complexity of nature, where a hundred species of plant might grow on a single acre, was traded for the simplicity of cultivation, in which a tiny handful of plant and animal species met all human dietary needs. Where nature had been too erratic, like a mad king that sometimes nurtures and sometimes destroys, cultivation seemed tame and reliable. By twisting and fettering nature, humanity seemed to find the key to prosperity. Forests could be sheared to clear land for crops. Rivers could be made to run into canals that watered thirsty fields. But by confining nature, the agriculturalists made it into a rival. They were forever working to conquer nature so they could wrest from it the things they needed for themselves and their domestic stock. The survival of wild plants and animals, once vital to humanity, no longer seemed to matter. Wild hoofed animals competed with domestic stock for grass. Wild plants encroached on croplands. Human society rapidly ceased to live in nature and came instead to defend itself against it.

Unfortunately, the sense that agriculture freed humanity from the rules of nature was an illusion. Eventually, though the process might take centuries, the natural laws would reassert themselves. At the dawn of agriculture, large regions in the Middle East were heavily forested. Rich grasslands, punctuated by small deserts in the most arid sections, also occurred in the Near and Middle East, extending into Mongolia and China as part of a great "dry belt" in which rainfall was limited. As the early agricultural communities grew and grew, they needed more and more land for cultivation and for pasture. The forests were cut for cropland. In later centuries, warrior herders conquered the crop-growing peoples and converted the farmlands to pastures. High densities of livestock overran the grasslands, eating the native grasses faster than the plants could reproduce. When livestock nibbled at the edges of desert pockets, the desert areas expanded across the depleted grasslands. This is why vast deserts lie today across North Africa, the Near and Middle East, and Asia in places that were rich in plant life 5,000 years ago. We cannot know precisely what the ruin of the forests and grasslands did ecologically, but doubtless some wildlife species, particularly those dependent on the forests, were lost as their habitat disappeared. The nature of the soil must have changed, becoming dry and granular and starved of nutrients. The amount of annual rainfall may have changed, too, declining with the disappearance of vast tracts of plant life that had cycled huge quantities of water through their leaves.

The destruction of native plant growth was not the only force that destroyed the Middle East's agricultural centers. Another factor was irrigation. By controlling the flow of rivers, early farmers sent waters laden with natural salts across their fields. When the water evaporated, the salts were left behind. Eventually they built up in the soil until they reached toxic levels and cultivation was brought to an end. Another cause of destruction was grounded in the demands of an increasingly urban life. As cities grew they needed building materials, including fuel to fire the furnaces that made iron and the kilns that made brick. It is likely that the building of the cities of Harappa and Mohenjo-daro, with their brick roads and structures, in India's Indus River valley led to the denuding of the region's forests—gone even today—and to the desertification of the region that lies along the Indian–Pakistani border, now covered by the Indian Desert.

Turning once-fertile wild lands into denuded and poisoned artifacts of farming was only a momentary problem for early agriculturalists. When they needed more land for crops or livestock, they had all of Europe to sweep across. One of the first agricultural migrations took place about 5,000 B.C. and led to the settlement of the eastern Mediterranean. Shortly after that, a wave of migration passed through Asia Minor and arrived along the Danube, where the people began to cut and burn the woods to create cropland. As the Danubian communities grew, segments of the population had to travel farther to find farmland. By 2,500 B.C. they were cutting the forests of northeastern France and northwestern Germany. Meanwhile, more land-hungry migrants were coming out of southern Russia, or moving out of the Mediterranean and up the Atlantic coast.

The destruction of woodlands and grasslands continued for centuries. During the Dark Ages, most of Europe's remaining old forests were cut and burned. The destruction was so complete and accomplished so long ago that modern German biologists are forced to examine medieval tapestries when they wish to understand the characteristics of their nation's pristine forests. This immense loss of a natural habitat, combined with poorly controlled hunting, had far-reaching effects on wildlife. A wide variety of European species were greatly reduced in the Middle Ages and before. Lions once occurred in the Middle East and even in Greece, but they vanished in Classical times. The medieval period of development led to the extinction of the aurochs, a type of wild cattle, and to the reduction of other species, such as the wisent or Old World bison and a host of predators, including wolves and brown bears. Without doubt, some forest-dwelling bird species were lost before they were ever known to any field of activity that could be called science.

The loss of native woods, grasslands, and wild creatures seemed to go unlamented, though it is hard to believe that not one witness to this widespread destruction ever felt a twinge of sorrow. Surely some ancient Roman centurion, some armored knight, some lady-in-waiting recognized the tragedy that lay in the ruin of the old wild lands. But no voice spoke of this concern. Nature, it seemed, was something to be overrun, molded. Forests were to be carved into plow frames and ax handles. Wildlife was to be reduced to meat and hides.

Imbued in this tradition, the first European settlers came to the New World. They were not aware of it, but in Central America the great Mayan civilization, which had peaked in A.D. 800, had collapsed a few centuries before when its agricultural base failed. But in the vastness of the New World, that was a minor, local incident. Colonists who arrived in North America saw before them a continent seemingly untouched by anything but the activities of peoples still living in the Stone Age. The settlers quickly changed that, clearing the forests to make room for crops. In order to grow large surpluses of crops for export, they farmed intensively, starving the soil of nutrients. Worse, with the forests gone, soil eroded in large areas. No matter, the settlers could move west, cutting and growing as they went. For the next two or three centuries they did just that. The canebreaks of the eastern Midwest and the Southeast, where bamboo-like plants grew ten feet tall and covered the earth for miles, vanished late in the eighteenth and early in the nineteenth centuries. Wetlands were drained, grasslands were plowed. In

Plains bison straggle through the hills of nineteenth-century North America in this painting by John James Audubon. The advent of the gun and the plow wiped out within a few decades the 50 million bison that crowded the Great Plains.

the arid Southwest, overgrazing by livestock turned grasslands into deserts.

Until the nineteenth century, no real concern for the destruction of the continent's natural habitats was expressed. All our natural resources seemed inexhaustible. There were always new lands to conquer. The tremendous impact that human development was having on the world was little noted until 1864, when George Perkins Marsh published his landmark book, *Man and Nature*. Marsh had grown up in the frontier state of Vermont and become a lawyer, historian, diplomat, and master of twenty languages. Appointed ambassador to Italy during the Lincoln administration, he kept that post until his death in 1882. He wrote *Man and Nature* while in Italy. It is a painstaking collection of information that showed how human actions were affecting the fate of forests, wildlife, rainfall, even climate. Marsh had a global view of the environment in an era when few people had even a national view. He identified the need for conservation in a time when all eyes were on development and exploitation.

The Turning Point

Throughout the bulk of history, human society has shown little or no concern for the fate of the natural environment or of wildlife. In preindustrial times, it must have seemed impossible that people could have a serious impact on the vast wildernesses of the globe. But finally, in the nineteenth century, change was so quick and sweeping that it could not be ignored, particularly in North America.

The rate of change was accelerated by the Industrial Revolution. The pace must have boggled the minds of nineteenth-century people. They had ridden into the century on horseback and on ships under sail, communicating with one another by letter and messenger. They left the century in automobiles, trains, and steamboats, communicating instantaneously by telephone and telegraph. The airplane was only three years away. But despite the progress and optimism to which the new technologies gave rise, before the close of the century a few visionaries were heeding Marsh's words and beginning to see some disturbing signs.

In the haste of settlement, much of the natural wealth of the continent had been plundered. By the closing decade of the 1800s, most of the forest lands had been cut, and nascent conservationists such as Theodore Roosevelt were concerned that the remaining stands would soon vanish. Wildlife had suffered tremendous declines. The 30 million to 50 million bison that crowded the Great Plains of the United States and Canada were reduced to a few hundred stragglers. The pronghorn antelope, once as numerous as the bison, was on the edge of extinction. Elk and moose had been wiped out over much of their original range, and the caribou that had once grazed in New England and the Great Lakes states was pushed back entirely north of the Canadian border. The Carolina paroquet of the southeastern United States, one of only two parrot species found in the United States, was wiped out by gunfire and habitat loss. The passenger pigeon, once so numerous that its numbers literally blackened the skies, was gone. Gone too were the Labrador duck, Atlantic gray whale, sea mink, great auk, and eastern mountain lion. Dwindling away were many species of goose and duck, the heath hen, wild turkey, grizzly bear, gray wolf, red wolf, ivory-billed woodpecker, California condor—the list is a long one. It seemed that most of the continent's large animals would soon be gone. To stop that decline, a handful of wildlife enthusiasts undertook a vast endeavor to change the nation's, if not the world's, outlook on wildlife. For the first time, people were calling for the protection of wild species and wild places, showing concern for and interest in the nonhuman world.

The Conservation Movement

The conservation movement began on several fronts. Many sport hunters were concerned that market hunting—the killing of wildlife so products made from it could be sold for profit—was going to wipe out the continent's game animals. They sought protection of animals hunted for sport, such as deer and waterfowl. Others were concerned that the killing of birds to supply the millinery trade with feathers and even whole bodies—some women's hats featured entire mounted birds—would wipe out the plume birds of coast and marsh, such as egrets and terns, and even songbirds. They shared with the hunters a desire to quash the meat markets. Another segment of the early conservation movement included people such as John Muir, dedicated to saving the land itself. Muir, founder of the Sierra Club, worked to save California redwoods and the mountainous region that today is Yosemite National Park.

Early conservationists could travel two roads in seeking protection for wildlife and habitat. One approach was to urge state legislatures to enact protective laws. The drive to do this was kicked off in the 1880s. One of its leaders was George Bird Grinnell, a leading conservationist of his day. Grinnell was editor of a popular hunting and fishing magazine, *Forest and Stream*. He was also a leading member of the American Ornithologists' Union, had traveled extensively in the West during the last years of settlement, and was an expert in the decline of the bison. He used his editorial voice in *Forest and Stream* to

A great blue heron peers from its roost to the water below, presumably in quest of food. Herons and other long-legged wading birds were nearly wiped out at the turn of the century by poachers who sold the birds' feathers to the millinery trade.

express his concern that many wildlife species would soon follow the bison into oblivion and to promote better laws for the protection of game and migratory birds. In the magazine, Grinnell suggested that bird enthusiasts should found an organization dedicated specifically to bird protection. He suggested that the organization be called the Audubon Society after famous wildlife painter and naturalist John James Audubon, whose wife had tutored Grinnell in his youth. The Audubon Society was so successful that within two years it had 50,000 members. Unfortunately, Grinnell and his staff could not meet the effort and expense needed to maintain the society, and the organization collapsed under its own weight.

However, the American Ornithologists' Union—an organization of professional bird experts—continued to propel efforts for bird protection by drafting a "Model Bird Law" that local bird enthusiasts sought to enact at the state level. To avoid alienating the hunting community by pushing for stronger protection of waterfowl, shorebirds, grouse, and other hunted species, the union's model

law limited protection from sport hunting strictly to nongame birds, such as the songbirds that were being killed in immense numbers for the meat markets. The law also banned the destruction of the eggs and nests of all native North American species.

The Model Bird Law drew opposition from some unexpected quarters. Many professional ornithologists opposed it because they were accustomed to shooting and collecting the birds they studied and also to collecting bird eggs. Taxidermists and amateur collectors also opposed the law.

The fight to pass state laws became a steep, uphill battle. Trying to promote state wildlife laws required conservationists to undertake one effort after another, state by state. Far simpler, it would seem, to follow the second road open to early conservationists: passage of nationwide federal wildlife laws.

But this was easier said than done. Under the Constitution, and by legal tradition, the states had control over wildlife. The states were quite willing to go to court to fight any federal wildlife-protection law on the grounds that it was unconstitutional, and often they did. Enactment of federal wildlife laws therefore required imaginative use of the legislative process.

One of the first sallies into federal regulation of wildlife came late in the 1890s. It was aided by a revival of the Audubon Societies. This revival was initiated in 1896, when William Brewster, one of the leading ornithologists of his day, helped organize the Massachusetts Audubon Society for the Protection of Birds, which continues to exist to this day. Other state groups soon organized, and they were at the forefront of an effort in 1898 to pass through Congress a bill that would have ended the importation, sale, or shipment of bird plumes within the United States. The millinery trade, whose use of feathers in hats was the target of the bill, organized opposition to it. Ironically, the death knell for the law was actually sounded by the American Ornithologists' Union, which refused to support the law because it believed the Audubon Societies were trying to stop the collecting of birds and eggs by scientists as well as market hunters.

More successful was another Audubon-supported bill, the Lacey Act of 1900, which made it illegal to import foreign wildlife without a federal permit and banned the transport across state lines of any wildlife killed in violation of state laws. The Lacey Act passed the test of constitutionality because it involved interstate commerce, which fell within the control of the federal government. However, a major weak point in the law was its reliance on state laws, since many states lacked any laws protecting wildlife. It was apparent to all but the most ardent protectors of states' rights that a more aggressive federal wildlife-protection law was needed.

Efforts to provide strong federal protection began in 1906 with a law that sought to impose direct bans on the taking of game birds. The law was designed to protect hunted species, such as the ducks and geese that market hunters were whittling away. It was introduced in Congress by George Shiras III in 1906. Shiras was one of the finest wildlife photographers working at the turn of the century and an ardent conservationist. As a Pennsylvania representative, he introduced in Congress a bill

that would have given the federal government the lead role in the protection of such migratory birds as ducks, geese, and wild pigeons. (Ironically, overhunting had already wiped out one species of wild pigeon, the passenger pigeon, once the most-numerous bird species in the world; however, in 1906 some ornithologists still held out hope that a few birds would be found in the wild.) The law was never a serious contender in the legal arena, though, because even congressional representatives who favored it doubted that it was constitutional.

Thus bird protection languished in the halls of Congress until 1912, when Representative John W. Weeks of Massachusetts and Senator George P. McLean of Connecticut introduced a bill patterned after Shiras's proposal. However, the Weeks–McLean bill went a step beyond Shiras's. Shiras's interest had lain primarily in protecting hunted spe-

A Canada goose cruises across a pond at Chincoteague National Wildlife Refuge in Virginia. The federal refuge system began as part of an effort to protect geese and ducks.

cies for the benefit of sportsmen. A bill of this sort compelled little support from those committed to the protection of songbirds, plume birds, and other species of little interest to sport hunters. Weeks–McLean was able to garner this wider support by including all migratory birds in its call for federal protection. Nevertheless, the bill looked as if it, too, would run aground on the question of constitutionality. Strong voices in Congress opposed the bill as an infringement on states' rights and suggested that if the law were passed it would soon lead the federal government to make other inroads on state authority. In all likelihood the Weeks–McLean bill would have died had it not been for the intervention of an ardent birder with a deep interest in natural history—Henry Ford. Ford sent one of his advertising men to Washington to shepherd the bill through Congress and used his considerable influence to engender support for the bill among his influential friends and associates.

The bill made it through Congress in 1913 and landed on the desk of President William Howard Taft as the Migratory Bird Act. Taft received the bill on his last day in office and signed it without reading it. He later declared that had he read the bill he would have vetoed it on the belief that it was unconstitutional. The law's success thus was founded on more than one layer of political whimsy.

The Migratory Bird Act was almost immediately brought to bay by court cases in which the states charged that the law was unconstitutional. But while conservationists concerned themselves with the court battles, developments were taking place on another front that would soon give birth to full federal authority in the protection of migratory birds.

Because migratory ducks and geese pass from Canada across the United States and into Mexico, the states had little interest in protecting the birds from hunters' guns. The birds were a sort of common property from which each governmental entity sought to get the biggest possible share. To get around the states'-rights issue and to ensure sound international protection for all migratory birds, including ducks and geese, the federal government in 1916 signed a migratory bird protection treaty with Great Britain, which acted in behalf of Canada. The treaty said that the United States and Canada would act together to coordinate closed seasons on migratory birds. After the treaty was signed, and while the constitutionality of the Migratory Bird Act of 1913 was being mulled over in the courts, Congress passed the Migratory Bird Treaty Act of 1918, which provided the legal basis for the treaty and gave the federal government the right to enforce closed seasons and limits on the take of migratory birds. The state of Missouri challenged the law in court, but the court ruled that the treaty-making power of the federal government superseded states' rights. As a result, cases involving the constitutionality of the 1913 law were dropped, and the way was opened for virtually all the federal wildlife laws and regulations that have followed since.

The first two decades of the twentieth century saw not only the passage of the first federal wildlife laws, but also the development of federal agencies set up to manage and protect public lands. These agencies also manage the wildlife that occurs on the public lands. The Forest Service was created in 1905 to administer the cutting of timber on national forests. The National Park Service was established in 1916 to manage the national parks that had been created in previous years, beginning with Yellowstone in 1872.

The federal role in wildlife conservation is led today by another agency, the U.S. Fish and Wildlife Service. The agency's roots date to 1871, when a Commission on Fish and Fisheries was created by Congress and assigned to find out why food fish were declining. In 1886, Congress created the Department of Agriculture's Division of Economic Ornithology and Mammalogy to administer studies on the relationship between agriculture and mammals and birds. From the fish commission and the bird and mammal bureaucracies developed the Bureau of Sport Fisheries in the Department of Commerce and the Bureau of Biological Survey in the Department of Agriculture. In 1940, the two agencies were merged and placed in the Department of the Interior. The merged agency was named the Fish and Wildlife Service.

One of the important tasks of the Fish and Wildlife Service is management of the National Wildlife Refuge System, which today includes some 420 refuges covering nearly 100 million acres. The refuge system, the only extensive system of public lands managed primarily for wildlife, dates to 1903, when President Theodore Roosevelt issued an executive order making federally owned Pelican Island, off Florida's east coast, a protected refuge for birds. For Roosevelt, that was only a beginning. By 1909, he had created fifty-two more refuges. Congress en-

This sign marks the entrance to a wildlife sanctuary operated by the National Audubon Society along the Platte River in Nebraska. Private conservation groups such as Audubon have been potent forces for wildlife and environmental protection.

tered the process in 1908, setting aside 12,800 acres in Montana as the National Bison Range, the first congressionally mandated refuge.

By 1920, the outlook for wildlife had changed. But the new laws and agencies were just a beginning. Although the federal government could create wildlife refuges out of its land holdings, it had no legal right to buy lands for refuges. Congress solved this problem in 1929 by enacting the Migratory Bird Conservation Act, which authorizes the federal government to acquire land for migratory bird protection. During the drought years of the 1930s, however, stronger federal commitment to wildlife protection was needed. The drought, in part a result of agricultural practices that turned prairies into dry, barren lands, destroyed many of the marshes that dotted the northern Great Plains of the United States and the southern plains of Canada. These

marshes were vital waterfowl breeding areas, and without them the birds were sure to fail.

Hunter concern about waterfowl was intense at the time that Franklin D. Roosevelt stepped into the president's office. One of Roosevelt's acquaintances was Joseph P. Knapp, the owner of *Collier's Weekly* magazine and some other popular magazines. He urged Roosevelt to do something about the waterfowl problem, and Roosevelt responded in 1934 by appointing a committee to look into the matter. The committee was chaired by Tom Beck, an editor for *Collier's Weekly*. Under him were Jay N. "Ding" Darling, a Pulitzer Prize–winning editorial cartoonist and conservationist, and Aldo Leopold, the man whose textbook, *Wildlife Management*, would help create a new science and make him the father of modern wildlife biology. The committee ultimately came up with a series of recommendations for improved wildlife management. Two of the most important recommendations were for a better-funded wildlife refuge land-acquisition program and for a federal program that would provide funding to the states for wildlife management.

As a result of his work on the committee, Ding Darling was made head of the Bureau of Biological Survey. He accepted the post only because he was promised increased funding for his agency. When the funding did not come, he complained to President Roosevelt. Roosevelt wrote him an IOU for $1 million and told him to take it to Harry Hopkins, a special assistant to the president. Hopkins recognized the IOU as one of the president's jokes. Despite such setbacks, Darling was ultimately successful in pushing through Congress two bills that instituted measures urged by the Beck Committee. One of these was the Migratory Bird Hunting Stamp Act, enacted in 1934. This law requires all waterfowl hunters age sixteen or older to buy a federal duck stamp, which they have to affix to their state hunting licenses. Funds from the sale of the stamps were used to acquire lands for the creation of wildlife refuges, primarily for the conservation of waterfowl. This was of inestimable help in the deadly years of the drought. The second important law was the Federal Aid in Wildlife Restoration Act,

which Darling helped shepherd through Congress in 1937. This law puts an excise tax on firearms and ammunition. Funds raised by the tax are distributed to the states for wildlife management, thus putting another of the Beck Committee's goals into operation. This provides the states with a large part of the money they spend on wildlife protection and has contributed immensely to the increasingly sophisticated role that the states play in conservation. A similar law, the Federal Aid in Fish Restoration Act, was enacted in 1950 to help state fisheries work by providing federal funds raised from a tax on fishing equipment.

During the first half of the century, important developments were also taking place outside the federal government. A variety of private wildlife-conservation groups was born during the first struggle to protect wildlife and the environment, and they grew with the conservation movement. One of the first was the Sierra Club, founded in 1892 by John Muir as part of his effort to save California wilderness. The Sierra Club continues to lead many efforts for sound protection of wild lands, but has broadened into a variety of other environmental issues as well.

The Audubon Societies that sprang up in the late 1890s combined in 1905 into a national group.

In addition to shepherding early conservation laws, the group also established wildlife sanctuaries and provided wardens for the protection of plume birds and other wildlife. The National Audubon Society has grown over the years to encompass such issues as population control, energy efficiency, and endangered-species protection. Today, its membership exceeds half a million, organized into 550 local chapters scattered throughout the United States and in other nations.

The biggest of the conservation groups is the National Wildlife Federation, whose roots lie in the hunting community. It started in 1936 as a confederation of hunting groups that united to seek common conservation goals. Today, the organization's horizons extend far beyond the hunting community, and it has some 4.5 million members.

Another leading group is the Wilderness Society, organized in 1935 to promote the protection of public lands, such as national forests, wildlife refuges, and parks. It has earned a reputation for in-depth economic analyses of various conservation issues. For example, its examination of logging on the national forests has revealed the tremendous financial loss that the federal government faces by continuing its current logging plans.

The full range of conservation groups has become quite vast. The *Conservation Directory*, published annually by the National Wildlife Federation, lists more than 400 organizations devoted to wildlife and habitat protection. They range from small specialty groups interested in the protection of a single species to organizations with international conservation goals. Organizations such as these shepherded through Congress much of the legislation that protects wildlife today, such as the Wilderness Act of 1964 and the Endangered Species Act of 1973.

The growth of private conservation groups, federal wildlife agencies and laws, and state wildlife management are all signs that we are living in a new era of human–wildlife relationships. After thousands of years of exploiting nature with little concern for the consequences, human society is becoming increasingly committed to the protection of the natural environment and wildlife. However, tremendous challenges remain. Many of our potentially powerful environment laws have been poorly enforced, and the old specters of excess and exploitation still jeopardize wildlife and the environment throughout the world. Fortunately, as the following chapters show, many individuals have sought successfully to alter the ancient course of environmental destruction. In this lies the greatest hope for both wildlife and human society.

WOLVES

Based on the Audubon Television Special by
Franz Camenzind and
Narrated by Robert Redford

LATE IN THE fifteenth century the wolves of North America were enjoying the final years of a pristine continent. Native Americans may have worn wolf hides, and the Aztecs may have kept live wolves in Montezuma's zoo, but activities such as these had little impact on the wolf. It roamed the entire continent at will, rarely challenged by any other species as it hunted the immense herds of hoofed animals that were its main source of food. Then, as the century drew to a close, three Spanish ships in the command of an Italian skipper started an avalanche of Europeans crashing into the New World. These were the people who had wiped out the aurochs, Europe's wild cattle, and nearly hunted to death the wisent, Europe's bison. In centuries past they had driven the lions of Greece into perdition and more recently had decimated the Old World forests. Now they were rushing into a continent brimming with wild things. In forest glades they found huge herds of grazing bison. Along woodland streams they tracked elk moving in groups of up to eighty animals. On open bays they found countless ducks and geese that took wing with the rumbling sound of thunder. And, resting at night from cutting trees and building homes, they must have heard from some dark place the distant, wavering howl of the wolf.

The link that exists between wolves and humankind is far older than history. Wolves have ranged throughout the northern hemisphere for millions of years, and prehistoric bands of humans must have clashed occasionally with packs of wolves, quarreling over who would feed on a freshly killed mammoth or woolly rhino much as a wolf pack today may try to wrest from an Alaskan grizzly a newly slain caribou. Early humans, or at least their offspring, may themselves have fallen prey to wolves. Such instances of predation may have been rare, however. Humans were, after all, armed predators, and top predators such as wolves and humans usually do not prey upon one another. Little reason exists, therefore, for presuming that Stone Age peoples harbored ill will toward wolves. Studies of living aboriginal peoples indicate quite the opposite. The Nunamiut Eskimos, for example, sometimes remove wolf pups from dens and play with them before putting them back unharmed. Similar contact between wolves and prehistoric humans must have occurred, too, because some time long ago wolves were made into pets and domesticated. The family dog, descended from the wolf, is the evidence that proves this.

Human Children Raised by Wolves

Stories about human babies being raised by wolves seem almost as old as history. Roman mythology tells us that the founders of Rome, Romulus and Remus, were cared for by a wolf. They were supposed to be the offspring of Mars, the god of war, and Rhea Silvia, the daughter of Numitor, a king in Italy. According to the myth, Rhea's brother overthrew Numitor and made Rhea a vestal virgin, one of the women who dedicated their lives to temple worship of the gods. When she gave birth to twins, she was put to death, and the babies were cast adrift in the Tiber. A she-wolf found them when they washed ashore, and she suckled them. Later, a shepherd and his wife took the children and raised them. Called Romulus and Remus, the children when they matured restored Numitor to his throne and founded the city of Rome. In a dispute over where to locate the city, Romulus killed Remus. Romulus ruled Rome for thirty-seven years as its first king and, when he died, was taken into the heavens by Mars. Statues of a wolf nursing twin boys were common in ancient Rome, symbols of the empire's beginning.

Many stories about wolves raising human babies have come from India and Africa, which also abound with tales of children raised by a variety of other animals, from gazelles to baboons. Perhaps the most famous story is that of Mowgli, written by Rudyard Kipling. Presumably based on stories that Kipling came across in India, the Mowgli stories tell of how the baby Mowgli was lost in the jungle and found and raised by wolves. He was also tutored by a bear, python, and black panther. His enemy was Shere Kahn, the tiger, whom Mowgli eventually kills. In the end, Mowgli marries a woman, and they raise their offspring among the wolves. The Kipling tale is an enduring story that has been made into a motion picture and a Disney cartoon. It is one of the few stories that show wolves in a positive light.

One obscure tale was related by Barry Lopez—with a measure of skepticism—in his book, *Of Wolves and Men*. It is particularly unusual because it takes place in America, along Texas's Del Rio. In this story, a girl born in May 1835 was left alone on a ranch, from which she disappeared. She was thought to have been eaten by wolves. Ten years later, a long-haired naked girl was spotted with several wolves attacking a goat herd. The girl was seen again during the following year, and finally a hunting party was set up to capture her. She was caught after a chase that lasted three days, and a wolf traveling with her was killed when it attacked the hunters. The girl was taken to the nearest ranch and locked up. A pack of wolves arrived that night, stampeded the livestock, and the girl escaped. She was seen for the last time in 1852, standing with two wolf pups on a sand bar in the Rio Grande.

This story rings false in two important ways. One is the attack of the first wolf on the hunters. A wolf that has been hunted down is very unlikely to attack its hunters. Trapped wolves usually cower when a human approaches, and old-time wolfers often killed wolves by clubbing them. The wolf attack seems so unlikely that it must be untrue. It is equally unlikely that a pack of wolves would approach a ranch house as described in the story.

The rest of the story is doubtless fiction, too. No authenticated report has ever been made of a human raised by wolves. However, the stories may have a remote basis in fact. Historical accounts of children who were thought to have been raised by wolves generally describe children who make animal sounds, crawl about on all fours, prefer meat raw, and attack their rescuers like wild beasts. These characteristics are found in autistic children. It is likely that tales of wolves raising children, if they contain any element of truth, are based on the discovery of autistic or disturbed children abandoned in the wilderness by their parents.

The turning point in relations between wolves and humans probably coincided with the development of agriculture, particularly the keeping of herds of domestic livestock. Peoples who abandoned hunting in favor of keeping livestock found the wolf a persistent threat because it sometimes killed and ate domestic animals. This changed the way humans viewed wolves, and so, at the dawn of civilization, the animals became specters prowling the boundaries of human safety. Ancient Greek and Roman writers portrayed wolves as evil and gruesome, and early Christians turned the table by portraying rapacious Romans as wolves. In the Dark Ages, a young nobleman's training included the hunting of wolves. Medieval Britons developed special breeds of dog for tracking and killing wolves.

The huntsman's spear and the gamekeeper's traps conspired with the destruction of European forests by agricultural development to wipe out most Old World wolves. The animals ceased to exist in England near the start of the sixteenth century. In Scotland they lingered until 1743, in Ireland until 1776. On the Continent they persisted longer, and some remnants survive even now in rugged parts of Spain and in the mountains of Italy and eastern Europe.

In a painting from the 1840s by John James Audubon, a black wolf runs across the prairie while other wolves pursue a bison in the background. Both the wolf and the bison would virtually disappear from the plains as human settlement arrived.

The Wolves of North America

Two species of wolf inhabited North America when the European colonists arrived. One of these, the red wolf, was completely new to the settlers. It had evolved in the New World and apparently represented a surviving line of primitive wolves that had ranged over North America a million years ago. It is a relatively small wolf, averaging at full growth about sixty pounds, roughly the size of a collie. It was first recognized as a distinct species by wildlife artist John James Audubon and his associate John Bachman in the mid-nineteenth century. It occurred then as far north as southern Illinois and Indiana but ranged primarily across the Southeast, from the Atlantic Ocean to east Texas. Presumably it lived in small groups of two or three animals. By the time modern science turned its interest to red wolves, the animals were so scarce that comprehensive studies could not be done. Apparently it preyed on small game, such as rabbits and beavers, and on deer. Government control programs, interbreeding with coyotes as the

A young eastern gray wolf pup nestles against its mother. Wolves establish close social bonds with one another. Young generally do not leave their parents until at least a year old, and may stay with the parents' pack for life.

wolf's numbers dropped, and development of wild lands for agriculture doomed the red wolf.

The other species was the gray wolf. The settlers knew this animal in the Old Country because it occurred throughout most of the northern hemisphere, making it perhaps the most widespread predator in the world. In North America it ranged from Newfoundland to the Pacific, including the islands of southeast Alaska, and from the table lands near Mexico City to within 400 miles of the North Pole. It lived virtually everywhere, avoiding only the most arid deserts of the Southwest.

Gray wolves come in a wide variety of colors and sizes, from black to white, from 60 to 120 pounds, with males averaging around 100 pounds and females around 80. The heaviest wolf on record, reported by Stanley Young and Edward Goldman in *The Wolves of North America*, weighed 175 pounds. The largest wolves come from the north end of their range, and this animal was no exception. It was from east-central Alaska.

Wolves were the ancestors of all domestic dogs— from Yorkshire terriers and Pekinese to bull mastiffs and Afghan hounds—and dogs in many ways still act like wolves. Consequently, we are all familiar with at least some types of wolf behavior. Anyone who has seen a growling dog defending its master's home has witnessed the wolf's way of defending its territory from others of its kind. Anyone whose dog has greeted him or her with bounding leaps and shrill yelps has seen how wolves greet one another after they have been apart. A dog's affection for its owner is nothing more than a modification of the wolf's affinity for its pack members. If wolves had been loners with little interest in social affairs, dogs would behave more like cats.

The most important social unit in the life of a wolf is the pack. Unlike wild cats, wolves are not equipped to hunt and kill large prey alone. With the exception of the African lion and the cheetah, cats hunt by stealth, as suits a solitary animal, and bear sharp claws for clinging to large prey that must be killed unaided. Because wolves also tend to hunt large prey but attack only with their jaws, it helps a great deal to have more than one wolf in on the kill.

Individual wolves have a large repertoire of vocal

sounds and body language that they use in communicating with one another. As in the dog, a wagging tail is a sign of friendly intentions, and a tail tucked tightly between the legs a sign of submission. Wolves also display submission by lowering themselves before a dominant animal, much as dogs do. In intense displays of submission, they will even fall to the ground and roll over on their backs. Facial expressions also exhibit a wolf's internal, or emotional, state. Ears laid back tight to the skull, accompanied by curled lips that reveal the teeth, are a clear sign of an animal that may attack, quite possibly because it is frightened. A snarl accompanied by erect ears is a sign of an aggressive animal that feels dominant and uncowed, a dangerous combination. Gradations in facial color, with light patches inside the ears, around the eyes, and along the lips, highlight the wolf's

facial expressions. Wolves also bark, growl, whine, and howl—all elements in their ability to communicate, a critical skill for any social animal.

Packs generally comprise a mated pair and one or more generations of offspring. Not all offspring stay with their parents. Some ramble off to find mates and begin packs of their own. Those that stay with their parents generally do not breed. Usually only the lead wolves, which wolf biologists call the alpha male and the alpha female, reproduce. They also set the pattern for most of the pack's activities, such as when and where to hunt. For example, a Minnesota pack switched from killing livestock to killing deer when the alpha members were trapped and killed, presumably because the alpha animals alone preferred to hunt livestock.

Pack size is probably dependent, at least in part,

Because they are social animals, wolves have a complex system of communication. Here a submissive wolf bares its teeth in an inhibited snarl, which shows the dominant wolf that the other animal will not attack. The pricked ears of the wolf on the right are another sign of its social dominance. Black lips against a white muzzle and light hair inside the ears and around the eyes help to heighten the effect of facial expressions.

on the availability of food. The more food there is to go around, the larger a pack can be. The largest pack on record, observed in Alaska, included thirty-six wolves. Packs in most parts of North America are likely to contain fewer than a half-dozen animals. In the Southwest and Mexico, the southern extreme of wolf range, prey species such as deer and peccaries were widely scattered, so packs rarely numbered more than three or four animals. Presumably, wolf packs strike the right balance of having enough animals to bring down prey but not so many that each member cannot get the eight to ten pounds of food it needs per day. When food becomes scarce, the alpha pair's reproductive rate often decreases. Either pups do not survive to adulthood or the poorly nourished adults do not produce robust litters. Reproduction usually rises again when food supplies increase. Under natural conditions, this birth control mechanism helps keep wolves from overpopulating their range and overhunting their prey.

Pups are born in spring, usually in underground dens, which they leave when eight to ten weeks old. After they leave the den the pups generally stay at rendezvous sites where the older animals gather after hunting. When prey is killed the adults usually bring food back to the pups, though sometimes the pups are taken to the prey. The site of a kill may then become a new rendezvous site, the pups remaining there while the adults hunt new food. By autumn the pups are big enough to travel regularly with the pack.

Wolf packs mark out territories and defend them from other wolves. The territories are marked with scent posts, usually some vertical object such as a tree stump or rock upon which the wolves spray urine. Scent posts are particularly numerous in areas where two territories border one another. The scent posts warn other wolves that this is the edge of a territory and under normal circumstances work almost like a fence at keeping other wolves from trespassing. Scent posts are long-term indications of territoriality. Howls are short-term, an immediate response to territorial encroachment. Howling warns other wolves away without the need for a possibly dangerous encounter. Scent posts and howling help distribute wolves evenly over their habitat wherever suitable prey can be found. Howling serves other purposes as well, such as allowing dispersed pack members to locate one another.

Individuals one or two years old may leave their packs and become lone wolves. The departure of lone animals peaks in autumn and during the mating season in January. Lone wolves wander over an area several times larger than the territory of a pack. They appear to be searching for mates and vacant areas. If a lone wolf's search is successful, it establishes a territory and may begin a pack of its own. The distant travels of lone wolves help ensure that the animals do not breed with close relatives.

The wolf was one of North America's consummate predators. Wherever it lived, it fed on the largest mammals—deer, elk, moose, bison, musk

A pack of eastern timber wolves engage in group howling. Howling serves a number of purposes, such as helping disbursed pack members find one another and warning off wolves that are not members of the pack.

oxen, caribou. As their wide range in a world not yet subjugated by humans showed, they were a highly successful species. North American wolves may have numbered as many as 2 million animals the day Columbus made his landfall in the New World.

The European settlers who came in Columbus's wake brought with them their ancient prejudice against wolves. As they colonized the Eastern Seaboard they rapidly diminished the wolf's natural prey by overhunting and by destroying habitat to create farms. When the settlers herded cattle, sheep, and hogs into pastures carved from eastern woodlands, the wolves, ever adaptive, turned from feeding on deer and elk to killing livestock. The colonists responded with alacrity. In 1630, scarcely two decades after the founding of North America's first English settlement, Massachusetts Colony enacted the first bounty against wolves. It was followed quickly by a Virginia bounty in 1632. By the middle of the seventeenth century most colonies had bounties. Some paid Native Americans for any dead wolves brought in. Delaware in 1654 even *required* natives to kill two wolves yearly. Fifty years later, wolf hunting was considered an aristocratic pastime among the gentry of Virginia. Farther north, residents of Cape Cod took a more practical look at wolf control by pondering the wisdom of raising 500 pounds to build a wolf-proof board fence across the Cape just above Barnstable.

The killing of a female wolf in 1739 near Pomfret, Connecticut, a village some thirty-five miles northeast of Hartford, shows not only the resolve with which the colonists pursued the destruction of wolves but also the esteem that wolf hunting could bestow upon an individual who succeeds in bringing a marauding wolf to bay.

Apparently, this wolf had been killing livestock in the Pomfret area for several years, leaving behind a recognizable track because she had lost the toes of one foot while escaping from a steel trap. The stockmen had tried to hunt her down, but never got within gunshot. Then one night she allegedly killed seventy-five sheep and goats that belonged to Israel Putnam.

Putnam had only recently moved to Pomfret from Salem. Just twenty-one, he was still years away from becoming the Revolutionary War hero who would agitate for a break with England and command troops at Bunker Hill. After losing livestock to the she-wolf, he joined with five of his neighbors in a plan to destroy her. They agreed to work in teams of two, hunting her alternately so she could not rest.

They gave chase when a light snow revealed the wolf's tracks. She retreated to the Connecticut River, then turned back toward Pomfret. At ten o'clock the next morning, bloodhounds cornered her in a den about three miles from Putnam's house.

Putnam and others from the community gathered by the den. For twelve hours they worked to get at the wolf. They tried to smoke her out with burning sulfur, but she would not budge. They sent dogs in after her, but the dogs came out badly wounded and would not go back in. Finally, Putnam asked one of his slaves to go into the den and shoot the wolf, but the slave refused. So Putnam removed his coat and vest, lit a birch-bark torch, and himself entered the two-foot-square opening of the den. Around his feet he had tied a rope so his neighbors could pull him out at a given signal.

He had groped his way some twenty-five feet down the narrow, rocky passage that led to the den when he saw the wolf in the glow of his torch. As soon as she growled he kicked his feet. The people at the mouth of the den hauled him out so quickly that his shirt was pulled off over his head.

Once his clothes were rearranged, Putnam loaded a gun with nine buckshot and again descended into the den. When he met the wolf she growled and appeared ready to leap at him. He aimed the gun at her head and pulled the trigger. The explosion stunned him and the smoke choked him, and once again he was dragged out with the rope. When the smoke had cleared and he had recovered from the explosion he went back into the den. The wolf lay motionless before him. He touched the torch to her nose and when she did not move grabbed her by the ears. He then kicked at the rope once more and was pulled for the last time from the den, this time with the dead wolf in tow and the crowd cheering. Because of this exploit, Putnam was a colonial hero long before the Revolution. A song written about his execution of the wolf was widely sung by schoolchildren for years afterward.

By the close of the eighteenth century wolves had been exterminated in most of New England. By the mid-nineteenth century they were rare anywhere in the East, and by the end of the century even the most rugged and remote parts of the Adirondacks and the Alleghenies had seen the last of them. The main front in the struggle against the wolf was now entirely in the West.

End of the Road

Explorer David Thompson journeyed to the Great Plains in the late 1790s, saw the myriad bison, pronghorn, and elk, and wrote, "Civilization will no doubt extend over these low hills; they are well adapted for raising of cattle; and when the wolves are destroyed, also for sheep. . . ."

Something in excess of three-quarters of a million wolves may have roamed the plains at that time. The Lewis and Clark expedition on July 14, 1806, saw twenty-seven wolves around the carcass of a single buffalo on the Sun River in western Montana. Artist George Catlin, when he returned from travels in 1835 among the Mandan villages of the upper Missouri River in North Dakota, claimed that he saw wolves moving in groups of fifty and sixty. John

Bradbury traveled the same area in 1810 and wrote that "some of them were almost constantly in sight, and so fearless, as to stand at no great distance to gaze." In autumn, he wrote, wolves would follow as Indians hunted and eat the refuse the Indians left behind. John James Audubon, painting mammals in the 1840s near Fort Union, on the eastern border of North Dakota, wrote, "The number of tracks or rather paths made by the wolves from among and around the hills to that station [a trading post] are almost beyond credibility. . . ." Lansford Warren Hastings wrote in 1843 that in traveling through the West "you will pass many hundreds of them, during the day, which appear to evince no timidity, but with heads and tails down, in their natural crouching

This 1840s painting by John James Audubon shows a white wolf scavenging at a campsite. In the early nineteenth century, wolves often gathered around hunters skinning game, waiting for a chance at meat.

manner, they pass within a very few rods of you.'' Wolves were common in Iowa, Nebraska, Kansas, Oklahoma, Texas, New Mexico, and Arizona and throughout the Rocky Mountain states.

The wolves followed the vast herds of wild hoofed animals and fed on the young, old, and weak. They stayed so close to bison herds that hunters took their appearance as a sign that bison were near. Their dependence on the bison, like that of the Plains Indian, made them vulnerable should the herds disappear. The disappearance began not long after the Civil War.

Until then bison had crowded the Plains. A single herd might extend for twenty-five miles. From a promontory over the Plains, 300,000 bison might be visible in one view. Experienced hunters could spot a herd over the horizon, if the weather was right, by the cloud of vapor created by the animals as they breathed. Near Great Falls, Montana, Merriwether Lewis wrote that both sides of the Missouri ''were crouded with buffaloe I sincerely belief that there were not less than 10 thousand buffaloe within a circle of 2 miles arround that place.''

In 1869 in Promontory, Utah, the last stake was driven into the line of railroad track that joined St. Joseph, Missouri, with the Pacific Coast. The railroad divided the 50 million bison of the Plains into two great herds and made them easily accessible to hunters. Six years later, the southern herd had been nearly exterminated. The northern herd faced the completion of the Northern Pacific Railroad in 1881. By 1888, it too was nearly wiped out.

As the bison were hunted out, increasing numbers of cattle and sheep appeared on the prairies. The cattle grew fat on the native grasses, but they were hunted and killed by wolves for whom the distinction between an ailing bison and a domestic cow was marginal. The livestockmen fought back with guns, dogs, traps, and poisons. They would sometimes burn river-bottom woodlands in hope of destroying wolf refuges. Woods burning was still being done as late as 1928 in some parts of the West and at about that time was considered for use on Arkansas' Ouchita National Forest, where cattle were being grazed on public lands. Wolf hunting even became a profession, often providing income for buffalo hunters, who no longer had any game to pursue. One professional wolfer in 1886 killed 146 wolves in one season in Montana. Another Montana wolfer that same year worked for one week in Yellowstone County and killed nine wolves and twenty-six coyotes, netting himself $118.50. Ranchers even formed clubs for the hunting of wolves.

Concerted action against the wolf did not take shape until early in the twentieth century. It began in 1907 with a study by the Biological Survey, a forerunner of today's leading federal wildlife agency, the U.S. Fish and Wildlife Service. The Survey called for a consistent program against wolves and other predators and provided ranchers and other interested citizens with information on how to trap and poison the animals. The Forest Service at about this time began killing wolves on national forests.

It was not until 1915 that the first federal funds were appropriated for the killing of wolves by federal agents. The bill, which provided $125,000 for federal wolf control, limited the operation to federal lands, such as national forests. However, the annual appropriation increased over the years and so did the role played by the control agents. In 1931, the Animal Damage Control Act was passed. It ordered the Department of Agriculture to destroy or control wolves and a variety of other animals—including mountain lions, jackrabbits, and gophers—on public *and* private lands.

By 1931 the wolf was in eclipse in the lower forty-eight states. Most of the few wolves that remained were on national forests. Persistent government trapping and poisoning programs scoured away the last western wolves. Today perhaps 1,200 survive in parts of northern Minnesota where human numbers are sparse. This is the only viable wolf population left in the lower forty-eight states. Perhaps twenty to thirty wolves have established themselves in Wisconsin, but because their numbers are so low their future is tenuous.

In recent years a few wolves have ranged from Canada into northern Idaho and northwestern Montana and have even bred in Glacier National Park. They continue to range back and forth across the Canadian border. The last known Mexican gray wolves—the same subspecies that once populated the arid portions of Arizona, New Mexico, and west Texas—are living out their lives in zoo cages and research kennels. And yet, despite the wolf's tenuous existence south of the Canadian border, at no time in the past century have wolf enthusiasts had better cause for optimism than they do right now.

The Times They Are A'Changing

Something happened to our attitudes about wolves during the 1960s. The wolf began that decade as a varmint species, still unprotected in most states, still the explicit target of the federal Animal Damage Control Act. By the end of the decade the red wolf and some subspecies of the gray wolf were on a federal list of vanishing species compiled under the Endangered Species Act of 1966. The act offered no protections for the wolves, but it did put the animals on a path that led to protection in 1973 with passage of a more potent version of the law. For the first time in its history, the government was in the business of protecting wolves.

Although the 1973 law catapulted wildlife conservation into a new era, an end to the outright persecution of wolves had been in the making for quite some time. It began with a federal publication by Adolph Murie, *The Wolves of Mount McKinley.* Murie was the first modern biologist to study wolves in the field and to learn the intricacies of their behavior. He was sent by the National Park Service to Alaska's Mount McKinley National Park (now Mount Denali National Park) in April 1939 to determine the effect that wolf predation had on the park's hoofed species, particularly the Dall sheep. The study was initiated because wolves had increased throughout most of Alaska since the late 1920s, which was a cause for concern among wildlife biologists. At that time wildlife management was still in its infancy, and the complexities of the relationship

The Status of Wolves in Canada and Across the Globe

Humans have persecuted wolves virtually everywhere that the animals occur. Consequently, wolves were extirpated long ago in most settled areas, such as the lower United States and Europe. Canada, however, still provides the animals with areas remote from human development and, consequently, is home to thousands of wolves. Here is a brief survey of wolf populations in the Canadian provinces.

Quebec: Wolves are no longer found south of the St. Lawrence River, nor along the north side of the river where forests have been cut for farming. They still occupy about 90 percent of their original range in Quebec, however. They can be hunted year round, except in provincial parks and reserves, where hunting is limited to moose season. Wolf control is used in some areas where deer numbers have declined. Some 500 wolves are killed yearly in Quebec for the fur trade. Exact numbers are not known.

Ontario: Wolves occupy about 85 percent of their original range in Ontario

Canadian timber wolves looking sharply alert with pricked ears and intense stares. Canadian wolves have fared better than U.S. wolves, surviving in healthy numbers in the remote regions of most provinces.

and occur throughout uninterrupted forest. Numbers have declined in some areas as deer and other hoofed animals have declined because of changes in regrowing forests. Wolves are still controlled in some areas to protect livestock and deer. Numbers probably exceed 10,000.

Manitoba: Original densities have declined in settled areas, and the wolf is missing from large sections in the southern part of the province. The animals can be hunted and trapped only during limited seasons, and government control is used only in response to complaints of live-

between a predator and its prey were not understood. Many wildlife managers thought that hoofed species—called ungulates by biologists—such as wild sheep and deer should be protected from natural predators. On some wildlife refuges and national parks, wolves as well as mountain lions and other predators were killed whenever possible in the name of game protection. What Murie discovered at Mount McKinley National Park would be used by the National Park Service in deciding whether wolves should be permitted to survive there. His work also was bound to have far-reaching implications for wildlife management elsewhere.

Murie found that Dall sheep constituted about 25 percent of the wolves' prey. But, he concluded, the wolves killed primarily very young, very sick, and very old animals. He believed that such predation "would seem to benefit the species over a long period of time. . . . " Although the wolves probably did hold the sheep population in check during the study period, he wrote, "If we were assured that there would not now be any striking reduction in sheep numbers, the wolf-sheep relationship might be considered a satisfactory one, especially to anyone who has seen the ungulate over-populations and the over-grazed big game ranges in the States."

Murie also studied caribou and believed that under "natural conditions the caribou herds are no doubt adjusted to the presence and pressure of the wolf." Moose, he discovered, had increased in the park and adjacent region even in "the presence of a large wolf population."

Murie's account of wolves and their prey was reasoned, logical, and biologically sound. His report became a classic within the school of field biology. Nowhere did Murie express an overt concern that

---

stock depredation. An estimated 4,000 wolves live in Manitoba. About 400 wolf furs are sold yearly.

Saskatchewan: Wolves still occur over most of their original forested range. No control measures are taken for protection of hoofed game, but the provincial government does initiate control in response to livestock depredations. However, livestock losses to wolves are uncommon. Wolves are protected from trapping during the closed season on furbearers, but they are not protected from other types of hunting. They are protected year-round in national parks and in provincial parks during seasons when trapping is not allowed. No surveys have been taken to determine wolf numbers.

Alberta: Predator control caused major declines between 1880 and 1920 and between 1952 and 1956. Control currently is practiced only in response to livestock depredations, which are statistically rare. An estimated 5,000 wolves remain. Wolf hunting is permitted only during big-game seasons, from September to May.

British Columbia: During the first half of this century, wolf control nearly wiped out the wolves of Vancouver Island and caused serious declines in mainland populations. It is now protected as a big-game animal, which means that it may be killed only during established hunting seasons. It is completely protected in national and some provincial parks. Some 6,300 remain. Up to 450 furs are sold each year. Predator control agents record an annual kill of 50 to 200.

Yukon Territory: Wolf populations in this remote area have been poorly surveyed. Hunting pressures are slight, but local livestock owners have sometimes pushed successfully for predator-control programs. Probably fewer than 100 wolves are killed yearly by hunters.

Northwest Territories: Wolves occupy 100 percent of their original range, but population densities have fluctuated over the years with the intensity of predator control. Some government control measures were initiated to protect caribou and bison, though the bison program was dropped when human hunters failed to limit their own bison kill voluntarily. The provincial government still uses control programs in areas where declines in hoofed game occur because of the combined effects of hunting by humans and wolves.

Newfoundland and Labrador: Wolves were last seen in Newfoundland in 1911. During the early part of this century they were very rare in Labrador, but since 1950 they have become common throughout the province. Apparently the increase occurred because Labrador caribou have recovered from overhunting and moose have moved into the area. Labrador wolves are classified as furbearers and are protected during the breeding season. No predator-control programs are underway.

Global Wolves: Wolves occur in extremely low numbers in the northern portions of Finland, Norway, and Sweden, but in high numbers across the northern Soviet Union. Scattered populations survive in Europe, mostly in the more rugged mountain ranges—perhaps 200 each in Poland, Spain, and Italy. In Italy, some wolves live near rural towns, even feeding in village garbage dumps. They are so secretive that many human residents do not even know the wolves are there. The only signs the elusive creatures leave is a dappling of footprints in winter snow. Small, scattered populations of wolves survive in the Middle East and in parts of India and China.

wolves would wipe out their prey. He suggested, instead, that it "would not be surprising if, in the course of the little-understood population cycles, the Alaska wolf again declines." Future biologists would corroborate much of what Murie's two-and-a-half-year study suggested: that wolves may suppress prey populations already reduced by other factors, such as severe winters or overhunting by humans, but will not wipe out their prey base, and that wolf populations may fluctuate in response to prey numbers.

The soundness of Murie's research and the measured conclusions he drew from it opened the door for a new attitude about wolves. The new attitude entered slowly, but increasingly it became clear that the wolf was not a rapacious despoiler of wildlife, not a "beast of waste and desolation," as Theodore Roosevelt had labeled it. It was instead an integral part of its ecosystem and engaged in a complex relationship with its prey, a relationship whose complexities still elude the full illumination of modern science.

During the next twenty years attitudes about wolves slowly changed. Some states still paid bounties for wolves, and Alaska continued to fund a wolf-control program, but both scientific and public support for such activities began to ebb. By the early 1960s at least one national hunting magazine was suggesting within its pages that the wolves that survived in the Great Lakes region should be legally classified as game animals. This would have been quite an elevation in the wolf's status, since throughout U.S. history it has been treated as a varmint that could be hunted year-round without limit. Game animal status would have meant that limits and seasons would be put on wolf hunting, offering the animal protection from year-round slaying. Given that many hunters, particularly around the Great Lakes, were strongly anti-wolf because wolves prey upon deer, this was a remarkably progressive stand for a hunting magazine to take toward wolves.

Meanwhile, more developments were afoot in the field. In 1957 Purdue University entered a cooperative agreement with the National Park Service to conduct a study of the wolf and its prey on Isle Royale National Park, an island in Lake Superior. The director of the study was Purdue wildlife ecologist Durward Allen, who was formerly an assistant chief of the Fish and Wildlife Service's Branch of Wildlife Research and author of the classic wildlife management text, *Our Wildlife Legacy*. In autumn of that year, Allen discovered a senior wildlife student at Cornell University who he believed should conduct the fieldwork. The student was L. David Mech, a self-trained woodsman who had worked for two summers on a New York black bear study. He accepted the assignment. His observations on the behavior and ecology of the Isle Royale wolves were submitted as a doctoral dissertation in 1962 and published four years later by the federal government as *The Wolves of Isle Royale*. Now, some thirty years after Mech began his wolf study, he is still studying wolves in the Great Lakes area. He has become the dean of U.S. wolf biologists. In 1970 he published his first popular book, *The Wolf*, which he dedicated to Adolph Murie. *The Wolf* compiled much of the new data that Mech and others were discovering through their field studies and made it available to the general public.

Biologists were aided immeasurably in their work by the development of a new technology early in the 1960s. This was the radio collar. To use it, biologists would trap a study animal such as a wolf and fix the collar around its neck. The collar contained a radio transmitter that emitted a signal that the biologists could pick up on a receiver. By tuning in on the signal, biologists could locate the animal and follow its movements. This permitted field researchers to determine the extent and frequency of an animal's movements and taught them incidentally about pack size, what wolves eat, where they den, and other important behavior. By using a different frequency for each of several animals collared in a study, biologists could even identify which animal they were following. Radio telemetry equipment has become a mainstay of field biologists, and transmitters have become increasingly sophisticated. Some, implanted in an animal's body cavity, even transmit heart rate and body temperature. They are used on everything from songbirds to the largest land mammals.

The information gathered by Mech and other biologists helped introduce the wolf to a public increasingly interested in wildlife. The researchers showed conclusively that the wolf was an intelligent species with a complex social life. As more was learned, it became clear that the wolf's social structure might mirror that of early human hunting bands. Like early humans, wolves live in groups based on family relationships. The animals hunt cooperatively, too, as prehistoric peoples doubtless

David Mech, one of the nation's leading wolf biologists, at work on the high arctic.

did. Need for cooperation and the common effects of a predatory lifestyle suggest that in the wolf's behavior might lie clues to our own hidden past. A creature such as this was bound to draw an avid constituency as people became more fascinated by the natural world. Early in the 1970s a recording of the howls of wild wolves was sold for popular con-sumption, permitting people to bring wolves into their living rooms. The growing public interest in the wolf helped stimulate ambitious plans within the scientific community for comprehensive, and even experimental, wolf conservation programs. One of these plans came to fruition in 1988 at a national wildlife refuge in the heart of the Old South.

Red Wolf Reintroductions

The red wolf made its last stand in the wild in the marshes and swamps of southeastern Texas and southwestern Louisiana. In the early 1970s a survey of wild survivors indicated that they were heavily infected with disease and parasites and in danger of extinction because of cross breeding with coyotes. The fact that the wolves were breeding with coyotes was itself a bad sign, since different species normally do not interbreed. That the wolves were doing so suggested that their social structure had broken down as the animals became scarce, leaving coyotes the only available mates.

In 1973 the U.S. Fish and Wildlife Service (FWS) completed plans for a red wolf captive breed-ing program and set out to capture as many pure-bred red wolves as possible. Eventually forty animals were captured and taken to the Port Defiance Zoo in Takoma, Washington. Only seventeen of these ani-mals proved to be true red wolves. The first pups were born in the zoo in 1977.

In 1980 the red wolf was declared extinct in the wild. Meanwhile, the animals bred so well in cap-tivity that offspring eventually were sent to other zoos and breeding facilities around the nation. This

A U.S. Fish and Wildlife Service biologist collects data for a red wolf restoration project. About forty red wolves—the last known survivors of the species—were captured in the early 1970s. Their descendants have become part of the first successful wolf restoration plan.

helped ensure that a single catastrophe, such as a disease epidemic, would not wipe out all the red wolves.

The red wolves quite possibly might have survived indefinitely in captivity. But captivity is not truly a safe haven for a wild creature. The hardships of nature—the need to forage and to survive in the wild—are the things that create species. Individuals that cannot meet the tribulations of life in the wild are culled out, and the better-adapted individuals survive. Without natural pressures to shape them, the red wolf gradually would have become a different creature, perhaps better adapted to cages than to woodlands. Consequently, FWS moved quickly to build up a large captive population so that selected red wolves could be released into the wild.

In the early 1980s FWS proposed to release red wolves into the Land Between the Lakes, a remote mountainous area in western Kentucky and Tennessee administered by the Tennessee Valley Authority. The proposal soon ran aground. This happened in part because FWS kept a low profile on the reintroduction project by negotiating quietly with the various state and federal agencies involved in managing the Land Between the Lakes and its wildlife. FWS did this to avoid arousing local opposition. Unfortunately, the strategy backfired because it gave local residents the impression that FWS was trying to hide something. Hunters, particularly, were concerned that the wolves would prey on deer and that hunting would be curtailed to protect the wolf. Some wildlife conservation organizations also opposed the reintroduction plan because it called for killing all the coyotes within the reintroduction area to prevent crossbreeding. Finally, the Tennessee and Kentucky wildlife agencies bowed to opposition from several livestock groups and withdrew their support of the reintroduction. Faced with such opposition, FWS eventually felt forced to abandon the plan.

At the time, some FWS officials worried that the failure of the Land Between the Lakes plan would set a precedent that would doom not only red wolf reintroduction, but also reintroductions of other species in later years. But at about that time, events in North Carolina were creating conditions that would lead to successful red wolf reintroduction. The crucial development was the opening in 1984 of Alligator River National Wildlife Refuge, some 140,000 acres of southern woodlands donated to the federal government by Prudential Life Insurance Company. Red wolf biologists recognized the new refuge as the perfect place for red wolf releases. Alligator River had no coyotes and virtually no live-

stock, it was not heavily hunted, the area in which it was located was inhabited by no more than 1,200 people, and it was surrounded on three sides by water, making it easier to control the movement of the wolves into other areas. FWS judged it a potential release site and set out to rectify the error it had made at Land Between the Lakes. Rather than quietly negotiating the wolf reintroduction with other government agencies, FWS went completely public. Refuge personnel visited schools and attended meetings of civic groups to explain the plan. They appeared on radio and wrote newspaper articles. They made sure that local residents knew that no recreational activities would be curtailed by the presence of the wolf and that the wolf would present no danger to people or pets. The service also promised to capture and relocate any wolves that strayed off the refuge or appeared close to villages.

U.S. Fish and Wildlife Service biologists put a radio collar on a red wolf prior to releasing the animal on Alligator River National Wildlife Refuge. The first release of captive wolves on the refuge occurred in November 1986. The animals have since bred in the wild.

The result was phenomenal. The local community has openly embraced the wolf reintroduction plan. John Taylor, manager of the refuge, says that North Carolinians take pride in the fact that their state is the only place in the world in which red wolves exist in the wild. Local residents often serve as volunteers for the reintroduction program by entering data on computers, building live traps, helping to track released animals, and collecting road-killed animals to feed to captive wolves being acclimated to life in the wild.

The kickoff for wolf releases began in November 1986, when eight red wolves that had been raised in captivity as part of an FWS captive breeding program were shipped to Alligator River National Wildlife Refuge. There the four pairs were housed in large pens built in four widely separated areas in remote sections of the refuge, giving them a chance to acclimate to their new surroundings. Their diet was switched gradually from commercial dog food to wild game. Contact with humans was kept to a minimum. One side of each pen was lined with plywood so the wolves would not see who fed them. However, some indications of human contact were evident. Each animal wore a radio collar. Each also bore the signs of a small abdominal incision where a

harmless radioactive implant had been made. The radioactive material would show up in the animals' droppings, giving researchers a chance to determine which wolf left the dropping and what each wolf is eating.

On September 14, 1987, the door of one of the pens was left open, and the wolves slipped off into the woods. The red wolf thus became the first species to be reintroduced to native habitat after it had become extinct in the wild. About two weeks later the other three pairs were released.

By the end of the summer in 1988, ten red wolves had been released at Alligator River and about a dozen more were being held there in pens. A mated pair had also been released early that year onto Bulls Island in South Carolina's Cape Romain National Wildlife Refuge. The pair was part of a plan to raise pups in the wild in an effort to propagate better candidates for release. Two pups born in captivity on Bulls Island were released at three months of age. They grew into healthy juveniles and were captured six months later in 1988. Their experiences in the wild indicated that the propagation plan was a success, and the pups were released at Alligator River the following January.

Although two wolves were killed by automobiles and a few were lost to other causes such as infection and injuries caused by other wolves, the release program has exceeded expectations. Two pairs of released wolves reproduced, the first ones to do so in the wild in more than a decade, and the first in North Carolina, Taylor says, in perhaps two centuries.

The initial phase of the red wolf reintroduction program will continue until 1993. Until then, FWS will keep radio collars on every wolf, if possible.

After that date, the service, with the cooperation of the state wildlife agency, will evaluate the program and decide what the next step should be. Says Taylor, if everything goes well, perhaps within the next decade the people of North Carolina can be persuaded to let the red wolf population expand off the refuge.

The red wolf program has set an important precedent for wolf reintroductions. It may prove crucial to the success of wolf reintroductions in the West.

Modern Wolf Wars

Wolves have been missing from the West since at least 1976, when a private trapper hired by Arizona ranchers dispatched what some people believe was the last wolf of the Far West. This animal may have been a straggler that wandered in from a tiny population of gray wolves that still survived in Mexico. Or, as some biologists argue, it may not have been a wolf at all, but a misidentified coyote or a cross between a wolf and a dog that someone had owned

as a pet. Only a few years before, gray wolves whose ancestry was verified by biologists were trapped in the Texas border country. These few meager incidents marked the end of the western gray wolf. The animal had been a resident of the West for at least a million years, but it could not survive a century of modern human settlement.

The last gray wolves in the Southwest belonged to a subspecies popularly called the Mexican wolf.

A female Mexican gray wolf dashing across her enclosure at the Rio Grande Zoo in Albuquerque, New Mexico. This wolf is one of about two dozen held in captivity for breeding. The subspecies may be extinct in the wild.

opposite: *A female Mexican gray wolf. This subspecies once ranged from Mexico through Texas, Arizona, and New Mexico, but intensive predator control programs drove it to extinction in the United States. The only known survivors are being held in captivity by the U.S. Fish and Wildlife Service.*

After its extirpation in the United States, the animal clung to existence in Mexico. No one can testify with any certainty about the number that survived there, but it must have been a scant handful, no more than fifty or so. Consequently, the Mexican wolf was added to the endangered species list in 1976. Three years later FWS created the Mexican Wolf Recovery Team. Believing that the few survivors were too scattered to offer any hope that their number would grow, FWS decided to capture as many as possible for captive breeding. Six were captured, and four bred successfully. Today more than thirty are held in zoos in the United States and Mexico and at the Wild Canid Survival and Research Center, a private wolf conservation group headquartered outside St. Louis. The wolves could have produced even more pups, but the facilities at which they were kept did not have enough room for them, and so for two or three years breeding was stopped. More zoos are joining the program, however, so breeding should resume soon. The captive wolves are a promise that wolves may once again take a place among the fauna of the West. The Fish and Wildlife Service has asked the wildlife agencies of Texas, Arizona, and New Mexico to provide lists of potential release sites for the wolves.

The history of the wolf in the northern Rockies, particularly its recent history, is a little more complicated than that of the Mexican wolf. Northern Rockies wolves were listed as endangered in 1973. Predator control programs were thought to have wiped them out nearly fifty years before that, but in the 1970s wolves were occasionally reported in the northern Rockies by nonbiologists, and tracks re-

This Mexican gray wolf lives in the Rio Grande Zoo in Albuquerque, New Mexico, but its offspring may once again run wild. The U.S. Fish and Wildlife Service plans to release the wolves in the Southwest. However, opposition from ranchers in Texas, New Mexico, and Arizona has stifled the plan so far.

Scenes of Glacier National Park in Montana, where wolves have bred in recent years. The gray wolf was driven to extinction in Montana decades ago, but wolves from Canada have been crossing the border into the park since the early 1980s. Glacier provides the wolves with a good food base, including deer and elk, as well as protection from hunters.

sembling those of wolves were sometimes discovered in winter snow. In 1973, biologist Robert Ream of the University of Montana started collecting and analyzing reports of northern Rockies wolves under the auspices of the Wolf Ecology Project, a private organization he founded. Within the next six years he collected more than 400 reliable sightings.

But the real evidence came in 1979, when a researcher with the Wolf Ecology Project found that a female wolf snared and radio collared in southern British Columbia was ranging back and forth across the border. She was the first wolf to be scientifically documented in the northern Rockies in half a century. Researchers have continued monitoring wolf activity along the border. In 1986 and 1987 they found that a pack of at least twelve wolves was living and breeding in Glacier National Park. But the wolves proved transient. In 1988, no wolf activity was observed south of the border, but three wolf packs are living just north of the border.

Why wolves have begun moving into the United States is not known. Perhaps wolf population pressures in British Columbia are forcing them south. Perhaps they are simply seeking easier game. North of the border, they feed mainly on moose and beaver. In the United States they have access to more elk and deer, which are easier to kill than moose and provide more meat than a beaver.

The natural reappearance of breeding wolves in Montana shows that parts of the Rockies are still suitable wolf habitat, despite human encroachment. This lends hope to a reintroduction proposal outlined in the Fish and Wildlife Service's Northern Rocky Mountains Wolf Recovery Plan.

The proposal has designated three potential gray wolf recovery sites in the northern Rockies. One of these lies in northwestern Montana and centers on Glacier National Park and nearby federally designated wilderness areas. Wilderness areas are vast tracts of mountain and forest in which the building of roads or permanent structures is prohibited. They could prove particularly valuable to wolves because the lack of roads limits human access to the region. The northwestern Montana area seems to meet all of the wolf's needs, including a good prey base of elk and mule deer, secluded denning sites, and sufficient space for minimal exposure to people. The recovery plan calls for a cooperative effort with British Columbia to promote the migration of wolves into the Glacier area and for monitoring the wolves' status. British Columbia opened wolf hunting in

Wolf country along the Kootenai River, Idaho, one of the regions in the northern Rockies first entered by Canadian wolves coming into emptied wolf habitat in the United States.

1987 for the first time in several years. In response to U.S. complaints after some border wolves were killed, British Columbia closed one area to wolf hunting, but left open another area used by one of the three border packs. Wolf hunting in southern British Columbia could limit the migration of wolves into the Glacier area.

The second proposed site is in central Idaho and encompasses four federal wilderness areas. No wolf pack activity has been reported there in recent years. Like the Glacier area, this site is mountainous and features an adequate amount of prey, primarily elk and mule deer. FWS is hoping that wolves will travel into the area from British Columbia without human intervention. If they have not done so by the early

1990s, the service may consider a reintroduction plan.

The last site, and perhaps the most important because it offers the best prey base, is the Greater Yellowstone Ecosystem, which includes Yellowstone National Park and adjacent national forests and federally designated wilderness areas. Some 20,000 elk winter in the park, and the number swells to 35,000 in summer. Some biologists believe that this many elk threaten vegetation with overgrazing. The seriousness of this threat is still subject to debate among wildlife biologists, but no one doubts that the elk could serve as an important food source for wolves. Moreover, the wolf could be a factor in keeping the herd healthy by culling weak individuals. Not to have predation on the elk is ecologically unsound, says John Weaver, who resigned in 1988 as coordinator of the Forest Service's grizzly bear habitat program in order to study wolf and prey interrelationships in Canada's Jasper National Park. His work there should help in predicting how wolves might become integrated into the Yellowstone ecosystem if they are ever released there.

Weaver says that restoring the wolf to Yellowstone would put a missing piece of the region's fauna back into place. The wolf was a Yellowstone native. The earliest report of wolves there dates to 1836. Through a liberal use of traps and rifles, Yellowstone rangers wiped out the park's wolf packs more than half a century ago. No wolves are known to survive there today, making the wolf the only large native mammal missing from the park. However, the park is so far removed from Canadian wolf territory that the animal will get there only if individual wolves are transplanted. The Northern Rocky Mountain Wolf Recovery Plan calls for doing just that by capturing wolves, probably in western Alberta, and releasing them in Yellowstone. These wolves, Weaver believes, are good subjects for Yellowstone restoration because they are accustomed to preying upon elk, moose, and mule deer and to living in mountainous terrain. They also constitute the closest viable wolf population.

The Odds Against the Wolf

A survey conducted by a private firm for the New Mexico Department of Fish and Game indicates that nearly half of all voters favor reintroduction of wolves. National Park Service director William Penn Mott in 1988 came out in favor of wolf restoration. Visitors to Yellowstone National Park also show strong support, and experience elsewhere suggests that wolves would be popular in the park. Every Thursday in August, rangers in Ontario, Canada's, Algonquin National Park take visitors into the field to hear the calls of wild wolves. In recent years nearly a thousand people have gathered together each Thursday night to participate.

Yet for the moment, the restoration plan for Mexican gray wolves is unlikely to succeed. The New Mexico Game and Fish Department has been lukewarm on the subject. It suggested one potential wolf release site, the federal White Sands missile range, a 4,000-square-mile plot of relatively pristine habitat that would be ideal for wolves. But the military turned down the proposal for security reasons. Since then, New Mexico has offered little hope for the wolf. Said the wildlife agency's director, Bill Montoya, "I hate to be negative, but if the critter is going to get any chance at all, it has to be on a place like White Sands." Anywhere else, he says, the wolves will be killed as soon as they are released. "The people sure aren't going to help them one damn bit," he believes.

The Texas Parks and Wildlife Department has refused to cooperate with FWS in wolf reintroductions, as has the Montana Department of Fish, Wildlife, and Parks. The Wyoming congressional delegation opposes reintroduction. An article that appeared in the Wyoming Game and Fish Department publication, *Wyoming Wildlife*, in March 1988 under Senator Alan Simpson's name indicated that he believes wolf reintroduction will result in the decimation of game animals and serious inroads on livestock. Montana Representative Ron Marlene said in remarks to the U.S. House of Representatives that "the wolf is in fact a very vicious killing machine and needs to be controlled." He also has said that reintroducing wolves to the Rockies is like releasing cockroaches in your own attic.

The opposition of the congressional delegations is at least in part a response to the concerns of two politically powerful portions of their constituency—hunters and ranchers. Many hunters fear that wolves will decimate the game animals they hunt, such as deer and elk. Virtually any biologist will argue that this is unlikely. Studies have indicated that although wolves can slow or stop the growth of a prey population that has already been reduced by some other cause, they are unlikely to reduce healthy prey populations. As Murie suggested decades ago, herds held in check by wolves may include healthier individual animals than larger herds that are not subject to predation. Game populations in the northern release sites are big and healthy. The best site, Yellowstone, offers tens of thousands of elk in addition to thousands of deer and bison. The 100 to 200 wolves that would live there if restoration were successful would have limited effect on these herds.

Federal plans to restore Mexican gray wolves to the wild have garnered a lot of public support. Here a billboard erected by the Mexican Wolf Coalition in Albuquerque, New Mexico, warns of the wolf's plight.

Coue's deer, a Southwestern subspecies of the white-tailed deer, was a primary prey of the Mexican gray wolf. The Coue's deer is a small subspecies, and the wolves that hunted them were among the smallest North American gray wolf subspecies.

Ranchers are the most influential opponents of wolf reintroduction, since they are extremely powerful in western politics. Although some stockmen support the wolf, the majority do not. Much of the ranchers' antipathy for the wolf is based on the belief that wolves will kill livestock in vast quantities. This belief is founded on records from the late nineteenth and early twentieth centuries. In the Southwest, for example, the large losses of stock that ranchers blamed on wolves stimulated the extensive government control programs that wiped out the Mexican wolf.

Biologists who have studied livestock depredations by wolves and examined the historical record believe that the ranchers' concerns may be groundless. They suggest that the historical evidence may have been biased. Most of the early data on wolf

opposite: *A Coue's deer in New Mexico. Deer are swifter than wolves, which help make up for this disadvantage by hunting in cooperative groups.*

diet, which suggested that a high percentage of wolves fed upon livestock, was collected by government trappers. This data would be skewed because the trappers were working exclusively in areas where livestock depredations were being reported.

James Bednarz, a biologist at the University of New Mexico, in a paper he prepared for the Fish and Wildlife Service, cites other possible reasons for high livestock depredations at the turn of the century:

> (1) natural prey populations were probably decimated due to unregulated subsistence hunting . . . (2) cattle were overstocked on most rangelands . . . resulting in widespread mortality and the availability of carcasses for wolf scavenging, (3) intense harassment of wolves disrupted natural social units leading to a high proportion of lone wolves that probably relied more heavily on livestock for nourishment, (4) by working areas

where depredations were reported, trappers were more likely to find individual wolves inclined to take cattle, and (5) some coyote and probably dog kills were attributed to wolves.

Data collected in recent studies suggest that wolf depredations on livestock are rare. Alberta, which has some 5,000 wolves, averaged fifty-four incidents of livestock killed by wolves yearly from 1974 to 1980, about one incident per year for every ninety-three wolves. In British Columbia, losses to its 6,300 wolves accounted for about a tenth of 1 percent of all livestock. A similar figure was found in Minnesota, where some 1,200 wolves live year-round among farm livestock. If livestock depredations are this slight in areas holding 1,000 to 6,000 wolves, they should be much less in reintroduction areas that will never have more than 200. The percentage should be even slimmer in Montana because livestock there is not as concentrated as it is in Minnesota. Also, because of Montana's severe winter weather, for all but three months of the year cattle

A white-tailed buck deer crossing Avalanche Creek in Glacier National Park. The white-tail is one of the species that provides food for wolves coming into Glacier from Canada.

and sheep must be taken out of the more mountainous areas where wolves range.

Even if overall livestock losses to wolves are slight, they can be a burden to individual ranchers. "It's like being hit by a car," says Wain Evans, assistant director of the New Mexico Game and Fish Department. "Very few people get hit by cars. But if you're one of them, it's a pretty big deal." Consequently, the federal plans for wolf restoration have tried to address the ranchers' concerns. Release sites would be divided into three zones. Wolves would be protected from all human activity only in the core of each release site. In the zone outside the core, wolf recovery would be encouraged, but problem animals such as those that prey on livestock would be killed or sent to research centers. And outside that zone would be an area from which wolves would be removed on sight.

Minnesota is a model for how wolf depredations could be handled. When predators kill livestock there, farmers call a federal predator control agent, who examines the kill. If it is determined that wolves are responsible, the agent sets traps for the animals and removes the likely culprits. A precedent for doing this in the West has already been estab-

lished in Montana, where six wolves implicated in livestock killings were trapped and killed in 1988. Transplanted wolves would be designated as an experimental population under the Endangered Species Act. This designation would allow depredating animals to be removed.

The federal government and several conservation groups are also considering the development of a compensation plan for ranchers who lose livestock to wolves. This would be similar to compensation plans in Minnesota and Canada, which pay farmers fair market value for any livestock killed by wolves. Defenders of Wildlife, a conservation group based in Washington, DC, has already begun a compensation fund in Montana. However, one of the biggest obstacles to compensation plans originates in the local culture. Unlike Minnesota farmers, western ranchers are uneasy about reimbursement. Compensation payments smack of welfare, they say. As for controlling wolves, ranchers will do it themselves using the "shoot, shovel, and shut up" technique, which means they will kill wolves on the sly. Some opposition is also bureaucratic. Says New Mexico's Montoya, compensation could prove simply too expensive in a time of tight budgets.

The Endangered Species Act

The federal Endangered Species Act of 1973 is one of the most powerful wildlife-protection laws in the world. If the law were carefully observed and implemented, the United States would be a haven for vanishing species.

The 1973 law had two forerunners. The first was the Endangered Species Preservation Act of 1966, which listed rare and disappearing species but gave them no protection. This was tantamount to publishing a list of murder victims but doing nothing to stop homicide. It did authorize the Secretary of the Interior to acquire habitat critical to endangered species, but the law made manage-

ment of the land for the benefit of listed wildlife secondary to other considerations. For example, the presence of an endangered species would not have stopped the cutting of trees on national forest lands set aside for logging. The law did nothing to stop interstate commerce in endangered species and gave no protection to foreign species.

In 1969 an endangered species law was enacted that increased the amount of money available to the Secretary of the Interior for habitat acquisition. The law also banned the import of species threatened with worldwide extinction. Real protection did not begin, however, until enactment of the 1973 law. Under this law, U.S. citizens are prohibited from killing or capturing listed species or harming them in any way, for example by

destroying their habitat. It also forbids federal participation in projects that jeopardize listed species. The law also calls for designation and protection of habitat critical to listed species and requires that the federal agencies in charge of listed wildlife develop "recovery plans" for each species, outlining the measures to be taken to restore the species to non-endangered status.

Plants and animals are listed under the 1973 law as either endangered or threatened. "Endangered" means that the species is in danger of extinction throughout all or in a significant portion of its range. "Threatened" means that it is likely to become endangered in the foreseeable future. Endangered species receive stricter protection than do threatened species. For example, in spe-

Wolves in the Future

About two centuries ago, one of the nation's leading livestock breeders—George Washington—complained to the president of the Agricultural Society of Great Britain that sheep could not be raised in Virginia because wolves slaughtered them. The wolves, Washington concluded, must go. The Englishman, Arthur Young, responded, "Wolves are named as a motive for not raising sheep: surely they cannot be serious, who urge it. They abound all over Europe: in France and Spain, among the greatest flocks in the world, and no wolf could get into my sheep houses, or at least, I may say, nothing is so easy as to keep him out."

Those who have endorsed Young's view of wolves have been largely ignored over the past 200 years. But that situation seems to be changing. The interest that Yellowstone National Park visitors have expressed in seeing wolves restored to the park is a sign of a wider interest among people throughout the nation. This interest has been translated into strong support for the wolf and has helped increase the odds that restoration will take place. In mid-1988 conservationists thought little chance existed for wolf restoration, but thanks to public support a congressional bill was introduced in the summer of 1989 that called for full implementation of the Endangered Species Act in behalf of the wolf, a move that would pave the way for restoration.

The wolf's howl is a haunting sound on still nights. But it is so fragile a sound that it cannot be heard above a slight wind. It loses all of its effectiveness as a territorial warning. The concern of many wolf advocates is like a howl. Sometimes it can scarcely be heard above the uproar of the opposition. That will have to change if the wolf is ever to be reintroduced in the West. Conditions for reintroduction are better now than they have ever been, but the issue will be resolved in favor of the wolf only if strong and vocal advocates steer bureaucrats and elected officials in the direction of wolf reintroductions. Otherwise, the fate of the wolf will lie, as it has for centuries, in the hands of those who see in the animal nothing more than a beast of waste and desolation.

---

cial cases, threatened species may be hunted for sport, provided that the hunt is held for the benefit of the species, such as when a local population has increased to numbers that exceed the ability of its habitat to provide for it. Individual populations also may be listed. For example, the wolves in Montana are listed as endangered and those in Minnesota as threatened, while Alaskan wolves are not listed at all.

Anyone may propose a species for listing. When doing so, one needs to provide the appropriate federal agency with material supporting the need to list. The Fish and Wildlife Service (FWS) handles the listing of land animals, freshwater fish, and plants, while the National Marine Fisheries Service (NMFS) handles ocean species. Oddly enough, sea turtles are managed by NMFS when in the ocean, but by FWS when on land.

When a species is proposed for listing, the federal agency examines the evidence and then announces either that the species will be listed or that it has been turned down. Once the species is a candidate for listing, the agency holds public hearings and listens to arguments for and against listing. If the agency chooses to list, the plant or animal receives the protections of the Endangered Species Act.

Some 480 U.S. species and more than 500 foreign species have been listed. But thousands more await listing. During the Reagan administration budget cuts slowed the listing process. Some species became extinct while waiting for the process to grind along. This is still a problem, because the small number of personnel involved cannot handle the great number of proposed species. However, the rate of listing has increased in recent years, primarily because of congressional commitment to the act.

On the other hand, the protections of the law have sometimes been nullified by congressional amendments that exempt listed species from protection from individual projects. For example, Congress may amend the act to say that a dam project that will destroy an endangered species can be built because the law no longer applies to that particular dam. This not only has weakened the law, but has made many conservationists reluctant to press hard for strict endangered-species protection out of concern that Congress would undermine the act if it were enforced vigorously.

SHARKS

Based on the Audubon Television Special by
Stan Waterman and
Narrated by Peter Benchley

THE SHARK'S STORY begins about 450 million years ago in a world vastly different from the one we know today. On the land there were no trees or ferns or other leafy plants. In the seas swam strange fish with eel-like bodies covered with bony plates. Across the ocean floor scuttled scorpion-like creatures that grew up to nine feet long. Even the face of the land was different. The continents we know today would not begin to take shape for another 250 million years, and the only landmass lay in the region of the southern pole. All the rest was sea.

It was in this lost world that the sharks first appeared, some 200 million years before the dinosaurs came to life. The earliest sharks show some of the physical characteristics of sharks today—stiff triangular fins and tails with upper fins slightly longer than the lower ones. Well-preserved fossils show that at least one species fed on fish which it swallowed whole, presumably after a short chase. Thus it seems to have lived, 4 million centuries ago, much as many shark species do today.

The primitive sharks that dominated the ancient sea apparently went through an evolutionary phase about 250 million years ago during which they lived on the ocean bottom, feeding on mollusks, crustaceans, worms, and other bottom-dwelling animals. During this period, the shark's mouth came to be located on the underside of the head, making the animal more efficient at plucking its food from the sand. These sharks started to die out about 135 million years ago and were replaced by the ancestors of the modern sharks. However, the new forms and most of their descendants retained the new mouth position.

The sharks that exist today have long biological histories. The newest evolutionary development was the hammerhead, which appeared about 25 million years ago. The mako shark, its meat now sold in fish markets, has existed for perhaps 100 million years. The great white shark dates back at least 60 million years.

Probably few sea creatures are as readily recognized as the shark. It is familiar to anyone who watches television or goes to movies or reads books and magazines. The basic physical appearance of the great white shark—or of the mako, blue, or tiger shark—comes readily to most imaginations: the triangular dorsal fin cutting across the surface of the sea, the creature below gliding on outstretched pectoral fins, moving swiftly like a

*A basking shark, its face distorted for dramatic effect, on display at a carnival in
California in the 1880s.*

living torpedo, powered by languid movements of
its tail, graceful, agile, sinister. This is the shark of
legend and nightmare, the consummate predator
and eating machine of best-selling novels. It has
given the shark its reputation. And yet it is only a
part of the story. Half of the approximately 360
species of shark that ply the world's seas are less than
three feet in length, and more than 80 percent do
not reach six feet. Only 4 percent exceed twelve feet
and three of these species, such as the twenty-foot-
long basking shark, feed on plankton and are harmless to people.

The largest shark is the whale shark, first discovered by scientists in 1828. The longest accurately
measured whale shark was not quite forty feet long.
However, living specimens observed at sea have been
estimated at nearly sixty feet, a size unmatched by
any marine vertebrate except whales. For all its bulk,
the whale shark is harmless to humans. Like the
basking shark, it feeds by swimming through the
water with its mouth open, filtering out small animals and plants by passing the water through its gills
and swallowing the organisms trapped in its mouth.
Whale sharks also swim straight up through schools
of fish until their heads are out of the water, then sink
back down with their mouths open so that water and
fish rush in.

Megamouth, another large shark that feeds on
small creatures, was unknown to science until 1976,
when researchers on a Navy vessel sailing off Oahu,
Hawaii, hauled in their anchor and found one entangled in the anchor cables. It was about 15 feet
long and weighed nearly a ton. Its mouth was huge,
lined with thousands of tiny teeth, and surrounded

by rows of luminous organs that presumably attracted the small shrimp and other animals upon which the shark fed. Only two other megamouths have ever been found. One was captured in 1984 in a gill net off Catalina Island, California. The other washed up on a beach in Perth, Australia, in the summer of 1988.

Another peculiar type is the frilled shark. Up to six feet in length, it looks more like an eel than a shark. Its body is long and attenuated and its fins long and low. It lives in depths greater than 400 feet, and little is known about its behavior. Odder still are the bottom-dwelling sawsharks, in which the snout is shaped like a blade and edged with needle-sharp teeth. The snout also bears a pair of barbels—antenna-like feelers—which presumably help the shark locate prey such as small fish and squids by touch. The snout itself probably is used to slash the prey.

Some types of shark belong in the realm of the grotesque. One is the wobbegong, with a body shaped like a club—bulbous at the fore end and tapering toward the tail. Its mouth is fringed with barbels, and it lives on sandy bottoms and on rocky and coral reefs, walking along on its pectoral fins as it searches for crabs, octopuses, and lobsters to eat.

Another grotesque species is the angelshark, with its body flattened and spatulate, its fins arranged around it like a border of pendulous lobes, and its eyes on the top of its head. It spends its days buried in sandy or muddy bottoms as much as 4,500 feet deep. More grotesque still is the goblin shark, which one author labeled "perhaps remarkable for being the ugliest of living sharks. . . . " Its long, dagger-like snout protrudes from its head like a unicorn's horn, and below the snout are jaws that resemble a parrot's beak. The jaws can be protruded and are armed with needle-like teeth. It, too, is a bottom-dweller.

One of the smallest sharks is the cigar or cookiecutter shark, which grows to nine or ten inches. It is a deep-water species that glows in the dark. Apparently it uses its luminescence to attract potential predators such as marlin, larger sharks, or whales. When it locates one of these larger animals, it turns the table, attaching itself by means of its large sucking lips to the body of the bigger predator. It then uses its sharp, buzz-saw dentition to cut a chunk of flesh out of its prey before swimming away. It is, in effect, a parasitic species, since it does not kill the animals upon which it feeds. Another species, the largetooth cookiecutter, grows to nearly

Megalodon: A Creature from the Past

Carcharodon megalodon was one of the most formidable animals that ever swam the seas. Known primarily through the thousands of massive, finely serrated triangular teeth it left behind, this shark was once thought to have grown in excess of sixty feet in length. Paleontologists based this estimate on the relative size of its teeth compared to those of living great white sharks, which rarely exceed twenty feet. A reassessment based on new fossil specimens and a better understanding of the relationship between tooth size and body length suggests that megalodon probably did not exceed forty feet in length, still nearly twice the size of the

This most recent reconstruction of megalodon jaws has reduced their size from older estimates, but nevertheless has left them formidable.

biggest great white. Its teeth could grow to more than seven inches long and lined jaws big enough to contain at least half a dozen people at once.

Megalodon vanished from the seas at least 50,000 years ago. It was not an evolutionary ancestor of the great white—which dates back some 60 million years—but the two species are close relatives. Megalodon and the great white both belong to a group of large, razor-toothed sharks that first appear in the fossil record at about the time the dinosaurs disappeared and mammals became prominent. Some paleontologists think the large sharks evolved to feed on big marine mammals. Fossil evidence supports this idea. Large numbers of fossil teeth from big sharks are found wherever the fossil bones of ancient marine mammals occur, and some of the bones bear gashes from shark teeth.

A Gallery of Sharks

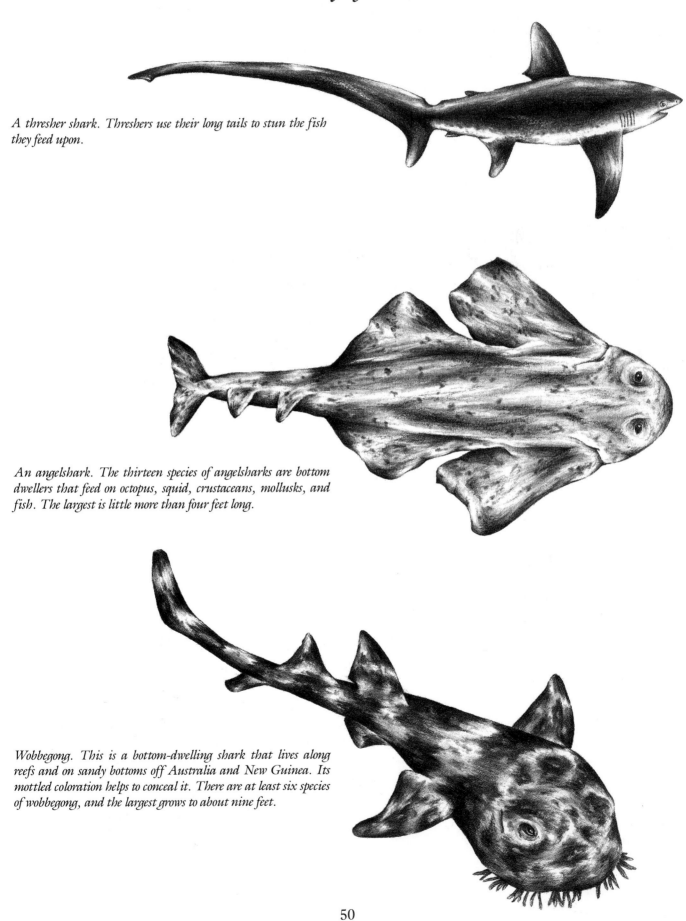

A thresher shark. Threshers use their long tails to stun the fish they feed upon.

An angelshark. The thirteen species of angelsharks are bottom dwellers that feed on octopus, squid, crustaceans, mollusks, and fish. The largest is little more than four feet long.

Wobbegong. This is a bottom-dwelling shark that lives along reefs and on sandy bottoms off Australia and New Guinea. Its mottled coloration helps to conceal it. There are at least six species of wobbegong, and the largest grows to about nine feet.

A goblin shark. The long snout and extendable jaws give this ten-foot-long shark its name. A bottom dweller, it lives on the continental shelf and outer slopes at depths in excess of 2,000 feet.

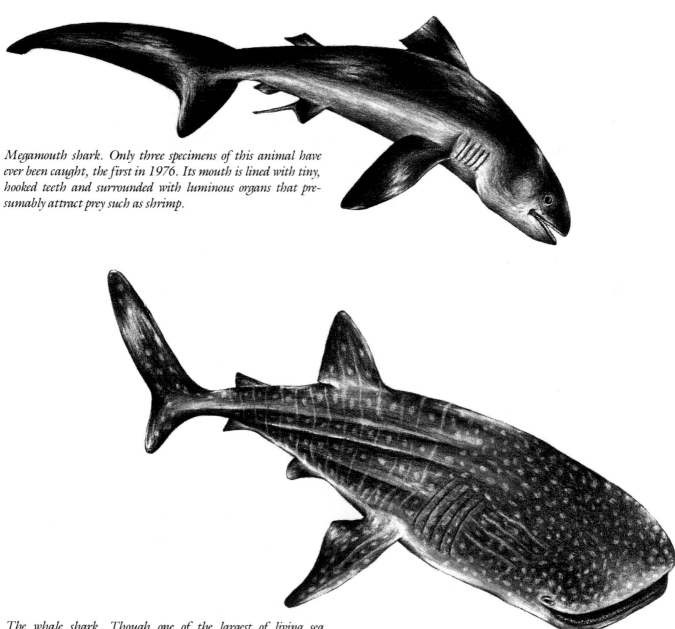

Megamouth shark. Only three specimens of this animal have ever been caught, the first in 1976. Its mouth is lined with tiny, hooked teeth and surrounded with luminous organs that presumably attract prey such as shrimp.

The whale shark. Though one of the largest of living sea creatures, the whale shark is harmless if left alone. It feeds on small crustaceans, algae, and fish.

A basking shark swimming with mouth open to engulf the small fish and crustaceans upon which it feeds. Because it does not prey upon large animals, it is not, despite appearances, dangerous to people.

eighteen inches. Its teeth, relative to body size, are the largest of any shark species, twice the relative size of the teeth of the great white.

The smallest shark is the pygmy ribbontail cat-shark, which grows to about six inches long. It lives in the western North Atlantic and in the west Pacific at depths of 150 to 2,300 feet. Its small body appears slender and lithe. It feeds on small fish, crustaceans, and mollusks.

Unfortunately, little is known about the be-havior of these various sharks. Creatures that live their lives entirely in the sea are difficult to study, and they keep their secrets to themselves. For many species lifespan is unknown, diet is barely understood, and the animals' travels, distribution, and reproduction remain largely unexplored. Perhaps it is this lack of knowledge that makes it difficult for science to dispell the many myths about sharks, to lay to rest the sinister image of the shark as the perfect eating machine.

The Anatomy of a Sea Predator

Sharks differ from bony fish to about the same extent that birds differ from mammals. Fish have air bladders that they inflate and deflate to alter their bouyancy. Sharks lack air bladders, but their oil-rich livers serve much the same function. Most fish have bony skeletons. The shark skeleton is primarily cartilage and consists of a skull and a vertebral column or spine, with pelvic and pectoral girdles and fin supports. The vertebral columns of some sharks are calcified, making them stronger. Sharks have no ribs,

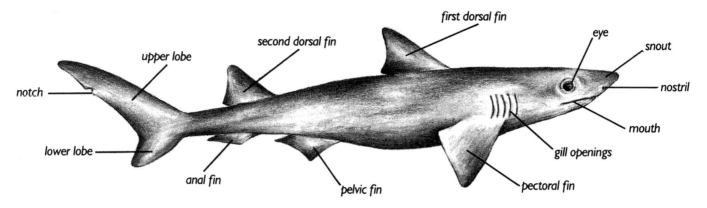

Anatomy of a shark.

so their muscles are often attached directly to the skin. Tiny calcified beads underlie the skin of some sharks, strengthening the support of the muscles.

The skins of fish are covered with scales. Sharks have no true scales. Their tough skin bristles with dermal denticles. *Dermal denticle* can be loosely rendered as "skin teeth," and in fact the tiny, pointed denticles that give sharkskin its rough surface are made of the same materials as shark teeth and grow in the same way. Like teeth, each denticle has a basal plate or root that lies under the skin surface and is capped by an enamel-like crown or spine. The denticles of fast, open-water sharks tend to be smaller than those of bottom-dwelling species and may help reduce the friction between the shark's skin and the water as the shark swims. Some species lack the abrasive spines, however.

The fins of fish usually are webbings of thin tissue strung across a series of rays or spines. The shark's fins are rigid, fleshy, and thick. In most fish, the upper tail fin is roughly equal in length to the lower. In sharks, the upper fin is usually longer.

In fish, the gills are usually covered by a bony protective shield called the operculum, whereas in sharks the gills are covered with flaps of skin. Fish lack eyelids; some sharks have a transparent membrane that can be closed over the eye.

Sharks also differ dramatically from fish in their reproductive methods. On their pelvic fins, male sharks have paired claspers, longer slender lobes that are inserted during mating into the female's cloaca, a single opening for the reproductive, urinary, and intestinal tracts. Only one clasper is used at a time to transfer sperm mixed with sea water down a groove in the clasper and into the female. Fertilization is thus internal. This contrasts with fertilization in most bony fish, in which females lay their eggs and males spray semen into the water over the eggs.

Female sharks of some species keep the semen in their bodies for many months before it is used. The eggs are fertilized when they pass the semen storage sacks while moving from the ovary down the female's reproductive tract through the organs that build the eggshell.

Shark eggs are usually laid in pairs and come in a variety of shapes. Some are rectangular cases with projections that grow like tendrils from two or more corners and help entangle the eggs in seaweed after they are laid. Others are spiral shaped and, laid on the sea bottom, bore into the sand when waves move them.

Not all sharks lay their eggs. Some hatch the eggs within their bodies, and the young are born live. Some sharks give birth to as few as two young, and a few, such as the tiger, may give birth to up to eighty. Most, however, produce fewer than ten young at a time.

Perhaps most fascinating of all, in some sharks that lack eggs the embryos develop a placental attachment to the mother, drawing nourishment from her body. Sharks developed the placental connection tens of millions of years before it appeared in mammals, the only other animals to establish such contact between mother and offspring.

Sharks live in a sensory world that we can never share and they perceive things we will never know. Their hearing is designed particularly for perception of low-frequency sounds, such as those made by a struggling fish. Sharks can tell the direction from which underwater sounds are coming, something submerged humans cannot do, and probably can hear sounds that originate as far as two miles away.

Jaws

About twenty-three years ago, Gordon Hubbell was wading with a friend in the waters near his home in Key Biscayne, Florida, when a baby lemon shark about three feet long came cruising into view. When Hubbell pointed out the shark, his friend vaulted without hesitation into their boat. For Hubbell, who is the veterinarian of Miami's Metro Zoo, the experience had a much different effect. It stimulated an interest in shark fishing, which in turn led Hubbell to start preserving the jaws of the sharks he caught. Not long after he had gotten into the habit of shark-jaw preservation, he adopted a friend's suggestion that he begin a collection of fossil teeth as well. In a short time, Hubbell amassed a number of fossil great white shark teeth. He noticed that the fossil teeth showed a great deal of variation, as if the species had not yet stabilized into its modern form. This led

Hubbell to start collecting the jaws of modern great white sharks. In pursuit of great-white dentition, he journeyed to Australia and traveled along the south coast, making contact with residents who still supply him with jaws.

Eventually, Hubbell's collection was so big that he had to add on to his house an entire room of roughly 450 square feet so he could store and display his shark artifacts. Teeth and jaws, both fossil and modern, are displayed in lighted cases with glass covers. Most of the fossil materials are labeled with information on species, where found, and how old. Hubbell now owns some fifty great white shark jaws. About eight years ago, he says, he had about twice that number, but he has traded some of them for fossil materials. He has about 50,000 teeth, fossil and modern. At one time he had close to 100,000.

Hubbell gets his jaws from importers. They arrive packed in salt from nations that fish sharks for food. He also

gets jaws locally. Restoring the jaws is no easy task, since they are made of cartilage, not bone, and each jaw bears several rows of teeth. Hubbell removes all the teeth in large specimens. He is careful about measuring the space between each tooth row and labels each tooth so he knows where it belongs in the jaw. After removing the teeth, he cleans the cartilaginous jaw, bleaches it, and dries it completely. He then glues each tooth—sometimes hundreds per jaw—back into place. He sells jaws mostly to museums, though he has also made sales to individual collectors. A medium-sized jaw is priced at about $2,300.

The biggest of Hubbell's great white shark jaws came from an animal caught off California that measured 18 feet 5¾ inches long. Its jaws, about 38 inches across and 30 inches high, are larger than those from another great white that measured 19 feet 6 inches long and which hang on Hubbell's wall beside the larger set.

Sharks possess a system for detecting vibrations in the water other than sound vibrations. This is the lateral line, a channel of nerve receptors that lies in loops around the top and sides of the head and in a line that stretches along the sides of the body and upper fin of the tail. When vibrations in the water, such as from a splashing fish, reach the cells of the lateral line, the cells send messages to the brain that tell the shark both the direction from which the vibrations came and the magnitude of the vibrations. During periods of violent movement, nerve impulses from the brain shut down the lateral line, presumably to prevent an overload of the receptors.

Sharks have a keen sense of smell. Sea water flows constantly over sensory pits on the shark's snout, where scent sacs enable the shark to smell extremely low levels of dissolved chemicals. Some sharks can detect traces as small as one part blood in a million parts water. Researchers have found that when a lemon shark first detects an attractive odor, its gills quickly take an extra beat, then momentarily shut down, clamping tightly against the body. This is thought to help streamline the body during the first few seconds of a chase.

The eyesight of predatory sharks is probably quite good. The eyes of sharks are lined with a reflecting layer that lies just behind the retina and reflects up to 90 percent of some colors of light into the receptor cells of the eye. The reflecting layer, or tapetum, causes the eyes of some sharks to glow an emerald green when a light is shined in them, much as the eyes of some mammals glow in light. Some species can darken the tapetum to reduce reflection in bright light. At least one species can see colors. The largest eyes relative to body size occur in the bigeye thresher shark, which lives in deep water where it hunts for fish and squid. The eyes may be as much as a fifth the size of the head and are directed upward, presumably so the shark can see prey silhouetted in the illuminated water above. Threshers are also unusual because their upper tail fins are nearly as long as their bodies and are used to strike and stun prey.

In addition to using sight, sound, and smell, sharks can detect weak electrical and magnetic fields. The receptors for these stimuli lie in a network over the shark's head and are called the ampullae of Lorenzini. It is possible that sharks can sense the Earth's electromagnetic field and use it to navigate. Experiments with wild dogfish, blue, and swell

The biggest teeth belonged to a megalodon shark, a giant, extinct shark that was even bigger than the great white, growing up to forty feet long. The largest megalodon tooth in Hubbell's possession measures 6¾ inches long, compared to the largest great white at 2⅝ inches.

About 100 species are represented in the collection. One of the finest specimens came not from a modern great white, but from a shark that lived about 5 million years ago. It is a nearly complete fossil white shark skull that Hubbell found south of Lima, Peru, near the town of Secauco. The ancient jaws lay in sediment about a quarter mile from the ocean. The jaws sit now in Hubbell's shark room, where he is slowly extracting them from the rock matrix in which they have been embedded for millennia upon millennia.

Gordon Hubbell and a small portion of his collection of shark jaws and teeth. The jaws came from great white sharks nearly twenty feet long. The teeth in the cases are all fossils.

sharks have shown that these species use the electrical sense to locate prey. They apparently can perceive the electrical impulses created by the beating of a fish's heart, even if the fish is buried under sand. Electrical perception is very limited, however. Sharks apparently cannot detect the electrical impulses generated by a human body beyond a distance of six feet.

All of these senses may be brought into play by a hunting shark. It may locate prey by hearing, track it by odor, and home in by sight and electrical sensing. It may brush against potential prey to get the feel of it, or take a sample bite for a taste test.

Sharks probably are not mere pawns moved about by the whim of their senses. Their brains are relatively large. A single lobe of a shark's brain is at least as big as the entire brain of a bony fish the same size. In fact, the brain to body ratios of some sharks are the same as those for some mammals and birds. Sharks may, therefore, possess some elementary form of intelligence. In captivity they have been trained to perform simple tasks, such as retrieving plastic hoops, that they learn about as quickly as would a rabbit or house cat. Some researchers have suggested that behavioral differences between adult and young sharks—the younger animals tend to be more unpredictable and aggressive—may reflect learning on the part of the older animals. Unfortunately, human understanding of shark behavior and motivation is still rudimentary. However, a number of dedicated biologists are attempting to plumb the mysteries of the sharks.

Biologists and Behavior

In his *Historia Animalium*, written more than three centuries before the birth of Christ, Aristotle attempted to classify all animals and discussed their origins and reproduction. Among the species included was the spiny dogfish, one of the smaller sharks. Aristotle described its reproductive system in recognizable detail and established that the spiny dogfish gave birth to live young.

Sonny Gruber, with the aid of his assistants, injects an adult lemon shark with a chemical that will allow researchers to study the animal's growth. Gruber's work has revealed new information on lemon sharks and indicated possible threats to the animals from people.

Though Aristotle is thought of in zoological circles as the father of biology, the natural sciences did not really come of age until the nineteenth century. As European nations established empires that stretched all over the globe, European naturalists were able to collect and classify animals with unprecedented vigor. One result was an extensive description and classification of the sharks, published in Germany in 1841. Despite this early effort, shark taxonomy has not been completely resolved even to this day, and many species have not yet been definitively classified. However, a recent revision of shark taxonomy by Leonard Compagno has helped clarify many shark relationships. His system was used to provide readers of this book with a list, in the appendix, of the scientific names for the sharks mentioned in this chapter.

Shark research is still in its infancy, and investigations into shark behavior have barely scratched the surface, providing little hints of things vastly interesting and mysterious in the world of sharks. One of the leaders in the field of shark research is Samuel "Sonny" Gruber, a marine sciences professor at the University of Miami's Rosenstiel School of Marine and Atmospheric Sciences. "Sharks are," he says, "more incredible than you know, more incredible than anyone can ever conceive of."

Bearded and slightly built, Gruber traces his professional interest in sharks to a day in 1958 when he went spearfishing in about thirty feet of water off Miami, Florida. He had speared several fish, and blood was in the water, when a hammerhead shark nearly fourteen feet long eased into view. "I pressed myself against the reef and drew my legs in toward my chest," Gruber wrote later. "I could hear my heart pounding and sensed the metallic taste of fear in my mouth. Although I expected to be attacked at any second, I was nevertheless struck by the grace and beauty of this great fish. It moved easily, almost lazily, through the water. I couldn't take my eyes off of it. Finally, the shark swam past me, about 5 feet from the end of my outstretched speargun, and disappeared into the blue.''

As a result of that encounter, Gruber left the premedical program at Emory University in Atlanta, Georgia, earned a degree in zoology, and went on to graduate studies on shark biology at the Rosenstiel School.

Thirty years later, Gruber is still pursuing his shark research in the azure waters off Florida. Much of his work is conducted in the shallow flats around Bimini, sixty miles east of Miami. The focus of his work is the lemon shark.

The lemon shark is a tropical species that seeks water warmer than 70 degrees Fahrenheit. Adults usually exceed eight feet in length. Gruber chose to study lemon sharks because they are large and abundant and the young adapt well to captivity, permitting him to conduct laboratory experiments.

Through his work, he hopes to elucidate the role a tropical marine predator plays in preserving the integrity of a lagoon ecosystem and to collect data that will lead to sound management and protection of lemon sharks.

Much of Gruber's work involves capturing, tagging, and releasing sharks. The tags are waterproof plastic cylinders that bear inscriptions identifying the individual shark and asking anyone catching it to return the tag to Gruber. The tag is attached by a six-inch-long piece of 200-pound-test line to a small, barbed stainless steel plate shaped like an arrowhead. When Gruber catches a shark, usually in a net, he makes a small incision just below its dorsal fin and inserts the arrowhead. He puts a second tag into the shark's body cavity via an incision he makes just behind the pectoral fin. The incisions heal quickly and become invisible within four days. Sharks, which usually bite each other while mating, do more

A passing motorboat sends an eruption of waves through the mangroves that grow off the Florida Keys. An increase in boating activity and damage to mangroves by recreational visitors are destroying trees whose root systems provide young sharks with vital shelter.

Biologists pursue a lemon shark in the waters around Bimini in an attempt to capture and tag the animal. Tag-and-release studies are providing the first reliable data on shark movements and habitat use.

damage to themselves during the breeding season than Gruber does with his tags.

Gruber also has tagged some sharks with ultrasonic transmitters that broadcast a recognizable signal. He is thus able to follow the sharks as they move in the waters of Bimini. He has observed sharks by following them in an ultralight aircraft, a flimsy vehicle in which the pilot sits fully exposed in a framework of sailcloth wings and tail that resembles a giant box kite. The ultralight plane permits him to fly more slowly, lower, and more cheaply than would a small conventional plane. He also has taken sharks into captivity for studies of eyesight and digestion.

Some of what Gruber has learned debunks the myth of the shark as eating machine. Eighty percent of the lemon shark's food is fish. The rest includes shrimp, crabs, octopuses, rays, and even a little seaweed, though Gruber thinks the seaweed he has found in shark stomachs may have entered via devoured fish. The young sharks digest their food at about a third the rate of a bony fish their size and—far from being continually on the prowl for food—tend to eat in four-day cycles. Even the quantities they eat are relatively small, the equivalent of only 2 percent of their body weight daily. This is about half of what a tuna would eat.

Gruber has also found that sharks may not be the solitary marauders they often are thought to be. Adults, though less social than juveniles, often move in small groups. At sunrise they swim away from the lagoon and onto the ocean reefs, returning to the lagoon and harbor at sunset. Lemon sharks also seem to associate with other fish, such as jacks, mackerel, barracuda, and nurse sharks. Gruber believes that the sharks are using the other fish as an extension of their own sensory skills. The smaller fish are more numerous and spread out more widely over the lagoon. When they find something that excites them, their movements send vibrations through the water and attract the sharks. Indeed, Gruber has found that if he floats motionless underwater, he is investigated first by these fish, and then by sharks.

During May and June, pregnant lemon sharks move into waters less than three feet deep at high tide and give birth to ten to twelve pups. For at least their first year or two, the pups are confined to the shallow waters of the mangrove stands. They feed there on the minnows, needlefish, grunts, snappers, and other small fish that circulate among the submerged roots of the mangrove trees. Young sharks also shelter beneath the roots. The young grow slowly. At birth they are about twenty-four inches long; at the end of the year about twenty-nine inches. Four out of ten lemon shark pups die during the first year, and most of the survivors eventually succumb to larger sharks.

Young sharks usually range over less than an acre of the lagoon. As they age they gradually expand their horizons. When five years old they may begin to leave the lagoon to feed on the deep reefs beyond it. When mature at the age of twelve to fifteen, they leave the lagoon entirely and travel as far as New Jersey and Brazil. At certain times the males go north and the females south, but the purpose of their travels is still unknown. The adults are all but lost to science until they return to Bimini in May, which is when Gruber begins to capture females with fresh scars caused by other sharks. This is evidence of mating, since males grasp females with their teeth and hold them while breeding. Young are born

*Biologist Jack Casey measuring a reef shark (*Carcharhinus perezi*) on board a National Marine Fisheries Service vessel.*

live a year after mating. During gestation, the embryos are nourished first by the yolk of the egg and then by a placental attachment to the mother.

Gruber has discovered that females breed only once every two years. The average mating thus results in only five young per year, or 2.5 young per parent. This is an extremely low rate of reproduction compared to that of a large marine fish such as the tarpon, which may lay as many as 100 million eggs at a time. The young sharks will not begin to replace themselves for more than a decade. The slow rate of reproduction and of maturation means that lemon shark survival is based on a relatively low rate of mortality. If anything should increase its death rate above a very low level, the lemon shark will in all probability quickly disappear.

Gruber often puts not only his own tags on sharks, but also those of another biologist, John Casey. Casey works for the National Marine Fisheries Service as chief of Apex Predators Investigation, headquartered in Narragansett, Rhode Island. Casey was introduced to shark work in 1961 after a bather at Sea Girt, New Jersey, was slashed by a shark. Commercial fishermen in the area, fearing that the dead fish, blood, and other byproducts of their work were attracting sharks, loaned one of their boats to the Sandy Hook Marine Lab so that researchers there could look into the shark question.

Casey was one of the researchers, and he was assigned to find out what types of sharks were working the fishing grounds. He set out to catch a sample of sharks on long lines, which are a series of baited hooks attached by wires to a single long line that lies along the ocean bottom. Casey set his lines every twenty miles from the eastern end of Long Island all the way down the New Jersey shore, more than two hundred miles. His catch was a real shocker even to the trained biologist. He brought in some 300 sharks, including great whites and 800-pound tiger sharks, both dangerous species. When the news reached the general public, the response was even more of a surprise. Sportfishermen were reportedly thrilled at the prospect of a new quarry to pursue.

Casey quickly integrated the sportfishermen into his research, building a relationship that continues to this day. He supplies the fishermen with tags that they use to mark the sharks they catch and release. They also help Casey recover tags. Similar tagging studies are conducted in Australia, Canada, Great Britain, Greenland, Ireland, Norway, South Africa, and South America, but Casey's is the biggest. More than 4,000 volunteers, mostly sportfishermen, are helping him collect data. During his first quarter-century of work, Casey and his volunteers tagged nearly 80,000 sharks of forty-three species. About 2,900 of them, representing thirty species, were recaptured by fishermen from thirty-four countries.

Casey's work may prove critical to efforts to manage the sport and commercial take of sharks, which totals some 100 million sharks yearly. His data indicate that many species cannot be completely protected by national regulations because they range widely. Blue sharks that Casey has tagged off New York have traveled as far as Europe, Africa, and South America. Thus, European fishermen who kill blue sharks are drawing upon the same population that is hunted off New Jersey, making it difficult for any one nation to take unilateral measures that will effectively protect sharks from overfishing. A similar situation exists for other species. Sandbar sharks move between the United States, Cuba, and Mexico. Night, blacktip, tiger, bigeye thresher, sandbar, and dusky sharks all travel between North America and the West Indies.

In addition to providing new data on shark distribution, tagging studies are also providing information on shark longevity. Apparently, as might be expected of an animal that breeds and matures slowly, sharks are long lived. Individual Australian school sharks have carried tags for more than thirty years, indicating that they may live as long as fifty years. A spiny dogfish was recaptured after twenty years, and a Greenland shark after sixteen.

Although shark movements and distribution are slowly being revealed by tagging studies, little work has been done on shark behavior. The obstacles to behavioral studies are great, since many sharks range widely and move swiftly. But the few studies being done on specific aspects of shark behavior have yielded some fascinating discoveries.

Most higher animals, in order to interact efficiently, have a system of signals with which they communicate their intentions to one another. Humans, for example, use not only spoken words but also a complex array of vocal tones, body postures, and facial expressions. Human communication depends so much on facial expression that humans tend to seek signs of feeling and emotion even in the faces of nonhuman animals. This works well with expressive creatures such as dogs, cats, and monkeys. However, few nonmammalian species have developed the facial flexibility and musculature needed for this type of communication. This is one reason that people find sharks and other facially immobile animals difficult to understand. Sharks, for example, do not snarl or frown in warning of an attack. They do not have ears to lay back or brows to arch. Nevertheless, they must in some way communicate their intentions to one another to avoid injurious encounters. Donald R. Nelson of California State University's Department of Biology has revealed some of the ways in which Pacific grey reef sharks do this.

The grey reef shark, which grows to about forty inches in length, is an unusually aggressive animal that has been implicated in a number of attacks on people. Evidence suggests that these sharks are territorial and that their attacks are motivated by territorial defense, not hunger. The sharks simply move in quickly, slash, and retreat.

Nelson has analyzed the behavior that precedes grey reef shark attacks and has found a consistent pattern that suggests that the animals give ample warning. Before attacking, the shark swims with its back hunched, its tail lowered, and its head raised. It

A hammerhead shark, its eyes on the ends of its distinctive head, moves through the sea as part of a large school. Because hammerheads often gather into large groups, they have developed a complex system of body postures that serve to communicate warnings, threats, and other information.

A sand tiger shark swims in a cloud of small fish. Though it looks fierce, the sand tiger shark has never been known to attack a human in U.S. waters.

also appears to bend its body at almost right angles when seen from above. In this posture it swims in an S-shaped pattern toward diver, shark, or other object that caused the warning display, switching to a figure eight swimming pattern as it closes in. The display becomes more intense as the shark is approached and is particularly intense if the animal is cornered or cannot escape. Another shark might retreat in the face of this display, avoiding a fight, but a human diver may ignore the posturing, press too close, and trigger an attack. Several other species—Galapagos, silky, blacknose, and bonnethead sharks—use components of this display to signal their intentions.

Another shark biologist, Peter Klimley of the Bodega Marine Laboratory of the University of California at Davis, has studied body language in hammerhead sharks, a species that frequently gathers into large schools made up of hundreds of individuals. Such a gathering would suggest a need for explicit forms of communication between sharks to avoid injurious conflicts, and explicit forms have evolved. Klimley has determined that hammerheads use at least seven body signals to communicate among themselves. As schools circle, larger, more dominant animals move to the center, forcing smaller sharks to the periphery. Large individuals express dominance by swimming up to a subordinate and bumping it with their lower jaws. They may also swim in tight loops as they move toward an opponent, flashing white bellies as a threat, warning, or challenge. Individuals show subordination by shaking their heads from side to side. It is quite likely that further research will show that other shark species have evolved similar means for controlling complex social interactions.

Although most sharks are unaggressive and usually avoid contact with one another, one aspect of behavior found in the sand tiger shark certainly lives up to the archetypal shark's reputation for savagery. This involves the sand tiger's embryonic development, which is being investigated by R. Grant Gilmore, assistant research scientist at the Harbor Branch Oceanographic Institution, Inc., in Fort Pierce, Florida.

Sand tiger sharks off the east coast of Florida give birth in February or March. After giving birth, the females mate again. The female has two reproductive tracts, and embryonic development occurs simultaneously in each branch. After fertilization, the eggs and embryos are encased in capsules and remain in the mother's uterus. The embryos live initially on the egg yolk and hatch in the mother's body when they have grown teeth and are about two inches long. After they hatch, uterine fluids increase. The embryos may draw nutrients and oxygen from this fluid by absorbing it through their filamentous gills. Meanwhile, the remaining yolk, still attached to the embryo, slowly shrinks as the embryo grows to four or five inches. At this time, the oldest embryo begins to attack the egg capsules with which it shares the uterus. It attacks only capsules that have embryos in them and eventually will eat all of its siblings. It then will begin feeding on unfertilized eggs. One biologist was bitten by a near-term young when he reached into the reproductive tract of a pregnant sand tiger shark.

The young complete development after nine to twelve months and are born in pairs, one pup from each branch of the uterus. Each is at least three feet long, with well-developed teeth. Gilmore believes that the large size of the sand tiger shark pups gives them several advantages. They are big enough to avoid falling prey to other predators, they are larger than the offspring of most other sharks with which they may have to compete for food, and they can take a greater range of prey. Moreover, the pups truly are born hunters. Their experiences in the uterus have conditioned them to hunt, attack, and eat prey. This may give them an advantage over other shark pups that may still have to learn the finer points of predation.

The idea that sand tiger sharks and some of their relatives engage in cannibalism prior to birth is a rather elegant predatory scenario and fits the image of the shark as a dangerous and cold-blooded predator, even if that image is poorly reflected in reality. The sand tiger shark, particularly, is not considered dangerous to human beings. No sand tiger shark in U.S. waters has ever been known to attack a human, even though divers quite frequently swim with them.

Sharks: Dangerous to Humans?

Every year about 100 people worldwide are attacked by sharks and about a third of those victims die, proof that sharks can be dangerous. However, given that millions upon millions of people wade in coastal waters and swim in deep seas each year, the odds of an attack in any given area are extremely remote.

Sharks make Australian waters among the most dangerous in the world for swimmers, but even there only about 250 attacks have occurred since 1901, with not much more than 100 deaths. A 1963 study of 2,500 incidents in which airplanes crashed at sea during World War II showed that sharks were seen

A diver is approached by a great white shark. Only professional divers and photographers very familiar with shark behavior should attempt this sort of contact. Although sharks of all species attack only about 100 people worldwide each year, with about a third of the attacks fatal, exposure of the kind illustrated here is not for amateurs.

Protection from Sharks

Sharks are probably the most feared creatures of the sea. Even though the average North American is about 15,000 times more likely to be killed in an automobile accident than in a shark attack, fear of sharks has stimulated an interesting array of efforts to keep the predators away from people.

One of the most persistent efforts has been an attempt to find a chemical repellent that will send sharks into retreat the way tear gas does humans. The search for a chemical repellent drew federal interest during World War II, when the military wanted to protect pilots and naval personnel lost at sea. Both the U.S. and British navies came up with formulas that included copper acetate and a dark dye. The copper compound was thought to repel the sharks, and the dye was supposed to diffuse around immersed individuals and obscure them from the sight of sharks. The repellent supposedly lasted for three or four hours and helped boost the confidence of personnel lost at sea. However, tests after World War II showed that the chemical had no effect on sharks. The Navy quit producing the "repellent" in 1976. Since World War II, hundreds of pilots have parachuted into the ocean, and only one has been bitten by a shark, and that incident caused no serious damage. Recently, shark biologist Eugenie Clark discovered that some Red Sea corals, the tiny animals that build coral reefs, produce a chemical that repels some fish. The chemical has shown some promise as a shark repellent, but as of yet no reliable chemical repellent has been developed.

However, other means have proved fairly useful. Effective means for keeping sharks at bay have been developed at beaches in South Africa, South America, and Australia. One of the best methods is the construction of steel fencing around the perimeter of a beach. This works well, but materials and maintenance are expensive. An alternative is the use of large-mesh gill nets. Nets up to 100 yards long are set up about 400 yards from shore in parallel rows. Sharks become entangled and suffocate. The nets have effectively reduced resident populations of large sharks in some areas but do not work well in others. The nets have a major drawback—they kill harmless shark species, marine mammals, and fish. Also, because most sharks are caught at night when they move toward shore to feed, the nets are killing animals that pose little threat because they appear at times when people have largely abandoned the shore. A great many animals are thus needlessly lost.

One form of protection that has received some promising reviews is a chain mail diving suit. The suit is made of nearly half a million steel links so small that a shark's teeth cannot penetrate it. The suits cost about $5,000 and protect the wearer from being cut by the bite of sharks up to six feet long. However, they do not protect from bruising and broken bones due to the pressure of the bite, or from internal bleeding if the chest is bitten. On the other hand, since most attacks are to a limb and since even broken bones are less likely to be fatal than heavy bleeding, the suits offer some protection.

Another device that has proved effective is the shark screen, which is a sort of large plastic bag—big enough for an adult to get into—with inflated rings around the opening. It folds up into a tiny package that pilots and sailors can carry with them. If they need it, they unfold it, inflate the rings, and climb inside. Because the plastic is dark and opaque, it obscures the person inside and apparently deters sharks. In tests, even dangerous sharks seemed reluctant to approach the bag. On land, the bags can even do double duty as sleeping bags.

A diver tests a chain-mail, shark-proof suit on a blue shark.

A great white shark cruises through the sea. The great white is perhaps the most dangerous of all sharks. However, most cases of attacks by great whites upon humans seem to be cases of mistaken identity—humans swimming at the ocean's surface resemble the seals and sea lions upon which the sharks usually feed.

by survivors in only thirty-eight cases and that only a dozen incidents resulted in injuries caused by sharks. One of the most famous cases was the sinking of the heavy cruiser *USS Indianapolis* in the Pacific some 200 miles from the Philippines. In the movie *Jaws*, shark hunter Captain Quint relates that some 600 sailors were killed by sharks after the sinking. In fact, 800 sailors jumped clear of the *Indianapolis* when she was torpedoed and were adrift at sea for four or five days. Five hundred of them subsequently died, but no more than eighty were killed by sharks.

In an average year, only about a dozen shark attacks occur in U.S. waters, and most of these occur off southern California and Florida, focal points of human beach activities. Only one or two of these attacks are fatal. Another hot spot is coastal New Jersey and New York, where hundreds of thousands of people take to the beaches every weekend of the summer. Most attacks occur on summer midafternoons in water four to ten feet deep, prime times and places for human beach activity.

Shark attacks are dreaded and feared all out of proportion to their frequency. This is due in part to their notoriety. The news media give a great deal of coverage to any shark attack, drawing public attention and creating mass anxiety. In South Africa, for example, in one weekend at one beach a single swimmer was wounded by a shark and fourteen people drowned, but the shark attack received most of the press coverage.

Certain characteristics of shark attacks doubtless

help compound human fear. For one thing, there is virtually no way to guard against an attack once in the water. Large sharks can attack in water as shallow as three feet, are rarely seen in advance by waders, and are invulnerable to anything an unarmed human can do to them. Some large sharks are swift, capable of speeding to twenty miles an hour, perhaps even faster. A nine-foot whaler shark can bite with a force of three or four tons per square inch, and large sharks can clip off a leg with a single pass. Moreover, sharks strike with no apparent emotion. Even an attacking grizzly gives some sign that it is angry, which is something humans can understand. But sharks—we are not even sure *why* they attack.

Some theories have been proposed, however. One analysis of 1,000 shark attacks showed that half had no connection to feeding and that three-quarters of the victims were struck no more than twice. Fewer than 30 percent were fatal, and studies of wound patterns showed that in most cases the sharks were not trying to eat their victims. One hypothesis, therefore, suggests that sharks attack in self-defense. Another theory suggests that since, in many cases, shark attacks tend to cluster within a short period of time, perhaps they are due to individual sharks that become rogues. Another possibility is that sharks sometimes mistake people for a food species and do not realize their mistake until they have attacked.

Several dangerous shark species—those with a record of attacks on people—occur in U.S. waters. Doubtless the most well known and dangerous, at least in temperate zones, is the great white, found along the coast from California to Alaska and from New Jersey to Maine. White sharks attacked about 100 people off California alone between 1950 and 1982. In many attacks the sharks took only a single bite, then moved on. A swimmer attacked by a great white in shallow water can often be rescued by other swimmers, since great whites seem to select a single victim and press the attack on that individual rather than attack other people randomly.

Surprisingly, even the great white can sometimes act with docility. Great whites often move in for a look at divers, then harmlessly cruise away. One eccentric story about an amiable great white was related by Valerie Taylor in the excellent book *Sharks*, edited by biologist John D. Stevens. Taylor, a renowned diver and underwater photographer, tells how, at the suggestion of her husband Ron, she once stood on the partially submerged diving platform of a charter boat and hand-fed fish to a mature great white.

> I offered a fish by leaning down and dangling it under the surface. Whitey cruised over. He seemed a rather clumsy eater, raising his pointy head up next to the fish rather than under it. I had to put the fish into his mouth. He took it nicely—no snapping about, just one big splashy bite. It was exciting, it was easy, it was fun. I gave him five more fish with a little pat on the nose each time while Ron filmed.
>
> There was no doubt the shark knew how the game was being played. I was totally vulnerable; he could have taken me at any time, but he didn't. He took only the fish. In about twenty minutes this giant marine predator had learnt a little trick. . . . "

She added, "What we do might seem crazy, and perhaps it is. But patting great whites and handfeeding tigers [tiger sharks] are skills that have been acquired only after years of patient observation and discipline. To try and copy us would very likely mean becoming another statistic in the shark attack files."

The bull shark is probably the second most dangerous shark in U.S. waters. It is very aggressive and can grow up to twelve feet long. It is the only shark species that regularly enters fresh water, traveling as far up the Mississippi as the Ohio River and as much as 2,000 miles up the Amazon. It frequently attacks people in Lake Nicaragua and along the Ganges River. The bull shark may be more deadly than official records indicate, since in many cases human deaths caused by bull sharks may have been attributed to other species. For example, in 1916 a series of shark attacks along the New Jersey shore, most of them in rivers and creeks, were blamed on a great white shark, which never enters fresh water.

One of the most dangerous species in U.S. waters is the tiger shark, which can exceed twenty feet in length. It is an entirely different creature from the apparently harmless sand tiger shark discussed earlier and to which it is not related. Unlike most sharks, the tiger is not particular about what it eats. Stomachs of dissected tiger sharks have divulged such items as paint cans, shoes, and car parts. Tigers also eat sea lions and sea turtles—animals that, when seen from below, closely resemble a human paddling on a surfboard or wearing a wetsuit for SCUBA diving. Though some sharks, including the great white, might not eat a surfer they have wounded once they realize their victim is not a seal or turtle, tiger sharks are known to deliberately kill and eat people. Three people shipwrecked off Australia in 1983 were re-

Hammerhead sharks often gather in large schools. Although the sharks have earned a reputation as man-eaters, recreational divers often swim unharmed among the large schools. However, the potential for attack is always present.

peatedly attacked by a tiger shark as they paddled for thirty-six hours toward land. Two of them were eaten. The tiger is considered the most dangerous shark in tropical seas.

Blue sharks and oceanic whitetip sharks also are potentially dangerous species, but they prefer waters more than 100 feet deep and so are unlikely to attack bathers. People swimming from boats in deep water may be in danger from them, however. Other species large enough to be dangerous but rarely involved in unprovoked attacks are the three large species of hammerhead sharks and the lemon, dusky, sandbar, blacktip, Caribbean reef, and spinner sharks.

Most shark attacks are provoked by people. Fishermen in the process of catching sharks are the most frequently bitten group. Divers who swim too close to sharks or try to hitch rides on them are the next most frequently injured category.

Perhaps the most remarkable thing about shark attacks is their rarity. People wade among sharks without any precautions or understanding. In most situations, waders cannot even see what is going on near them underwater. This is akin to hiking blindfolded among a pride of lions. Perhaps we should wonder not why sharks attack at all, but why they attack so rarely.

Blue sharks in the open sea. Though aggressive, blue sharks usually occur far from shore, where they pose little danger to people. However, they can be a threat to shipwreck victims.

Sharks: Are Humans Dangerous to Them?

The answer is an unqualified yes. Some of the dangers humans pose to sharks are indirect, says Grant Gilmore. For example, pollution of estuaries may be reducing populations of mullet, a major food fish not only of sharks but also of ospreys and dolphins. Thousands of acres of estuaries used by fish as nursery grounds have been destroyed from Cape Cod to Louisiana. For example, most of the wetlands of Florida's Indian River lagoon have been diked, hampering movement of young mullet into important nurseries. Also, increased human recreational activities in areas such as the Florida Keys are reducing mangrove stands that harbor and feed young sharks.

At present, however, the primary danger to sharks is fishing. Sport and commercial fishermen kill perhaps 100 million sharks yearly. Indeed, shark biologists are increasingly worried that many shark species will soon be devastated by overfishing in the same way that whales were nearly wiped out by whaling.

People long ago found commercial uses for sharks. In the seventeenth century, sharkskin with the denticles intact was used as a covering for jewelry boxes and other containers and for book bindings. In feudal Japan, sharkskin was used to provide a nonslip surface for samarai-sword handles. Dried sharkskin, called shagreen, was used throughout the world as an abrasive in the way that sandpaper is used today. Because sharkskin is tougher than cowhide, it is still used, with the denticles removed, for shoes, boots, and other expensive leather goods.

Sharks are fished for meat, and their fins are the primary ingredient in sharkfin soup. Sharks' fins presently sell for about $22 a pound. Some U.S. fishermen have entered the sharkfin market, catching sharks, lopping off their fins, and releasing them alive but doomed. Since some sharks, particularly open-sea species such as the mako and porbeagle, have to swim to keep water moving over their gills and to keep their hearts pumping, these sharks soon die. Even those that can respire without moving need fins for balance and propulsion and will either bleed or starve to death.

In the 1930s and 1940s, sharks were heavily hunted for their livers. Oil from the liver was richer in vitamin A than cod liver oil. The shark-oil industry collapsed when synthetic vitamin A entered the market, but other extracts from shark liver are still employed in cosmetics and pharmaceuticals.

Sharks also are being used for a variety of medical purposes. Shark corneas have been transplanted to human eyes to correct corneal problems. Shark corneas work particularly well in transplants because vertical fibers within the corneas prevent swelling and rejection. In addition, chemicals extracted from shark cartilage have killed cancerous tumors in laboratory animals, suggesting a potential treatment for cancer. Also, sharks possess powerful immune systems, so their blood is being studied in connection with research on AIDS.

Many sharks are killed just for their teeth and jaws. The jaws are used as ornaments, and the teeth are often fashioned into jewelry. Tons of sharks are killed simply for fun. In Key West, Florida, boats take people out to the flats, where young sharks are among the most common fish caught. Some fishermen take their catch home for food, but many simply throw them away.

Increased interest in sharks for meat and sportfishing have put new pressures on shark populations. Nearly a billion pounds are being caught yearly, most of it by sportfishermen. In the U.S. alone, sportfishermen bring in about 22 million pounds each year. The kill involves about two-thirds of all shark species. Hundreds of thousands of sharks are taken accidentally by commercial fishermen in pursuit of other species and simply thrown away.

Because sharks mature and reproduce slowly, they fall easy victim to overfishing. Several populations have already collapsed, usually within a short time after exploitation began. The Scottish-Norwegian stock of the spiny dogfish was commercially wiped out in this century to supply the British fish and chips trade. In the 1950s, the fish-oil in-

Help! Help! Shark! What to Do When You're Swimming with Sharks

At our current level of understanding, shark behavior is unpredictable. People in water with a potentially dangerous shark can never make themselves completely safe. However, here are some guidelines from National Marine Fisheries Service shark biologist Jack Casey that may help reduce the chances of attack.

1. Remember that shark attacks of any kind are extremely rare. In most cases the shark will completely ignore you. So remain calm. Sudden movements or thrashing may draw a shark's attention.

2. Swim in calm, rhythmic movements back to your boat or to land.

3. Keep the shark in sight, particularly if you are a diver underwater. Sharks seem to shy away from people who look directly at them. Also, remember that in almost all shark attacks, the victim did not see the shark beforehand.

4. If all else fails, try to act prepared, to be aggressive. (Note that Casey says, "All bets are off if the shark is a great white and you look like a seal and it plans to eat you.")

Casey also recommends taking these preventive measures:

- Do not carry dead fish when swimming or diving.
- Stay out of the water if sharks are spotted.
- Do not swim at night.
- Stay out of murky water.
- Do not wear contrasting colors or any flashing objects.
- Avoid wading or swimming in offshore sloughs or channels, in harbor entrances, and in waters that drop off steeply to greater depths.
- Never molest a shark of any kind, regardless of its size.

A mako shark shows the look that typifies sharks in most human imaginations. Makos can be dangerous to people, but people are far more dangerous to sharks. Fishing kills about 100 million sharks yearly, and in some areas shark populations have collapsed because the slow-breeding animals could not keep up with the losses. The mako is a popular seafood species.

A sign outside a Key West restaurant advertises shark meat. Increased demand for shark meat is threatening shark populations throughout the world. Federal shark experts say that a lack of data on shark catch and population levels makes it impossible to establish sound protection. Many shark populations have already collapsed.

These sharks were caught by half a dozen people off Key West during a half-day of sport fishing. Most of the fishermen discarded their catches at the dock. Because data for the management of shark catches is limited, both sport and commercial fishing pose threats to shark populations.

dustry nearly destroyed the basking shark population off Scotland by slaughtering about 2,000 of the animals yearly. Overfishing has also depleted the North Atlantic's porbeagles and the soupfin sharks of California waters. School sharks off Australia were depleted in the 1950s and still have not recovered. When a school of thresher sharks was spotted by airplane recently off California, a fleet of commercial vessels raced out and fished the sharks intensively for several days. It is not known what percentage of the eastern Pacific thresher population this school represented or whether the school or population could sustain the take.

Data from the western Atlantic and the Gulf of Mexico suggest that large sharks in those seas are being exploited excessively. Gruber says that he has no hard data to prove that a decline has occurred in his lemon sharks, but he observed that in 1979 it was not hard for him to tag 1,000 shark pups, whereas now it is impossible to reach that number within a single year. By interviewing shark fishermen, Grant Gilmore has learned that single catches of sandbar and blacktip sharks totaling several thousand pounds are not uncommon off Florida. Gilmore believes the take is reducing those species. The sandbar shark's low reproductive rate makes it

impossible for the species to withstand heavy fishing pressure, he says.

Shark declines may have unknown effects on the entire ocean ecosystem, because sharks are important predators at the top of their food chain. Too little is known about them, however, to determine how shark declines affect prey species. Unfortunately, little can be done to stop shark declines. The public, bureaucrats, and politicians have shown little interest in sharks. Presumably, the shark's image is just not one that attracts a constituency strong enough to move bureaucracies toward better shark protection. Consequently, little funding is available for shark research and little is known about shark populations and how they are being affected by fishing. In 1986 a special panel of shark experts was appointed by the federal government to investigate the effect of fishing on sharks and to make management recommendations. The panel concluded that there is not a single shark species for which enough information exists to permit the creation of a sound management plan. Under the current regimen, shark populations will doubtless collapse at various sites throughout the world. Off Australia, even the great white shark may be dwindling. Humankind has proved itself the most dangerous creature on the open seas.

SEA TURTLES
ANCIENT NOMADS

Based on the Audubon Television Special by
Robert Nixon and Karen Kelly and
Narrated by Jane Alexander

SEA TURTLES, in those rare moments when they come ashore to lay eggs, seem slow and cumbersome creatures. As they drag themselves laboriously across the sand, they look like boulders into which some torturous life has been breathed. Viscous tears pour from their eyes. The tears are part of a process that removes salt from the turtles' bodies, but they were long thought to be a sign of the sorrow and agony that sea turtles endured on land.

Perhaps because they are so cumbrous and lumbering during those rare times when we see them on land, sea turtles have rarely attracted the broad, enthusiastic interest that people have devoted to more dashing creatures—tigers, wolves, cheetahs, grizzlies, even whales. But that is a failing more of the human constitution than of the turtle's. If people could take to the sea as turtles do, they would see the creatures transformed. Underwater, sea turtles become winged beasts flying through the medium of the sea. They propel themselves with powerful thrusts of broad front flippers, moving the flippers much as birds in flight move their wings. They glide and hover, they dart like swallows and swoop like hawks. They become masters of great distances, swimming thousands of miles across trackless oceans. Guided by signposts still unknown to humankind, they can navigate unerringly to tiny bits of land not five miles long, awash in the middle of the ocean. They have plumbed the great depths of the sea.

Sea turtles are among the Earth's oldest creatures. They have plied the seas for nearly 90 million years, and their ancestral lineage dates back to twice that age. They were contemporaries of the dinosaurs, and they have outlasted tens of thousands of other species. They are biological mysteries. People have hunted them for centuries and science has pursued them for decades, but until recently we knew hardly more about them than we do about fossilized creatures that vanished 100 million years ago.

Like all turtles, sea turtles are reptiles, related to lizards, snakes, crocodiles, and alligators. What sets turtles apart most obviously from the others is the shell. The upper and lower shells are created by a broadening and fanning out of the turtle's ribs to form a solid box of bone around the internal organs. The skin that covers this box of bone has evolved in most species into horny plates. The soft-shelled turtles, such as the leatherback

Sea Turtles of the World

There are eight species of sea turtle. The largest is the soft-shelled leatherback (*Dermochelys coriacea*), which can exceed half a ton and measures up to six feet long. It ranges throughout the Atlantic, Pacific, and Indian oceans as far north as Alaska and Labrador and as far south as the Cape of Good Hope. This puts the leatherback in cold seas, but unlike other sea turtles it is able to maintain a body temperature that is warmer than that of the environment. It dives more deeply than any other sea turtle, with a known record of 4,000 feet. Individual leatherbacks are known for their farflung travels. One tagged in Surinam on the eastern coast of South America was recovered 3,600 miles to the north. Leatherbacks subsist largely on jellyfish, and it may be the pursuit of this food that takes them so far north, where the cold waters are particularly productive of jellyfish. One arctic jellyfish grows up to ten feet in diameter.

The green sea turtle (*Chelonia mydas*), found in most tropical and sub-

A leatherback sea turtle drags itself ashore to nest. This is the largest species of sea turtle, weighing up to 1,000 pounds.

sea turtle, are exceptions. Their protective boxes are made of thick skin and flexible cartilage.

The first turtles were land animals. To carry the weight of their armor, their legs evolved into ponderous columns of muscle and bone. Those that turned to living in the sea were reshaped by evolution. Their shells became lighter and more compressed, giving them a streamlined contour suited for cutting smoothly through water. Their limbs were flattened into flippers. That this pattern has worked for millions of years is a sign of the sea turtle's evolutionary success.

All sea turtles lead similar lives, with the sea meeting nearly all their needs. They bask at the water's surface, warmed by the sun, and feed upon the living things the sea produces. They even mate in the sea. But the females must return to shore to lay their eggs. The shell-encased eggs that they lay, an inheritance handed down by terrestrial ancestors, cannot survive in water. They are part of an immutable chain that binds the sea turtle to land.

When a female returns to shore—perhaps even to the very beach on which she hatched—she must drag herself up the beach beyond the reach of the waves. As she moves along she pauses occasionally to press her snout into the sand, as if checking its taste

tropical waters, is perhaps the species most important to commerce. Its meat and eggs were eaten during the colonial era, and even today the animal's commercial value threatens its survival in some areas. The skin of its flippers is made into leather, its eggs are used as food, and its fat is the main ingredient in turtle soup. It is named for the color of its edible fat. Among the hard-shelled sea turtles, it is matched in size only by the loggerhead. It weighs up to 400 pounds and grows up to 3.5 feet long. A carnivore for the first year or so of its life, the green sea turtle soon switches to a diet of plant matter. Because of its dependence on plants, it tends to live in shallow waters with an abundance of seagrasses. Consequently, it congregates in coastal waters, where it falls easy prey to hunters.

The loggerhead sea turtle (*Caretta caretta*) grows to nearly four feet long and more than 400 pounds and ranges throughout the world's tropical and subtropical seas, ranging in the United States into the northeastern Atlantic. Its major New World nesting beaches are in the Caribbean, Central America, the Yucatan, and the southeastern United States. It was named for its relatively large head. One immense skull measured nearly twelve inches wide. The skull is large because the bones must provide attachment sites for the heavy jaw muscles the animal needs for crushing mollusk shells. Loggerheads also eat crustaceans,

fish, and jellyfish. One loggerhead reportedly chomped through a clam shell that was a third of an inch thick.

The relatively small hawksbill turtle (*Eretmochelys imbricata*)—it weighs from 80 to 250 pounds, and measures from two to three feet long—is the source of tortoise shell. It occurs only in tropical seas, where it stays around reefs and rocky areas in search of the sponges that make up most of its diet. It also eats mollusks, crustaceans, jellyfish, and algae. Its concentration around reefs makes it vulnerable to hunters.

The small Pacific or olive ridley (*Lepidochelys olivacea*) is found throughout the Pacific and Indian oceans and in the Atlantic off South America. Stray individuals sometimes are picked up along the east coast of Africa. It is probably the most numerous of all sea turtles, but heavy hunting in some Latin American nations soon may wipe out some populations. Though its skin is used for leather and its eggs are eaten, little is known about its biology and behavior.

The most endangered and the smallest sea turtle—it rarely reaches 100 pounds—is the Kemp's ridley (*Lepidochelys kempi*). It nests primarily along a small stretch of beach on Mexico's Gulf Coast. Young Kemp's are thought to be omnivorous, but the adults are strict carnivores, feeding mainly on blue crabs but also on crustaceans, jellyfish, fish, mollusks, and even starfish. Their jaws are

strong enough to crush almost anything that will fit into their mouths.

The flatback turtle (*Chelonia depressa*), like the Kemp's ridley, has a limited range. It is found only along northern Australia and the adjacent waters of the continental shelf. It is jeopardized by uncontrolled and excessive predation of eggs by native people and by introduced species that have become feral, such as hogs and foxes. Development has disrupted some nesting beaches, shrimp trawlers capture and drown the turtles in nets, and native people kill some nesting females—all tolls that could severely affect the animal's survival. Nevertheless, it is the only sea turtle that is not on the federal endangered species list, though it has been proposed for listing.

The eighth species is the black sea turtle (*Chelonia agassizi*), a native of the eastern Pacific. Not all biologists are agreed that this species is distinct from the green sea turtle. Some treat it as a subspecies and call it the east Pacific green sea turtle. It weighs 100 to 150 pounds, compared to the green's 250 to 400, but the two animals look much alike. Though it nests along the coasts of Central and South America and in the Galapagos, its largest nesting site is in the Mexican state of Michoacan. The black sea turtle has been found as far north as Alaska. Little is known about this animal, but it is thought to feed on various seagrasses, algae, and invertebrates.

or odor, until finally she selects a place and digs a hole into which she deposits her eggs before burying them. Then she returns once more to the water. The whole trip may take less than an hour, certainly less than two.

The unguarded eggs often are dug up and eaten by any of a wide range of predators and also succumb to drowning tidal surges and hurricanes. Eggs that survive hatch, usually at night, about two months after they are laid. The baby turtles, about 100 the size of silver dollars in the average hatch, find themselves buried under two feet of sand. They have to dig to the surface. To discover how they do

this, researchers have transferred entire clutches into boxes with glass sides and buried the eggs as they would be in nature. Watching through the glass, the researchers saw how the hatchlings dig out. The first to hatch lie still until others have finished breaking free of their shells. Eventually, contact among the piled hatchlings causes them to begin thrashing with their flippers. Those on top chip away at the ceiling of the nest, and those on the sides dig into the walls. The sand that falls in upon them sifts down to the hatchlings below, whose movements send the sand ultimately to the bottom of the nest. As the turtles cut away at the ceiling, the floor rises, and the

Green sea turtles mating at the water's edge.

A sea turtle lays its eggs. The turtles dig out the nests with their rear flippers, then cover the eggs by throwing sand over them with their front flippers.

turtles reach the surface as if riding in an elevator. If those on top stop digging at any time, those underneath soon begin to squirm. The topmost respond with renewed thrashings that send down another cascade of sand. The group effort is important to hatchling survival. Researchers found that if they buried single eggs in a viewing box, few of the solitary hatchlings made it to the top. In one test, only six out of twenty-two succeeded without human help. By the time they reached the surface, they were too tired to crawl down the beach and into the sea.

Once free of the sand, the hatchlings make a mad dash to the water. Great numbers immediately fall victim to land crabs and other carnivores. Apparently, traveling in a group helps some baby turtles survive this challenge, too. If a group member stops, others soon run into it, stimulating it to get moving again. Consequently, members of a group spend less time sitting still than do single hatchlings released experimentally. This makes the turtles less vulnerable to predators. The mass movement also has another effect on predation, called *swarming*. Apparently, most predators cannot hunt successfully unless they can pick out an individual to chase. When large numbers of prey are moving about all at once, predators find it difficult to pick out a target, making it seem that there is indeed safety in numbers. Swarming is used by a number of species to reduce predator success. For example, arctic caribou in some areas all give birth within a single three-week period, presumably because the appearance of thousands of calves at one time makes it harder for wolves to chase any single calf.

When they reach the water, the hatchlings catch an incoming wave and immediately switch from scuttling to swimming, moving their flippers frantically as they move toward the sea. They ride the waves and dive into the undertow, which pulls them beyond the breakers. At this point, swarming may help the hatchlings survive the gauntlet of hungry fish they encounter during their initial contact with the ocean.

Despite the great odds against any individual sea turtle—probably not more than one in 100 survives, maybe as few as one in 10,000—the survival of the various species over millions of years is a testimony to their biological fitness. They have surmounted

A green sea turtle hatchling makes its way in a rush to the sea.

Hatchling sea turtles, racing from nest to sea, face a variety of predators. Here, a hatchling is killed by a crab.

every obstacle that has threatened their existence during the past 900,000 centuries and more—from global climate changes to the moving and shaping of whole continents and seas. But nothing in the past prepared them for the specter that now threatens to drive them into oblivion. They are creatures on the very edge of doom, and the specter looming over them is humankind.

The Legacy of Destruction

Sea turtles occurred in tremendous numbers in the coastal waters of the New World during colonization. The Spanish named one group of Caribbean islands the Tortugas, after the green turtles that swarmed in surrounding waters. Green turtles were abundant as far north as Massachusetts. Off Cape Hatteras in North Carolina, a solitary fisherman could land 100 in one day. But too many turtles were taken from those and other waters very early in New World colonization. In 1620 the animals were already so clearly in decline that the Bermuda Assembly passed a law that banned the killing of young sea turtles and fined violators fifteen pounds of tobacco. That law and any that followed must have been too little or too late. Green sea turtles no longer breed in Bermuda and, except for a few limited sites in the Southeast, have forsaken U.S. beaches.

The story is much the same elsewhere. In parts of Europe sea turtles were quickly extirpated because females were caught as they came to nest and were killed before they laid their eggs. In the Seychelles and Bahamas they were harpooned. In China and Mozambique hunters released remora-like fish with sucking disks among basking sea turtles. When a fish attached itself to a turtle's shell, the hunter reeled it in with a line attached to the fish by a ring.

The turtles were able to sustain losses to hunting in places where human numbers were low, just as they could sustain losses to gulls and sharks. But where hunting pressure mounted, the turtles soon declined. For example, the Miskito Indians of Nicaragua traditionally hunted turtles at sea, chasing after them in open boats and taking only what they needed to feed themselves. It was a limited take, and Indians and turtles both prospered. But the tradi-

tion came to an abrupt end after World War II, when commercial demand for the turtles increased worldwide and spurred the Indians to more intensive efforts. They began to hunt in fleets of large boats, taking every turtle they could get. As hunting for food turned to hunting for money, docks and processing plants were built to accommodate the burgeoning catch and the turtles dwindled. The same has happened wherever subsistence hunters have found a commercial market for shell, leather, and meat or where human populations have become too dense for the turtles to meet the market demand. The extent of the decline cannot even be measured, because without doubt many turtle populations vanished long before science knew they existed. Historical accounts show that beaches which

These old sea turtle kraals at Key West, Florida, are proof that trade in turtles once flourished throughout the Caribbean. These kraals—Afrikaans for pens—*were built in the 1920s to hold sea turtles caught from as far off as Nicaragua and the Cayman Islands. The turtles were processed into soup or shipped to the Northeast.*

today never see a nesting sea turtle in the past were crowded with egg-laying hordes during breeding season.

The many causes of destruction in league against the sea turtle have yielded predictable results. All species but the flatback—which may be listed soon—have been listed by the federal government as endangered or threatened species. Their plight, however, has not been ignored. Intensive efforts are being made to save them.

Archie Carr: The Leading Pioneer of Sea Turtle Researchers

One man who looked at the destruction of the sea turtles and thought something must be done to stop it was Archie Carr. His career began in 1937, when he became the first student to receive a doctorate in zoology from the University of Florida. His initial interest was in freshwater turtles, but late in the 1940s, while writing a handbook on North American turtles, he became aware of how little was known about sea turtles. He started searching the Caribbean for a place to study sea turtles and came, in 1953, to Costa Rica's Tortuguero Beach, a wild, twenty-two-mile stretch of coast. It was, and remains today, one of only two major green sea turtle nesting sites in the Caribbean. The other, Aves Island, a tiny bit of land in the Leeward Islands some 100 miles off Monserrat, appears to be sinking slowly into the sea, making Tortuguero critically important.

When Carr first arrived at Tortuguero, its turtles were beset by people who took eggs and killed turtles for meat and by packs of wild dogs that ate eggs and hatchlings. Carr feared that eventually even this last stronghold would be lost. However, his writings attracted the interest of Joshua B. Powers, a publishing house representative with an interest in the Caribbean. Powers organized a group of influential peo-

Archie Carr on the beach at Tortuguero, Costa Rica, with a green sea turtle, the creature to which he devoted much of his professional life.

ple into the Brotherhood of the Green Sea Turtle, which devoted itself to saving the animal. A Tallahassee, Florida, philanthropist named John H. Phipps joined the brotherhood and subsequently financed the Caribbean Conservation Corporation, a nonprofit group dedicated to preserving the Caribbean's natural resources. The corporation funded Carr's efforts to study and protect the green sea turtle. In 1955 Carr set up a permanent camp on the Costa Rican beach and, over the years, this grew into the Tortuguero research center.

The Costa Rican government helped out, too, initially by banning the taking of eggs and turtles along the first three miles of nesting beach and eventually by protecting the whole Costa Rican coast and declaring Tortuguero a national park. Among the earliest protective measures was extirpation of the dogs that plagued the nesting grounds.

By digging up eggs and feeding on hatchlings, the dogs posed one of the most immediate threats to sea turtle survival at Tortuguero. Wrote Carr in *So Excellent a Fishe*,

the government sent in posses that shot every dog they could hit. . . . It was a dismal time, but it is hard to think what else could have been done to save the Tortuguero turtles. Hateful as the sound of the old Enfields and Tommy guns was, it was they, and the new laws prohibiting turtle-turning [the killing of turtles for meat], that saved this last of all the green turtle beaches of the western Caribbean Sea.

In the early days at Tortuguero, researchers stayed in huts borrowed from local people and lived on rice and beans supplemented occasionally by the meat of a peccary, a type of wild pig. "You had none of the blessings of civilization," Carr recalled, "if blessings you insist they are." Carr went to Tor-

Tracking Sea Turtles with Satellites

Satellites are the newest technology used by biologists in their efforts to learn more about sea turtles. Tracking sea turtles with satellites is still an experimental procedure, says Jack Woody, the U.S. Fish and Wildlife Service's top sea turtle researcher, but the technique promises to offer biological insights that have eluded scientists for 200 years.

To track sea turtles with satellites, biologists attach radio transmitters to the turtles. The transmitters emit bleeps that are picked up by an orbiting satellite which transmits the signals to Earth. Biologists contact the receiving station by using a computer telephone modum, which allows them to access data from the sea turtle radios on their own computer screens. They can even print out the information for study.

One of the problems with the technology is lack of a safe and reliable method for attaching transmitters to the turtles. Researchers have tried putting radio harnesses on leatherback sea turtles, but these chafed the relatively tender

leatherback and were difficult to recover. They also tried attaching radios to long wires and bolting the wires to the turtles' shells so that the swimming animals would tow the radios behind. The bolts were designed to rust away in eight to twelve months, about the life expectancy of the transmitter. But this technique was abandoned because "we didn't want them dragging dead radios," Woody says. Also, in some turtles, notably the Kemp's ridley, the edge of the shell itself tended to break off. "Now we're trying fiberglass glue," Woody says. Initial experiments showed that the glue held for at least two months on a wild turtle and five months on a captive animal. Though the glue shows promise for work on hardshelled species, a safe, functional method has yet to be found for the soft-shelled leatherback turtles.

Woody says the satellites are providing information never collected before. In the past, he says, hundreds of thousands of turtles were marked with metal tags, which showed the location of the tagging and asked anyone who found the animal to return the tag to the researcher. The problem with that technique, Woody says, is that you need someone to re-

cover the tag, and then all you know is where the turtle was first marked and where it was last seen. You do not know what happened in the months or years between. The radio-tracking method is changing that.

The radios show the location from which the turtle is transmitting and how often it is diving. The technique is being further refined to show diving depth. From these data a great deal more information can be deduced. If you find that an animal is diving a lot, you can presume it is feeding. If you know where it is diving and how deep, you can check maps or visit the site and find out what kind of habitat it is using and what it is eating. You can also tell by a turtle's diving patterns when it is most active and when it is resting or just drifting with the waves.

The satellite method has some drawbacks. In order for the satellite to receive and transmit data, the turtle must be on the surface, its radio antenna must be above water, and the satellite must be overhead. Despite this, the technique is a major success and, as it is perfected, promises to provide information vital to the better protection and management of sea turtles.

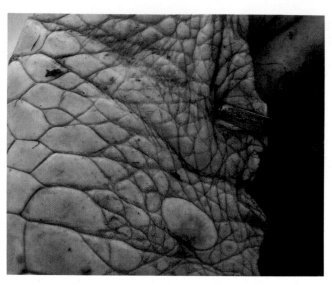

The tagging projects pioneered by Archie Carr are still being used. Here is a metal tag attached to the flipper of a green sea turtle caught in Florida's Indian River by University of Central Florida sea turtle biologist Llewellyn Ehrhart.

tuguero each year during the University of Florida's summer break. There, during the first decade of work, he and his students marked more than 3,000 nesting green sea turtles with numbered metal tags. The numbers identified individual turtles so that Carr could chart their movements if they were later captured elsewhere. To help ensure some measure of success, the tags bore instructions promising anyone who caught one of the turtles a five-dollar reward if the tag were turned to Carr in Florida.

The tagging program has paid off. Tags have been returned from as far away as Venezuela. The locations from which tags were returned indicate that after nesting, green sea turtles travel north into Nicaraguan waters and south past the coasts of Panama and Colombia. There they feed in the seagrass beds, migrating back to Tortuguero when it is again time to breed. Thus, Tortuguero was proved to be the source of most of the green sea turtles that swam the Caribbean. If Tortuguero should ever fail as a nesting beach, most of the Caribbean's green sea turtles presumably would be lost.

In addition to exploring the movements of adult turtles, Carr also sought to discover where hatchlings go during their first years of life, a period he called "the lost year" because the hatchlings seemed to disappear into the sea, reappearing later as juveniles. Since it would be impossible to establish a comprehensive turtle conservation program without knowing where the turtles spent the first year of their lives, Carr spent a great deal of time and energy trying to solve this mystery. His work, along with research conducted by other biologists, brought several interesting points to light. Hatchlings, the biologists found, enter the sea with enough yolk attached to them to survive without food for two or three days. Also, they enter a sort of swimming frenzy when they hit the water, paddling like mad toward the open sea. The frenzy and the yolk both run out when the hatchlings are about fifty miles out to sea, where in some areas huge rafts of sargassum seaweed drift on the currents.

Carr guessed that the rafts were the hatchlings' destination and proved to himself experimentally that captive hatchlings, if given the choice, would rather stay near or under chunks of seaweed than float in open water. He also looked at the prevailing currents in the Caribbean and found that they would be likely to carry the hatchlings to the sargassum rafts. This mosaic of evidence led Carr to conclude that the young turtles drifted with the rafts and fed on animal matter until they reached the age and size at which they were ready to move out to the reefs and shallow-water "flats" that surround islands and adopt an adult herbivorous diet. Observations by fishermen corroborated Carr's idea, but it is still not entirely accepted in the scientific world. Some biologists believe that the evidence for the sargassum rafts is circumstantial and proves only that the rafts are home for at most some Atlantic green sea turtle hatchlings. These biologists believe that convergence zones, where two ocean currents meet and provide a denser food supply than most open-sea regions, are the more likely destinations of the young turtles. Skeptics are even less convinced that sargassum plays a critical role in the lives of Pacific sea turtles. Additional research may resolve the conflict.

Carr's work on turtle migration attracted the interest of the U.S. Navy, which thought it might learn something about navigation from an animal capable of traveling hundreds of miles through the sea to zero in on a few miles of beach. The Navy even permitted Carr to use its planes to travel around the world in search of information about turtles. It also played an instrumental role in Carr's efforts to reestablish green sea turtles on Caribbean beaches where nesting sites had been wiped out by colonial hunters. To do this, Carr collected and hatched thousands of eggs from Tortuguero and transferred the hatchlings to other beaches, where he released them with the hope that they would mature in the sea and return to the new beach when the time came to breed. This would not only reestablish the turtles on lost beaches, but would provide back-up breeding areas to help ensure that the animals would not be wiped out completely if a major catastrophe destroyed Tortuguero. In pursuit of this goal, the Navy helped Carr transport as many as 20,000 Tortuguero hatchlings a year to sites scattered around the Caribbean, the Bahamas, and southeast Florida. None of the turtles have yet returned to those beaches, but then, green sea turtles may take thirty, forty, perhaps even fifty years to reach breeding age. The success of Carr's relocation program is still uncertain.

Carr did not restrict his work to the green sea turtles of Tortuguero. He also played a role in studying and protecting other species. One was the Kemp's ridley sea turtle, and it provided Carr with what must have been one of the most exciting moments in his life, a moment that, in the way Carr later described it, showed his unbridled enthusiasm for the creatures that he made into his life's work.

Until the early 1960s no one knew where the Kemp's ridley sea turtle nested. This was a critical gap in our knowledge, since nesting beaches provide biologists with the best opportunity they have for taking some measure of sea turtle populations and getting some sense of whether the creatures are sinking or swimming as a species.

Of course, Carr could not be expected to ignore

Dispersal of Kemp's ridley sea turtles from Rancho Nuevo. It is not certain that turtles that move east and north past Florida ever return.

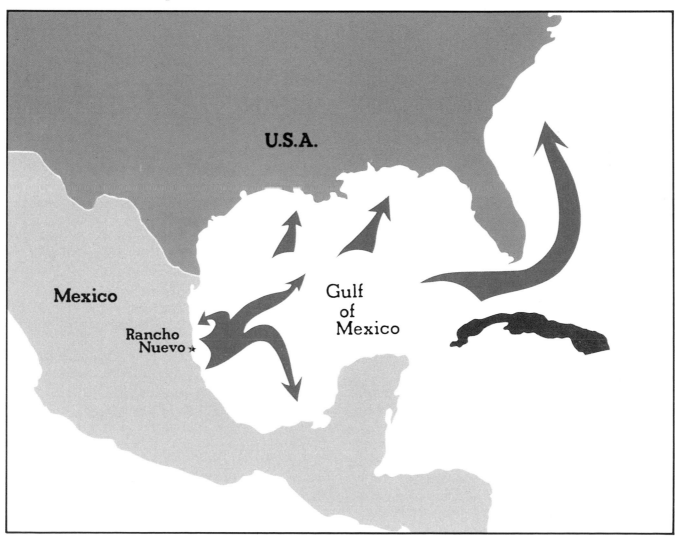

this lack of knowledge. For two decades he searched for the Kemp's ridley nesting ground, scouring Caribbean shores as well as beaches as far away as Africa. "I spent literally over a dozen summers trying to locate a place where people would admit this turtle bred," Carr recalled. "I never found it." Some biologists even speculated that the Kemp's bred at sea and gave birth to live young, a pretty far-fetched idea given that no turtle of any kind is known to give live birth.

The breakthrough came in 1961. For Carr, it was announced by a phone call from biologist Henry Hildebrand of the University of Texas in Austin. Hildebrand invited Carr to see a film he had discovered during a trip to Mexico. The film had been taken in 1947 by Andres Herrera, a Mexican architect who had made a hobby of searching for the Kemp's ridley nesting ground. It was taken on a secluded twenty-mile stretch of beach near Rancho Nuevo, a village on Mexico's Gulf Coast some 200 miles south of the U.S. border. It showed a vast number of Kemp's ridleys coming ashore to nest in daylight, contrary to all other sea turtles, which nest at night. The film was the first record of a Kemp's nesting ground. Incredibly, it had lain stored on a shelf for thirteen years while Carr and other biologists were searching the globe for the nesting site that the film showed so clearly.

Hildebrand planned to introduce the film to the scientific community at a meeting of the American Society of Ichthyologists and Herpetologists in Austin. But, just before the meeting, he called Carr and offered to give him a preview.

The phone call brought Carr to a darkened classroom at the University of Texas, where the film was to be run. He was keyed up, bearly able to contain his excitement about the movie. But delays seemed legion. There was trouble getting a window shade to close, and some problems with having the wrong-size film spool. Wrote Carr, "The tension about what I had been told I would see had already grown too tight."

The tension mounted as the film finally rolled. At first there was no view of the nesting ground, just footage of a turtle here, a turtle there; footage of grown men standing on the backs of turtles, trying to go for a ride. "Finally," Carr wrote in *So Excellent a Fishe*, "when I was ready to rend my garments, the cameraman tired of the horseplay. He turned his lens down the shore. And there it was, the *arribada* as the Mexicans call it—the arrival—the incredible

crowning culmination of the ridley mystery. Out there, suddenly in clear view, was a solid mile of ridleys"—some 40,000, Hildebrand estimated, and Carr saw no reason to dispute the figure. "The customary metaphor to use in telling of great abundance of beasts is to say that one might have walked across a lake (or stream or plain) on their backs, or could have walked a mile without touching the earth," Carr wrote. "In the film you could have done this, literally, with no metaphoric license at all. You could have run a whole mile down the beach on the backs of turtles and never have set foot on the sand."

"For me really, it was the movie of all time," Carr recalled.

> For me, personally, as a searcher after ridleys for twenty years, as the chronicler of the oddness of ridleys, the film outdid everything from *Birth of a Nation* to *Zorba the Greek*. It made Andres Herrera in my mind suddenly a cinematographer far finer than Fellini, Alfred Hitchcock, or Walt Disney could ever aspire to be. . . . It still is hard for me to understand the apathy of a world in which such a movie can be so little celebrated. . . . To me Andres Herrera is a man who ought to be knighted, or to get a Nobel prize, or some kind of prize. And he would, too, if the ridley were only DNA, or a UFO, or something more negotiable.

Unfortunately for the Kemp's ridley, its nesting ground had been known to egg gatherers and turtle hunters long before it was known to science. In the 1940s eggs and turtles were being devastated. By the time the film reached Austin, the Kemp's was in decline, and the big *arribadas* were over. Since the 1960s the turtles have been subject to an intensive effort to preserve them, but their numbers have remained low. Rancho Nuevo is still the only known major nesting site. If others ever existed, they were wiped out long ago.

Once the nesting site was found, Carr, his students, and other biologists turned their attention to finding out where the Kemp's went after hatching and where they lived as adults. The range of the adults proved to be fairly discrete. The species appears to have two major feeding grounds, one off Louisiana and one in the Campeche-Tabasco area off Mexico's Yucatan peninsula. From these they go to Rancho Nuevo to breed.

The activities of the young were harder to nail down. Apparently, some remain in the Gulf of Mexico off the coasts of Mexico and the United States. Others, however, travel widely, cutting around Florida and moving north to New England. A very few go to places as distant as the coasts of Portugal and Africa. It is not clear whether the young turtles that go beyond the Gulf ever come back. Most biologists believe the wanderings up and down the U.S. Atlantic Coast are part of the turtle's normal travels and that the animals eventually return to the Gulf. Others believe the wanderers were swept out of the Gulf involuntarily by strong currents, never to come home again. Carr was reluctant to write off the wanderers as lost, but nevertheless the fate of the young turtles, critical to Kemp's conservation, remains unknown.

The success of Carr's work at Tortuguero is less in question. His research center helped stimulate the interest of the Costa Rican government in green sea turtles and won them the government protection that has helped save them. Were it not for Carr's presence at Tortuguero, the greens that nest there might have vanished years ago into the oblivion that swallowed their kind elsewhere in the Caribbean. Equally important, Carr's work showed that sea turtle conservation would require international cooperation. The oceans are too vast for any one nation to hope by itself to protect the creatures that live there. As Carr asserted in the Audubon television film, "You've got a bobtailed and doomed-to-disaster effort in conservation if you can't get collaboration among various nations whose boundaries are crossed by the species in question."

Today, thousands of green sea turtles go each summer to nest at Tortuguero—more of them, it seems, than when Carr first started the research center. Carr, however, has paid his last visit to the beach. He died in the spring of 1987. But what he started survives, carried on by his students, and the man himself is not likely to be forgotten. Wrote biologist David Ehrenfeld in memoriam to Archie Carr,

> Some of us who continue his work will pause at times to read a passage from his writings that describes, with the full intimacy of love and genius, a landscape or a part of wild nature or human culture that has vanished beyond recovery. To experience the world through his words is also to understand why his like cannot pass this way again. . . . He was one of the last great minstrels of wilderness, singing a song of joy mixed with abiding melancholy, a song that saddened his listeners as it gave them heart to fight, as he did, against the unthinkable outcome.

One of Carr's favorite beaches was at Cape Canaveral, Florida, one of the last undeveloped nesting beaches of the loggerhead sea turtle in the United States. He took his students there to train them and many times strolled the cape's shores looking for sea turtles. The National Audubon Society is supporting a growing movement to have land south of Cape Canaveral, where 10,000 loggerheads nest each year, designated as the Archie Carr National Wildlife Refuge. It would be a fitting tribute to a man who devoted much of his life to sea turtles.

But perhaps another, equally fitting tribute is already in the making someplace where seas run warm and green sea turtles feed among coastal grass beds. There, sometime early in the next century, scores, hundreds, perhaps even thousands of maturing green sea turtles may feel for the first time the calling of the years, the old urge to come back to shore, and will return across ocean miles to nest on beaches selected for them, half a century before, by a man named Archie Carr.

Swimming in Dangerous Seas

Despite the scientific interest that sea turtles have enjoyed for the past three or four decades, the plight of the sea turtle has not abated. If anything, the sea turtle's future is more tenuous today than it has ever been. Most populations are seriously depleted; breeding adults are being slaughtered for meat, leather, and shell; and many of the nesting beaches that remain are being destroyed or the nests raided for eggs. Efforts to protect sea turtles are being outstripped by commercial interests in the de-veloped nations and by the poverty that inclines Third World peoples to kill sea turtles for money rather than save them.

The hunt for sea turtles goes on exhaustively. Most of the shells and hides are funneled into Japan. The Japanese have accounted for the deaths of some 2 million sea turtles since 1970. Each year they import more than 35,000 hawksbill turtle shells alone. The bulk of these are reduced to shell for ornaments. About 8,000 juvenile turtles are stuffed

These sea turtle products—purses, a golf bag, and stuffed hawksbills—were seized by U.S. Fish and Wildlife Service agents at an international port of entry in New Orleans, Louisiana. Trade in such products, legal in many nations, accounts for thousands of sea turtle deaths each year. Import of the goods into the United States is illegal.

and lacquered to be hung on walls. Ironically, the Japanese view the stuffed bodies of these sea turtles—killed before they were old enough to breed—as a symbol of longevity.

Coastal development also threatens turtle survival. Beach resorts and construction of all kinds ruin beaches for turtle nesting. Eggs are crushed by human activity, and babies that do hatch face a strangely altered environment in which their instincts malfunction. Turtles hatch at night and, driven by innate urges, move in the direction of the brightest light. Under natural conditions this would move them toward the sea, which is brighter than the land because it reflects moonlight and starlight. But where condominiums now stand sentinel at the water's edge, lights from streets and buildings lead the hatchlings to destruction on highways and walkways.

Some turtles simply abandon beaches after development. Florida once provided nesting sites for

thousands of green sea turtles, but, says Llewellyn Ehrhart, a University of Central Florida biologist who has studied sea turtles since 1973, greens abandon beaches after people move in. Today, he says, probably no more than 500 female Florida green sea turtles survive.

Pollution of the seas is also taking a toll of sea turtles. Millions of tons of refuse are dumped into the sea yearly, including plastic materials that pose threats to sea turtles and an array of other animals, from sea lions to dolphins. The plastics come in a great variety of forms, from sandwich bags to plastic sheeting, from cushioning pellets to fish nets. They persist for years, perhaps centuries. Plastic fishing nets that have been lost or abandoned each year entangle and drown sea turtles as well as millions of birds and thousands of sea lions.

Plastic objects have been eaten by green, loggerhead, leatherback, hawksbill, and Kemp's ridley sea turtles. Plastic bags and sheets, apparently mistaken for jellyfish, squid, or some other food, are the most common items eaten, followed by tar balls and plastic pellets. Ingested plastic objects can block sea turtles' digestive tracts and cause ulceration and starvation. Ingested foam plastics may increase a turtle's bouyancy, inhibiting the turtle's ability to dive in pursuit of prey or to escape predators.

The death toll due to ingestion of plastic materials is unmeasured, but some evidence suggests what the limits may be. Of fifteen dead leatherbacks found on Long Island, New York, during a two-week period, eleven had eaten four eight-quart plastic bags each and one had eaten fifteen. Another had swallowed nearly 600 feet of plastic monofilament fishing line. A leatherback that washed ashore along the New Jersey coast in 1988 had died after ingesting one of the hundreds of thousands of balloons released yearly at sports events and other outdoor functions. One twelve-pound juvenile hawksbill found in Hawaii had eaten nearly two pounds of plastic items, including a bag, golf tee, sheeting, monofilament fishing line, artificial flower, bottle cap, and comb.

Even the sargassum rafts and convergence zones that are thought to provide many hatchlings with food and shelter may be turning into death traps. Pollutants such as tar pellets are carried to the rafts by currents, just as the hatchlings are, and pose a danger to the turtles. "Baby turtles eat almost anything, including tar," Archie Carr had observed. "When they do that, it either gums their jaws shut or the tar goes down a way and stops their digestion. It is a very pathetic sight and it kills untold thousands of turtles, up and down the Atlantic Coast and probably every coast."

Chemical pollution is also a suspected problem. About half the juvenile green sea turtles caught in recent years in Florida's Indian River, really a lagoon on the East Coast, bear papillomas on their flippers and heads. These are tumorous growths, Llewellyn Ehrhart says, presumably caused by a virus and perhaps related to chemical pollution. The papillomas,

A hawksbill turtle adrift underwater. The hawksbill is heavily pursued for its shell, which is used in jewelry and ornamentation. In Japan, mounted juvenile hawksbills are sold as symbols of longevity.

Deerfield Beach south of Boca Raton, Florida, illustrates the type of beach development that is jeopardizing sea turtle survival. Even if turtles can nest on the heavily trafficked beaches, the hatchlings, distracted by bright city lights, tend to move toward doom on inland highways rather than toward the sea.

some the size of tennis balls, make it easier for turtles to snag in fishing nets, and they become sites for abrasion and infection.

One major problem for sea turtles may have an easy solution. This is the loss of turtles to the trawl-net fishing industry, in which powerful boats drag trawl nets through the sea, and the nets scoop up everything in their paths. The target is shrimp, but the catch includes millions of pounds of unwanted fish and thousands of sea turtles. This bycatch is simply thrown overboard. Because most of the fish bycatch dies, the U.S. shrimp fleet in the Gulf of Mexico and the Southeast destroys 1.5 billion pounds of fish every year, about 10 pounds of by-catch fish for every pound of shrimp landed. The fleet also catches about 45,000 sea turtles, more than 10,000 of which drown. Most of the captured turtles are juvenile loggerheads, but nearly 1,000 Kemp's ridleys drown in the southeastern fishery each year, too. Each turtle, says Ehrhart, "repre-sents one in a thousand, perhaps one in ten thou-sand hatchlings that came off a beach somewhere. This is the one that the population is counting on to be a breeder in another five or six years. Killing an

animal like this is as important to the population as losing ten thousand hatchlings."

The shrimp-fishing industry continues to kill sea turtles and waste fish bycatch even though the National Marine Fisheries Service (NMFS) sought an end to the killing by requiring trawl fishermen to use a turtle excluder device, also called a trawling efficiency device or TED. This is a mechanism that, attached to the trawl nets, permits sea turtles and much of the other bycatch to escape. There are several different models, but all function in much the same way, releasing unharmed roughly eighteen to twenty of twenty trapped turtles in experiments.

A TED resembles a square cage attached to a net. A set of bars inside the cage allows shrimp to pass through, but deflects large fish or turtles out through a trap door. Smaller fish that are not de-flected by the bars escape through another opening. Some TEDs reduce the bycatch of fin fish by up to 70 percent and virtually eliminate turtle drownings. The TEDs should have provided a rare opportunity for wildlife conservation. "It's very seldom that you run into a situation with an endangered species where there's a technological solution," says Mike

Weber of the Center for Marine Conservation, in the Audubon television program. "With sea turtles, however, we've been in a position of saying, 'We know what the solution is, so what's the problem?'"

The problem is that many shrimpers consider the TEDs a nuisance and resent being required to use them. "The economic impact to the fisherman and just the aggravation of the thing is going to be hard to swallow," the captain of the *Georgia Bulldog*, one of the boats used by NMFS for testing various models of TEDs, told Audubon television filmmakers. However, conservationists argue that the TEDs do not cost all that much, about $200 or less. That is roughly 1 percent of a shrimp vessel's operating costs over the two-year life of the TED.

Weber believes that other factors are more influential in fueling the fishermen's opposition to the TED. "Those factors range from the fact that it was developed by the federal government—and fishermen generally don't get along very well with the federal government—to just not wanting to

Thousands of sea turtles, trapped like this one in a fishing net, drown every year. Such deaths are part of a mounting toll caused by pollution of the sea, loss of nesting areas, and shrimp trawling.

This sign on a Boca Rica, Texas, marina signals the shrimper's opposition to the turtle-excluder device, gear designed to free sea turtles trapped in shrimp nets before they drown.

change," Weber says. Peer pressure against the TEDs is tremendous. In Louisiana some captains were told their boats would be burned if they used TEDs. In addition, many fishermen do not believe that their activities harm sea turtles. One fisherman estimated that in twenty-eight years of fishing he had killed only two sea turtles. Anecdotal comments such as this tend to ignore the data showing that many fishermen kill more turtles than that and also overlook the cumulative impact that results from the large number of people who fish.

Louisiana has been quite a hotbed of opposition. Fishermen there went to court to stop the federal regulation requiring use of TEDs, which was supposed to go into effect in 1987. Implementation of the regulations was halted during the court case, but in the end the fishermen lost. However, the fishermen's influence was felt in Congress, too, where amendments against the TEDs tied up reauthorization of the Endangered Species Act in 1987 and 1988. Texas Representative Solomon Ortiz tried to attach to it an amendment that would

have delayed implementation of the TED regulation. The House of Representatives voted down the amendment by a substantial vote of 270 to 147, but Gulf State senators also held up reenactment of the Endangered Species Act in a dispute over the use of TEDs. In the end the amendments were dropped, but debate about them still held up implementation of the rule. Offshore fishermen were not required to use TEDs until May 1989, nearly two years after the regulation was first issued. Inshore fishermen escaped the regulation until May 1990.

Although the rule is now in place, resistance to it may make it ineffective unless the federal government strictly enforces it. One fisherman echoed the opinion of many when he said, "The TEDs ain't been proven to work and whether anybody is going to pull them or not, I don't know." Without the use of TEDs, the future looks dire for some sea turtle species. Said Archie Carr, "If we don't get the TEDs on, if we don't get the incidental catch by trawling cut down, the Kemp's ridley will disappear within ten years."

What Is Being Done

The United States and Mexico are engaged in several programs for the protection of sea turtles. Perhaps foremost among them are the Kemp's ridley beach-protection and head-start programs.

Protection for the Kemp's got under way in 1966, when the Mexican government sent federal fisheries personnel to Rancho Nuevo to study the turtles and armed Marine guards to protect them. Four years later, the turtle was listed as endangered by the United States.

The big push began in 1978, when the Mexican and U.S. governments initiated a cooperative program that could have been modeled after Archie Carr's attempts to relocate green sea turtle hatchlings on new nesting grounds. Under the program, the United States agreed to assist Mexico in Kemp's management and research in exchange for 2,000 to 3,000 Kemp's eggs each year for a ten-year period. The eggs are taken to Padre Island, a barrier island along the Texas coast, as part of an experimental effort to establish a new Kemp's nesting beach. Biologists hope to establish the second colony to help alleviate the turtle's susceptibility to being wiped out all at once should a major disaster, such as an oil spill or hurricane, destroy Rancho Nuevo.

The eggs are collected as they pass from the female's body and are placed directly into a plastic bag. Special care is taken to avoid contact with Rancho Nuevo sand because biologists suspect that contact between egg and sand may imprint the smell of the sand in the memory of the developing hatchling. If this suspicion is correct, then, years later, turtles imprinted on Rancho Nuevo sand would return to Rancho Nuevo by, in effect, following the scent of the beach. As a precaution the eggs are packed in sand from Padre Island. If the developing hatchlings imprint on this sand, then, when they reach maturity a decade or more later, perhaps they will seek out Padre Island for nesting.

Once placed in Padre Island sand, the eggs are flown about 200 miles to the Padre Island National Seashore, where they are turned over to the care of the National Park Service. The park service incubates the eggs in Padre Island sand and releases the hatchlings on a Padre Island beach, where they are allowed to scuttle across the sand and into the sea in an effort to duplicate the normal course of events after hatch-ing. A taste of the water, too, may imprint the young turtles on their new home.

After the hatchlings have had their first whiff of the sea they are netted, boxed, and shipped to a National Marine Fisheries Service laboratory in Galveston, Texas. There they live in buckets for the next year, growing to about ten inches across. In nature only a small percentage of the hatchlings would live through the first year—perhaps as few as 1 percent—but in the experimental program the survival rate is 95 percent. In addition, biologists hope that the year's delay in release will give the turtles a head start on life. As tiny hatchlings about the size of a silver dollar, the turtles' chances in the ocean were slim.

Llewellyn Ehrhart sketches a green sea turtle's belly as an aid to identification should the turtle be recaptured. Before he releases it, Ehrhart will measure and weigh the turtle and attach a numbered tag to its flipper.

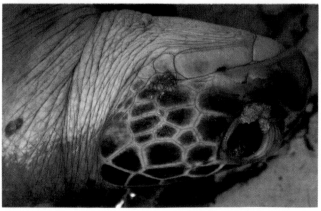

left: *Barbara Schroeder, a biologist from the Florida Department of Natural Resources Sea Turtle Project, assists Llewellyn Ehrhart in weighing a young green sea turtle caught in Florida's Indian River.*

below left: *About 50 percent of the turtles caught in Indian River have tumorous growths, possible evidence of serious pollution problems. This green sea turtle has small tumors around the eyes. Some tumors are the size of softballs.*

Grown to the size of dinner plates, they presumably will be better equipped to escape sharks and other predators.

The juveniles are returned to Padre Island and released from boats directly into parts of the Gulf of Mexico inhabited by young Kemp's that hatched naturally at Rancho Nuevo. The head-start turtles will have to survive in the Gulf for a least ten, or more likely fifteen, years before they will be ready to breed. Within the first ten years of the program, not a single one of the 13,000 head-started Kemp's returned to Padre Island to nest. The relocations were terminated in 1988. Scientists are waiting to see if any turtles return before releasing more, in part out of concern that the head-start turtles are simply becoming new victims of human tampering, no matter how benevolent the intentions.

Despite the risks, most biologists thought the head-start program a worthwhile endeavor. The Rancho Nuevo population remains low. In 1988, only 655 females came ashore at Rancho Nuevo throughout the nesting season, only 1 percent of the 40,000 that crowded just one section of the beach four decades ago. The chance of developing a second colony offered one promise of increasing the animal's numbers and perhaps saving it from oblivion.

Although Kemp's ridleys are now well protected against egg and turtle hunters, this is not the case for other sea turtle species at other Mexican beaches. One example is the olive ridley of the Pacific Ocean. It is under direct assault from commercial exploitation, particularly on Mexico's Escobilla Beach, one of the olive ridley's largest nesting grounds in the western hemisphere. There, as the Kemp's once did, the olive ridleys gather in massive *arribadas*, thousands on one beach at a time. This makes it easy for local fishermen to catch and slaughter large numbers of the turtles quickly and legally, for Mexico is one of the major exporters of turtle skins.

The Mexican government monitors the annual kill and, in an effort to conserve the olive ridleys, reduced the annual quota from 100,000 in the late

1970s to 23,000 today. No data exist, however, to show whether this is a safe number to take, creating a dangerous situation for the turtles. Says Georgita Ruiz, a biologist and veterinarian who is trying to determine the effect of the hunt on the turtles, "From the biological point of view, we know little about the population—how many there are and what they're doing and how much exploitation this population can stand. We are in fact taking adult females from a reproductively active population . . . so this is bound to have a detrimental effect on the population."

Despite the damage that the hunt may be doing, Ruiz does not advocate a total ban on turtle killing because that would deny local residents an important source of protein and income. Instead, she hopes that by monitoring nests and hatchings she can determine the level of catch that will permit the turtles to survive and yet will provide food and income for Escobilla's human residents. Jack Woody, who heads up the U.S. Fish and Wildlife Service's sea turtle programs and also acts as a counselor on international efforts, says that Ruiz and Mexican Federal Fisheries researchers have spent a decade trying to piece together a comprehensive management plan for the government, the same decade that saw the commercial harvest of hundreds of thousands of olive ridleys. Many more years will be needed before population counts will show whether action has been taken in time. The most optimistic note is that the work here is attracting attention throughout Mexico.

By attracting attention to the olive ridley's plight, Ruiz has helped bring more researchers into the program. Most of these are university students who give up vacation time to help count and tag turtles. Since the hatchlings are attracted to any light, the volunteers place lanterns in the middle of hatchling traps. The hatchlings come to the lights, and the volunteers count them. Once tallied, the hatchlings are released. The task is immense. Two million hatchlings emerge each year at Escobilla, and during the hatch the beach is hot, even at night, and the humidity hovers at 100 percent. Sand flies swarm, mosquitoes drone annoyingly, and the count goes on.

The Mexican government has provided strong support for turtle conservation, including full-time military protection to keep poachers away from the turtle eggs. "One reason we are seeing so many positive changes is because of public awareness," says Ruiz. "Turtles have become a symbol of conservation in Mexico. The international importance of

Kemp's ridley sea turtle hatchlings being released on Padre Island, Texas, as part of a federal conservation project. Under an agreement with Mexico, the U.S. government released about 10,000 Kemp's ridleys on Padre Island during a ten-year period that began in 1978.

the species is also making us as Mexicans realize that we're not the sole owners of the resource."

Another sea turtle being studied at a nesting ground on Mexico's Pacific Coast is the black sea turtle, perhaps the least understood of all New World sea turtles. Even its classification as a distinct species or as a subspecies of the green sea turtle is up for grabs. Ranging the Pacific from Chile to Alaska, it nests mainly in Mexico and the Galapagos Islands and is heavily exploited for eggs and meat.

A major nesting site of the black turtle is Colola Beach in remote Michoacan. The beach is protected by the Mexican government. There, male and female black turtles mate offshore, swimming together at the water's surface and thus offering researchers and students from the University of Michoacan a unique research opportunity.

With rare exceptions, male sea turtles of all species never leave the sea. Consequently, very little is known about them. The only way to study them is to find them in the water and bring them up for tagging. That is nearly impossible when the turtles are in the open sea because they swim too fast to catch. But biologists at Michoacan have an unsur-

passed opportunity to make contact with the males when the turtles are mating. The researchers speed up to the breeding animals and catch the males at the surface before they can release the females. The males are then measured and tagged. As with Archie Carr's green turtles, repeat catches of the males will help show how widely they roam.

The director of the program is Javier Alvarado. He at first set out to study sea turtles, but finds himself, as Archie Carr did, increasingly involved with turtle protection. At Colola Beach, turtle and egg poaching is a constant concern, and Alvarado's work on male black sea turtles now shares his time with efforts to save the animals.

Black turtles come up on Colola Beach at night during the five-month nesting season. Each one arrives alone, making it difficult for the Marines to patrol the beach thoroughly. Poachers slip in at night and follow turtle tracks to the nests. They even take eggs as they are laid. Ironically, when Alvarado and his volunteers catch an egg poacher, they may not press charges. Mexico's economy is very bad right now, and many egg poachers are just trying to get food for their families. The turtle re-

Eggs from sea turtle nests are carried to protected sites and surrounded with wire mesh to keep out predators in this Mexican conservation program designed to reduce egg poaching.

This arribada *of olive ridley sea turtles took place in August 1982 on Nancite Beach, Costa Rica. The turtles here are females coming ashore to breed. It is the only time sea turtles return to land.*

searchers therefore are sympathetic toward the egg poachers they apprehend and may let the poachers keep some of the eggs. However, they encourage turtle conservation by getting the egg poachers to put the remaining eggs into protected areas on the beach. This quells any resentment the poachers might feel toward the researchers or the turtles and teaches that sea turtles must be protected if they are to be used, a sound conservation lesson.

Alvarado is also working on a new way to beat egg poaching. He is enlisting the help of local children in gathering eggs from the beach and bringing them to a small, fenced area where he can bar human and nonhuman predators. The work makes the chil-

dren into friends of the turtles long before they will have thoughts about poaching them. He gives prizes to the children who bring in the most eggs, making the quest into a sort of Easter egg hunt. When the hatchlings emerge, the children return to help with the counting. "If you could only see the expression of joy on the children's faces when they are releasing the hatchlings coming from the eggs that they themselves helped transplant to the hatcheries," Alvarado says. "It makes us feel that our efforts are worthwhile." It is his hope that the children will grow up to understand the needs of the black turtle and to protect the resource so that they can later catch turtles in balance with nature.

And What About Tomorrow?

Sea turtles are among the most difficult animals to protect. There are a number of reasons for this. Perhaps foremost among them is the fundamental

problem of locating and working with turtles. As Archie Carr pointed out in the Audubon television program, "The young of all species, we're now con-

97

vinced, are out in the open ocean isolated from the kinds of help that we normally think we can give." Moreover, though young turtles may swim beyond the helping hand, they are well within reach of such destructive forces as ocean pollution and fishing bycatch.

Another obstacle is the many habitat and behavioral shifts that the turtles make during their lifetimes. They need not only safe beaches, but also clean open oceans and rich seagrass beds and protected reefs, all widely scattered. The problem is compounded because most sea turtle species occur throughout the globe, so each species is subject to different problems in different places. To protect these species will require development of a large array of conservation programs that meet the needs of specific geographic areas. The programs will also have to take into account the differences in the various human cultures that use sea turtles. In addition, most sea turtles migrate across international boundaries, making it impossible for one nation to protect the species in the way that the United States might try to protect, for example, its wolves, condors, or grizzlies.

In one of his scientific articles, Carr pointed out another major problem. "To make valid judgments of the survival outlook of a species, and to devise programs of conservation, the sizes of breeding populations must be known, at least approximately." But making biologically sound estimates of sea turtle populations has so far proved elusive. Landing records of commercial turtle operations are inadequate for making population estimates, and the difficulty of monitoring individual turtles makes it impossible to count them in their feeding areas. The best opportunity for making population estimates would be the nesting beaches, provided that all females in each colony bred each year and always returned to exactly the same beach. Unfortunately for turtle tabulators, most of the evidence suggests that females do not nest in consecutive years and may even go for several years between nestings. At Tortuguero, fewer than half the tagged females are seen a second time. Carr was never able to figure out where the missing turtles went. The situation appears even worse for some other species. Of 1,835 adult leatherback sea turtles tagged in Surinam as part of a study of their species' wide-ranging travels, only six were seen again. Of

10,000 adult leatherbacks tagged in French Guiana during the late 1970s, only one long-range recovery was made. The lack of returns and the uncertainty of the fate of the missing turtles makes sound population estimates based on nesting beach counts difficult at best.

Another problem is that we have started so late. Years of research are necessary to establish the baseline data needed to determine whether a population is increasing, stable, or declining. The rates of turtle exploitation and beach destruction today make it difficult to collect population data in time to take measures to protect declining colonies. The difficulty is compounded because sea turtles are so long lived. Females that do return to nesting beaches may do so for years, making the population appear stable when in fact no young turtles are being added to the colony. The decline would not become apparent until the old adults died off and the whole population collapsed.

Archie Carr believed that we have an obligation to protect the sea turtle, and in the Audubon television program said, "The obligation to save the turtles is very real, just as we have a very real obligation to save whales and condors and all the rest of wild nature and wild landscapes, [because of] the mere fact that they are there, that we don't know what we're doing when we remove them, that it is distressing to many of us to see them gone." But the world has rarely, if ever, been run by men and women who feel obligations toward sea turtles and responsibility toward condors and whales. The fate of the sea turtle therefore lies heavily on the shoulders of those who want to know that sea turtles will forever ply the world's oceans. Congress needs to be swayed to provide funding for long-term sea turtle research designed to provide data on ways to ensure sound turtle protection. Congress also needs to be urged to seek international treaties that coordinate the sea turtle management efforts of several nations into a consistent and effective plan, much as the treaties won by conservationists eighty years ago laid the basis for international migratory-bird protection. If just these two things can be accomplished, then perhaps the sea turtle will have a future that will match its long, long past.

IF DOLPHINS COULD TALK

*Based on the Audubon Television Special by
Hardy Jones and Julia Whitty and
Narrated by Michael Douglas*

AMONG THE THINGS left to us by the ancient Greeks is this story:

> The boys who attended the gymnasium at Iassos used to wash daily in the sea. One day a dolphin came up to them and fell in love with the finest of the boys. At first the boy feared the dolphin, but with gentle behavior the dolphin won the boy's love. The two became inseparable, and the boy would meet the dolphin each day and ride it out to sea. But then once, when the boy was very tired, he threw himself carelessly down upon the dolphin, and its upraised fin impaled him. As the dolphin took the wounded boy out to sea, it saw the billowing blood and felt the boy's limp weight and realized he was dead. In sorrow, the dolphin bore the boy to shore and threw itself upon the beach, and there in the sand it lay beside the dead boy until it too died. The people of Iassos built the dolphin and the boy a tomb where they could lie together for eternity, and in front of the tomb they erected a monument graven with the image of the boy on the dolphin.

The story may have been based on fact, for dolphins frequented the unsullied shores of the Classical Mediterranean, and stories abound of dolphins and children playing together in that lost time when seamen believed that evil would haunt a man who killed a dolphin.

Here is a true dolphin story from modern Japan:

> For centuries, the fishermen of Iki Island, 40 miles off the Japanese mainland, earned their living by fishing with hook and line. After World War II, fishing intensified because the waters around Iki provided some of the best fishing in Japan. At the same time, industry sprang up on mainland Japan, polluting the coastal waters. In the face of these two pressures, fish and squid populations around Iki began to drop off. But the fishermen blamed the declines on the bottlenose dolphins and false killer whales—another dolphin species—that live off Iki. In February 1978, the fishermen herded more than 1,000 of the animals into a shallow bay and slaughtered them with clubs, guns, and knives. The sea turned red with blood. Despite scientific evidence which shows that the fishing declines are due to overfishing, the slaughter became an annual event. The kill was repeated the following year, and in 1980 about 800 dolphins were killed and their bodies ground into fertilizer. The seamen of Japan apparently have concluded that it is bad luck *not* to kill dolphins.

What has happened at Iki is unique only in its overt goriness. The destruction of dolphins has become increasingly common in many of the world's seas.

The Origin of a Species

Dolphins are descended from an ancient family of extinct hoofed animals called Mesonychids. These animals lived throughout the northern hemisphere many millions of years ago, in a time when the great Tethys Sea still covered most of the world, when South America, Antarctica, and Australia were still joined in one big continent. Some Mesonychid species were the size of cocker spaniels, some were as big as bears. Though they walked on hooves—five little hooves to each foot—unlike modern hoofed animals they were not all herbivores. Their fossilized teeth show that some species ate meat.

Paleontologists believe that some of the smaller predatory forms lived on fish and other animals that they found in the shallow, nearshore waters of the Tethys Sea. As natural selection worked its biological miracles, the hoofed creatures became more and more suited to life in the sea. From looking much like wolves they evolved through a stage at which they were much like sea otters, and then seals, their feet transformed into flippers. Time passed, and their tails flattened to form flukes. Their muzzles became longer, and their nostrils after thousands of generations of natural selection moved from the tip of the muzzle to the top. Fifty million years ago, the Mesonychids had given rise to the earliest whales, which may still have been clad in fur and had four flippers, though the hind limbs were probably quite small. Later whales were still more like those alive today—the nostrils moving above the eyes, the hair vanishing, the hind limbs disappearing. Like their land-dwelling, hoofed forebears, they lived entirely in the northern hemisphere.

And then, about 30 million to 40 million years ago, South America and Australia broke away from Antarctica. The climate of the southern seas changed, and the primitive whales moved into them. As they spread over the globe, they evolved into new forms suited for new niches, until, 25 million years ago, they had radiated into a large variety of species. From these evolved the modern whales, a group that includes the dolphins. The dolphins had appeared by 12 million years ago and subsequently gave rise to more species than any other group of toothed whales, a sign that they are biologically very successful.

Because the study of dolphins is such a young field—only in the past two or three decades have scientists been able to investigate sea creatures with anything akin to thoroughness—the exact number of living dolphin species is not certain. The figure is probably about forty. Taxonomists—biologists who study the classification of species—are still in the process of classifying the various species.

Dolphin taxonomy suffers from some fairly fundamental problems, since even the term *dolphin* is used imprecisely and is often interchanged with *porpoise*. Scientists place the animals in a group called the Cetacea, which includes the big whales and encompasses about seventy-six species. The cetaceans are broken into two groups—the baleen whales, such as the humpback, and the toothed whales, which includes the sperm whale. Dolphins and porpoises are classified as toothed whales. However, the word *whale* is usually applied only to large members of the group, including the killer whale or orca, which is really a type of dolphin.

Some modern biologists have tried to restrict use of the term *dolphin* to the members of the family of animals called Delphinidae and to the family of river dolphins, the Platanistidae. They have tried to restrict the term *porpoise* to members of the Phocoenidae family, which includes the Dall's porpoise and the harbor or common porpoise (which, one source points out, is neither common nor found very often in harbors). Other biologists have suggested that all the small toothed whales be called porpoises, in order to avoid confusion with a species of fish called a dolphin. This approach seems simple and logical, but nevertheless it failed to gain any currency. The result of all this is that there is simply no rule of thumb for determining which animals to call dolphins and which porpoises. Of course, for scientific purposes the confusion caused by common names was more or less solved about 200 years ago by Carl Linne, who developed a now worldwide system that assigns each species an unambiguous Latinized or Greek name. To avoid confusion in this chapter, the appendices include a list of the common names used here with the more precise scientific names.

Dolphin anatomy.

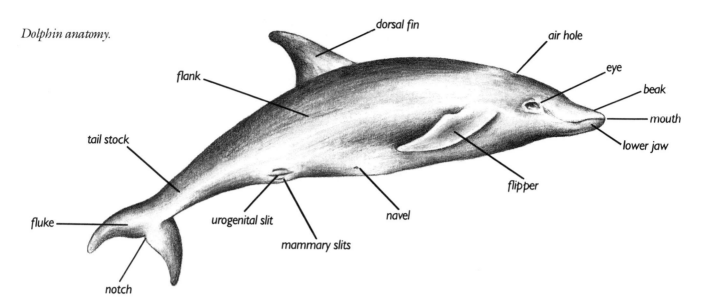

The World of the Dolphin

The dolphin is a mammal adapted to life in the sea. Because it lives in a world so alien to humans, its secrets have only recently, and then only partially, been revealed to science.

Dolphins and porpoises are air-breathing animals, but life in the sea has caused them to evolve more efficient respiratory systems than those found in land animals. Bottlenose dolphins can exhale and inhale in roughly a third of a second and can stay underwater for at least a quarter of an hour, though they usually do not stay under for more than half that. More impressive are the diving times of some of the large whales. Sperm whales can stay under for up to an hour and a half. The mechanism that allows such prolonged dives is much the same in great whales and in the smaller species. The animals are able to take deeper breaths than land mammals and can absorb more oxygen per breath. Also, pound for pound whales have about twice the blood of land animals, with relatively more red blood cells for oxygen absorption. Moreover, the muscles absorb oxygen from the blood much more efficiently than do the muscles of land mammals. In addition, the heart rate of dolphins and porpoises during submersion may be only half of its peak rate when breathing.

As might be expected of an animal that lives in water, the dolphin's sensory world is much different from that of a land animal. Because dolphins have to be able to see well both in and out of water, evolution has bestowed upon them powerful muscles around the eye that can change the shape of the focusing organ, the lens, so that the animals can see well in either environment. Dolphins and other whales apparently have lost, or have largely lost, the sense of smell. This was caused partly by the migratain nerve endings that allow the dolphin to maintain a posture that keeps water flowing over the body in a pattern that is suitable for most efficient swimming.

Dolphins and porpoises outstrip all land mamplex nerve endings found in the skin around the blowhole may tell a dolphin when the blowhole is above water so that it can be opened for breathing. When investigating strange objects, dolphins often touch the objects with the tips of their lower jaws, suggesting that nerve endings on the "chin" might be sensitive to touch. The skin may also sense the speed at which a dolphin is traveling and may contain nerve endings that allow the dolphin to maintain a posture that keeps water flowing over the body in a pattern suitable for most efficient swimming.

Dolphins and porpoises outstrip all land mammals, with the exception of bats, in their acoustic and auditory abilities. They have refined biological sonar to the point that they can virtually "see" with sound.

Perhaps the first to study the dolphins were the fishermen of ancient Greece. In *The History of Animals* Aristotle wrote that the dolphin "lives for many years; some are known to have lived for more than twenty-five, and some for thirty years; the fact is fishermen nick their tails sometimes and set them adrift again, and by this expedient their ages are ascertained." In marking dolphins and releasing them, the ancient fishermen anticipated by several centuries the tag-and-release studies that have revealed so much about the lives of dolphins, sharks, sea turtles, and other ocean creatures.

Knowledge of the real nature of dolphins was slow to accumulate. Aristotle, writing half a millennium before Christ, thought dolphins were fish that breathed both air and water. Some 2,000 years later, Herman Melville, despite Linne's declaration in 1776 that whales and dolphins were not fish, wrote in *Moby-Dick*, "Be it known that, waiving all argument, I take the good old fashioned ground that the whale is a fish, and call upon the holy Jonah to back me. . . . To be short, then, a whale is *a spouting fish with a horizontal tail*. There you have him."

Melville also had this to say: "Porpoise meat is good eating, you know." In this, Melville touched upon perhaps the earliest interaction between humans and dolphins, the exploitation of the animals by people. Long before anything was known about dolphin biology, people were taking the animals for various uses. Melville declared, "A well-fed, plump Huzza Porpoise will yield you one good gallon of good oil. But the fine and delicate fluid extracted from his jaws is exceedingly valuable. It is in request among jewellers and watchmakers. Sailors put it on their hones."

Even today dolphins and porpoises are exploited more than they are understood. In Japan, about 50,000 a year are killed for food. Only in the past twenty or thirty years have scientists begun to get more than a glimmering of knowledge about live dolphins.

Dolphins and porpoises look much like fish because all three are adapted to the same environment. They live in a weightless, watery world, where limbs are not needed to support heavy bodies. Consequently, the hind limbs have disappeared and the front limbs have evolved into small appendages with broad surfaces that can be used to control movement. The dolphin's tail has become a powerful engine that propels the animal through the water. Its body has lost virtually all of the hair that characterizes other mammals. Its skin has become smooth and its body fusiform to reduce friction when the animal is moving through the water. Even the breasts of the females are concealed inside the body, opening into small slits on either side of the genitals.

When dolphins lost their hair as an adaptation to aquatic life, they had to evolve some other means to keep body heat from escaping. The solution was a layer of fat that envelopes the body. Called *blubber*, this fat is a good insulator, so good that another mechanism has evolved to keep dolphins from overheating when in warm water. Blood vessels pass from the deeper parts of their bodies through the blubber and into the surface of the skin. When a dolphin is warm, blood flows to the skin, where contact with the water cools it. When the animal needs to conserve heat, the vessels constrict and the warm blood is kept within the body.

Dolphins and porpoises lost external ears as part of the evolutionary process of streamlining. The openings of the ear are also tiny, in many species only two or three millimeters in diameter. Biologists have not determined exactly how the ear functions. The animals certainly hear well underwater, and apparently at least some species can hear well in air, too. In order for the ear to function underwater, it must be filled with water, because the difference in density between air and water makes it difficult or impossible for sound to transfer from water to an air-filled ear. Similarly, when the animal is above water, its ear must be air filled if it is to hear sounds transmitted through the air. How dolphins and porpoises are able to hear in both environments is something of a mystery. Some scientists believe that the ears are vestigial and useless, that the animals hear only through their lower jaws. In some species, fat deposits along the lower jaw run up to the inner ear, and the jawbone near the deposits is very thin—nearly transparent. The thin bone and the fat deposits may transmit sound to the inner ear.

More certain than how sound is heard is the importance of sound to dolphin lives. Dolphins, porpoises, and other toothed whales emit pulsing sounds as they swim underwater. When the sounds

Biologist Bernd Wuersig tracks radio signals from tagged dolphins off Patagonia, Argentina. A receiver is used to pick up beeps transmitted by a radio that has been attached to a dolphin's dorsal fin (inset). Radio tracking helps reveal dolphin movements and periods of activity, but many of the animals' deeper secrets remain unexplored.

hit an object in the water, they bounce back to the animal that emitted them. The animal can tell what objects lie ahead by the way the pulses bounce. This is called *echolocation*, and it gives dolphins much more information about their environment than vision can do. Sounds give the animals data on an object's size, shape, texture, internal structure, and even the material the object is made of.

Biologists have not yet determined how dolphins and porpoises make sounds. The animals have no vocal cords, so it has been hypothesized that at least some cetaceans make sounds by moving air through the nasal passages. Scientists believe that once the sounds are produced, they are "focused" into a directional beam by a ball of fat—old-time whalers called it the *melon*—that lies in front of the braincase. The sounds then strike their target and echo back to the dolphin, where they are picked up by the fat deposits around the lower jaw and trans-

mitted to the ear. The role of the melon and the fat deposits of the lower jaw has not really been determined with any assurance, but the position of the deposits, the composition of the fat, and the presence of the deposits in every toothed whale ever examined suggest indirectly that the deposits are used in echolocation.

Using echolocation, blindfolded bottlenose dolphins can distinguish plates made of copper, glass, plastic, and aluminum. Some dolphin species can detect objects only three-quarters of an inch in diameter. Experiments have shown that bottlenose dolphins can detect a 10 percent difference in metallic balls, differences in thickness of 0.1 centimeter in metal disks, and differences in the shapes of plates. Blindfolded bottlenose dolphins can track and locate pieces of fish that float past them, provided that the pieces do not fall below the level of the dolphins' upper jaws. They can also navigate without any apparent difficulty. However, not all dolphin and porpoise species are equally adept at echolocation. The common dolphin, for example, tends to become disoriented in a tank filled with cloudy water. When a captive Pacific white-sided dolphin was blindfolded experimentally, it ran into the walls of its tank and required several days before it could navigate without vision. The best echolocation probably is to be found in species that live in waters where visibility is limited.

Evidence suggests that some cetaceans use pulsing sounds to stun prey. One researcher discovered that when he put his hand on the forehead of a young sperm whale, the animal made a low sound forceful enough to push the hand away. Sperm whales are thought to stun squid by bombarding them with pulsing sounds. Some species of dolphin and porpoise are thought to use sounds to stun fish.

Dolphins produce other sounds in addition to those used in echolocation. Each bottlenose dolphin apparently has its own unique, individualized "signature" whistle that identifies it to other dolphins. Presumably the individuals of other species have signature whistles, too. Newborn bottlenose dolphins begin almost immediately to whistle, and mother dolphins may recognize their own offspring by this sound.

Dolphins and porpoises seem to use vocalizations to reveal their emotional states, too. Juveniles separated from their mothers, one researcher observed, "often whistle constantly for hours, even days, a behavior which suggests emotional unrest." A mature female that had spent ten years in captivity with one male bobbed in the center of her tank and vocalized for two days and three nights when the male was removed. She also refused to perform tricks she had been trained to do. She returned to normal behavior when the male was put back.

The dolphin's ability to use echolocation certainly has captured the interest of the human imagination. The military has even studied cetaceans to learn more about radar and sonar. The amount of

A blindfolded bottlenose dolphin retrieves rings tossed by a trainer in a study on echolocation conducted at Marineland of the Pacific in Los Angeles. Not all dolphin species are equally adept at echolocation. Some can hardly navigate if blindfolded.

attention that echolocation has drawn, however, is rivaled or exceeded by the attention drawn to dolphin intelligence.

Dolphins and porpoises have relatively large brains. The brain of a bottlenose dolphin weighs about 3.5 pounds, larger on average than the typical three-pound human brain. However, brain size alone is not necessarily an indication of intelligence. The structure of the brain is also important. Human and dolphin brains are similar in having large cerebral hemispheres that are complexly folded. However, the outer covering of the brain—the cortex, where the centers of conscious control lie—is thinner in dolphins than in humans. Also, the pattern of folding in the cetacean's cerebral cortex is more like that of such hoofed animals as deer, but this may be more a sign of the cetacean's early evolu-

tionary ancestry among hoofed stock than proof of a lack of intelligence.

Perhaps also important to levels of intelligence is the size of the brain relative to body size. The average human brain may weigh slightly less than that of a bottlenose dolphin, but on the other hand the average human body weighs a good deal less than the average adult bottlenose's 500 pounds. The brain-to-body-size ratio of the human is about 2 percent, compared to slightly less than 1 percent for the bottlenose.

Why dolphins and porpoises have relatively large brains is subject for speculation. They may need large brains for processing all the information they receive from echolocation. Researcher Francis Crick, who won the Nobel Prize for his work in genetics, has formulated a hypothesis that may answer the

At Marine World in Vallejo, California, a researcher records data on dolphin sounds as part of a study on dolphin communication. Dolphins and porpoises apparently use vocal sounds to communicate among themselves, and scientists are beginning to unravel the mystery of dolphin calls.

riddle of dolphin brain size. He has discovered that animals—such as dolphins—that have high metabolic rates and lack or experience little dream sleep tend to have relatively large brains. He has suggested that the large brains help the animals cope with large amounts of unnecessary information that other animals erase while they are dreaming. On the other hand, it is quite possible that the large brain size of animals such as the bottlenose dolphin is exactly what it appears to be on the surface—a sign of high intelligence.

Perhaps the biggest problem in determining whether this is so is the difficulty of measuring intelligence. Even the IQ tests administered to people have been seriously questioned as valid measures of human intelligence, particularly when the individual being tested comes from a culture different from the one that created the test. Psychologists know that problem solving, one sign of intelligence, is governed among humans by cultural factors. For example, a test based on problem solving performed by an individual working alone does not give a valid measure of intelligence for individuals from a society in which all problems are solved by people working in cooperative groups. An individual human may therefore fail a test not because of a lack of intelligence, but because the test did not ask the right question or put it in the right context. Given that it is difficult enough to measure human intelligence in any reliable, cross-cultural way, it is easy to see that valid measurement of cetacean intelligence is nearly impossible if only because dolphins live in an environment vastly different from that of humans and have vastly different sensory inputs. In any test of dolphin intelligence, how can scientists be sure they are asking the right question? Or asking it in the right way? A useful, universal definition of intelligence, one that applies equally well to all species, has never even been formulated. Is it foresight? Is it insight? Is it memory? And what are the signs of intelligence? Is one sign the possession of a behavioral flexibility that is based more on learning than on instinct? Whatever intelligence is, it certainly must be adaptive to an animal's needs. And if that is true, then how does biological adaptation affect the signs of intelligence?

Clearly, investigations into dolphin intelligence are hampered by lack of consistent methods of measurement and by the differences that separate human from cetacean. Nevertheless, work on dolphin and porpoise intelligence has led to some fascinating discoveries. At the University of Hawaii, Louis Herman and his associates have studied dolphin intelligence for more than two decades. Early in his research Herman concluded that captive dolphins perform badly in tests of visual memory because they are oriented toward a more auditory interpretation of the world. Their scores improved dramatically when visual elements were connected to an auditory code. Using sign language and sounds, Herman and his colleagues have discovered that dolphins can be taught syntax, semantics, and such concepts as up and down. By training bottlenose dolphins to associate certain sounds or hand signals with corresponding objects and teaching them a variety of verbs, Herman has been able to teach dolphins to respond correctly to complicated commands, such as "bring the ball to such and such a trainer" (as opposed to any trainer at random) or "touch the triangle with your tail."

Herman and other researchers have also found that dolphins are great mimics of both sounds and actions. They often mimic the sounds of motors and other noises. A bottlenose dolphin was observed to copy the leaping technique of the Pacific spinner dolphin after seeing it done once, even though the leaps are not normal behavior for the bottlenose. A captive female bottlenose mimicked the swimming technique of a fur seal with which she shared a tank. She and another female also used a piece of glass to scrape the sides of their tank after watching a human tank cleaner at work. A six-month-old captive female once watched a visitor blow cigarette smoke against the glass of her tank. She then swam to her mother, took a mouthful of milk, returned to the visitor, and released the milk, which swirled around her head like smoke.

Some things that dolphins do in the wild also could be interpreted as signs of intelligence. Orcas, also called killer whales but really a type of dolphin, cooperate in hunting large whales. They even prevent the big whales from surfacing to breathe. Sometimes, in their attacks on whales, orcas throw themselves over the heads of their prey, perhaps in an effort to cover the blowhole. Perhaps most remarkable of all, a herd of orcas off New South Wales, Australia, reputedly helped whalers by driving large whales into Twofold Bay and keeping them at the surface, where they could easily be harpooned. The whalers let the orcas eat the lips and tongues of

A trainer at Marine World in Vallejo, California, communicates with a dolphin by using hand signals. Some dolphin and porpoise species are easily trained and quickly learn complicated sets of commands.

whales killed. One family of whalers worked with the orcas for nearly a century in a tradition apparently handed down through generations of both whalers and whales.

Bottlenose dolphins also cooperate in the herding of fish. Bottlenose dolphins that live off the southeastern United States have learned to enter estuaries, where they herd fish into shallower and shallower water until finally they force the fish to come ashore. The dolphins then beach themselves, coming almost entirely out of the water, in order to eat the stranded fish. Bottlenose dolphins have also learned to untie the knots that fishermen use to draw together the ends of purse-sein nets.

Although all of these behaviors seem signs of intelligence, they can also be explained by other means, such as conditioning or genetically innate behavior. In any event, it is quite likely that all species are not equally intelligent, just as all primate species—monkeys, apes, and humans—are not equally intelligent. This complicates the matter of measuring dolphin intelligence even more. Clearly, far more research is needed before anything certain can be said about the level of dolphin intelligence.

A Sampler of Dolphin Species

Because dolphins and porpoises, like other sea creatures, are difficult to study, little is known about most species. However, some dolphins and porpoises have been relatively better studied than others because they live along coasts, or do well in captivity, or are part of a fishery operation that puts them into contact with humans.

One of the best known is the bottlenose, the

112

species that starred in the television series *Flipper*. The bottlenose is found in most of the world's coastal and offshore waters and was one of the first dolphin species kept in captivity. In 1913 five bottlenose dolphins were dragged by ropes around their tails from nets off Cape Hatteras and taken to the New York Aquarium in boxes filled with enough water to support them. Apparently none survived the next three years. Despite this early beginning, the real impetus for keeping dolphins in captivity

Human meets bottlenose dolphin. Although wild dolphins can sometimes be approached closely, divers usually should let dolphins make first contact. Dolphins sometimes resent human intrusion.

did not come until the 1930s, when the leaps and play of dolphins at Marine Studios, the precursor to Marineland, in Florida caught the attention of the staff. After World War II, Marineland established a colony of captive bottlenose dolphins. Some of the animals even bred there. Today the captive population worldwide probably exceeds 500 animals. Because the bottlenose lives in nearshore waters and adapts well to captivity, it has been more studied than most other species.

Bottlenose dolphins are big animals. A very large one can reach thirteen feet long and weigh in excess of 1,000 pounds, though most are around 500 pounds and nine feet long. Wild groups have been studied off the United States, Argentina, South Africa, Australia, France, and England. In some areas they have voluntarily made contact with people in ways similar to those described in the stories of ancient Greece. A lone male that appeared off the north coast of Cornwall in England in 1981 began making contact with people in 1983. He seemed to choose certain individuals for contact and became

River Dolphins

Although we usually associate dolphins with oceans and seas, four species live exclusively in rivers. The largest is the Amazon River dolphin (*Inia geoffrensis*), which lives in the Amazon and Orinoco rivers and their larger tributaries, feeding on fish and crustaceans. Adults are up to ten feet long and weigh as much as 200 pounds. It is usually pinkish, though sometimes the back is gray. Its eyes are small, as might be expected of a creature that lives in dark waters with limited visibility, but they are functional. It lacks a distinct fin on its back, which instead bears a high ridge that peaks over the center.

Two river dolphins ply the waters of southern Asia, the Ganges River dolphin (*Platanista gangetica*) of the Ganges, Brahmaputra, and Karnaphuli rivers of India and Pakistan, and the Indus River dolphin (*Platanista minor*) found in Pakistan. The two species are much alike. They bear only a vestige of a fin on their backs and characteristically swim on their sides so that one of the front fins drags along the river bottom, presumably stirring up organisms for the dolphins to eat. They are nearly sightless, their tiny eyes capable only of distinguishing light from dark. They navigate entirely by echolocation, feeding on shrimp and such bottom fish as carp and catfish. Females grow to about six feet in length, about 25 percent larger than males.

The Chinese River dolphin (*Lipotes vexillifer*) is found only in the mid to lower

Chinese River dolphin.

portions of the Yangtze River, where it apparently feeds on fish. It lives in cloudy waters, so its use of echolocation doubtlessly is highly developed. Adults are a little more than six feet long. It has a low fin on its back. Called *baiji* by the Chinese, this dolphin was listed in 1986 by the International Union for the Conservation of Nature and Natural Resources as one of the world's twelve most endangered species. It disappeared from the upper reaches of the Yangtze around 1970 and numbers only some 300 animals. The population seems to be declining even further. About half the deaths are caused by snagging in fishing gear, though other deaths are attributed to injuries from boat propellers and river pollution. Shipping traffic on the river has increased about eightfold in thirty years and is still rising. The Chinese goverment has undertaken a plan to protect some of the animals in captivity until their habitat problems can be solved. However, fishing and shipping are almost impossible to control under current conditions.

friendly with at least one diver. However, he discouraged close association with many other people, butting them or biting them lightly. Once he even forced his diver "friend" out of the water by grasping the diver with his jaws and dragging him to his boat so roughly that the diver bled. The dolphin became increasingly aggressive as he achieved celebrity status and more and more people came to see him. He disappeared in 1984. At Monkey Mia on Western Australia's Shark Bay a group of dolphins has become friendly with beach visitors, allowing people to pet them and even letting children ride on their backs. The animals also take fish from people's hands and sometimes reverse the situation by bringing fish to people. The Monkey Mia dolphins are the only herd—some twenty animals—to become friendly with people. Other cases have always involved individual dolphins.

When humans have chosen to make contact with dolphins, the result usually has not been pleasant for the animals. Oil rendered from the jaws of porpoises was used in the nineteenth century to lubricate watches. In the 1880s bottlenose dolphins were hunted off Cape May, New Jersey, and Cape Hatteras, North Carolina. Wrote British naturalist Richard Lydekker in the 1890s,

> It appears that these dolphins are abundant off the coasts of Hatteras, in North Carolina, and associate in schools of considerable size. On the 19th of May fourteen of these animals were secured at one haul of the nets in the morning, while in the afternoon of the same day no less than sixty-six were taken . . . between 15th November 1884 and the middle of the following May, no less than twelve hundred and sixty-eight of them were caught at Hatteras.

Lydekker also described how Native Americans hunted porpoises by shooting at them with shotguns from boats, then rowing up to the wounded animals and spearing them. To be a successful porpoise hunter required years of training. "Boys, ten or twelve years of age, are taken out in canoes by the men, and thus early trained in the pursuit of that which is to form their main support in after years. Porpoise-shooting is followed at all seasons and in all kinds of weather—in the summer sea, in the boisterous autumn gales, and in the dreadful icy seas of mid-winter." A good hunter was said to kill 100 to 150 porpoises each season.

Wild bottlenose dolphins may live alone or in groups numbering more than 1,000. The social patterns within the groups vary. Clear dominance hierarchies exist in captivity, with males dominant. Presumably this reflects dominance hierarchies that occur in the wild. Wild dolphins that follow behind fishing boats cadging scraps of food also show a dominance hierarchy topped by males. However, social order within wild bottlenose groups is fluid, depending on the type of habitat in which the group lives. Individuals seem to switch from group to group. Large herds of several hundred bottlenose dolphins seem to be made up of numerous stable subgroups that join and leave the larger groups at will. For example, a herd off South Africa that sometimes swelled to 500 animals seemed to be made up of many stable groups of 25 to 50.

Some groups seem to be exclusive. A herd of 100 in Florida Bay kept within a range of some thirty square miles, never mixing with bottlenose dolphins outside their range. In Queensland, Australia, a herd of bay dolphins never mixed with coastal bottlenose that lived outside the bay. Such exclusivity may have evolutionary significance. Bottlenose dolphins that live nearshore tend to be smaller than those that live offshore, and may represent different species or subspecies. They may even provide an example of how animals of a single species might become reproductively isolated and gradually evolve into separate species.

Bottlenose dolphins subsist on a variety of bony fish and also eat sharks and squid. Probably anything edible that a dolphin can catch is considered fair game.

Bottlenose dolphins seem to have highly active libidos. Although they do not mature until about twelve years old, males only six months old have been seen trying to initiate sexual activities with other dolphins. In fact, in captivity they do not seem particular about the sex or even the species of the animal they approach, since young males will court other males as well as dolphins of other species and even sea turtles. It is not clear whether they would engage in sexual behavior so intensely in the wild.

Gestation in the bottlenose lasts about a year. The young is about 3.5 feet long at birth and swims unassisted to the surface. Mother and offspring maintain vocal contact with whistling sounds. The bond between them is close, and the young nurse for about eighteen months, though some may nurse nearly a year longer. The animals probably live no more than twenty-five years.

Another dolphin species that has been studied

extensively is the orca. It is the largest of the dolphins, reaching in excess of thirty feet and nine tons. Adult males may be distinguished from adult females by the larger fins on the males' backs. In females, the fin is curved. In males it is erect and up to six feet long.

Orcas are found worldwide in both nearshore and offshore waters. Traditional wisdom says that they live in cold coastal waters, but recent sightings show that they occur around Hawaii and in the Mediterranean. Historical reports also locate them in freshwater, including the Thames, Rhine, and Seine. Studies in Washington State's Puget Sound and in waters around Canada's Vancouver Island have indicated that orcas live in herds, or *pods*, of up to fifty animals. The social bonds that hold the pods together are poorly understood. Some pods seem to lose and gain members periodically, whereas the membership of other pods is unchanging. Also, some Puget Sound pods seem to be resident units; other pods are transient. One hypothesis suggests that the transient pods are made up of individuals rejected from the resident pods and that transient individuals will never reproduce. If this hypothesis is correct, then the transient pods are biological dead-ends.

Members of stable resident pods apparently are related. Some pods combine with other pods to form larger aggregations which some biologists call communities. Each pod seems selective about which of the other pods it will join with. Pods from different communities do not mingle.

Individuals communicate vocally, and all the pods in a single community seem to share a set of similar calls, though each pod apparently uses the calls in its own pod dialect. Moreover, orcas from different communities have different sets of calls.

Orcas feed on a wide range of prey, including fish, squid, other dolphin species, and large whales. They hunt cooperatively. Biologists have watched them kill blue whales which they attacked in packs and fought for hours. They sometimes circle around smaller dolphins, herding the animals together the way the bottlenose and other smaller dolphin species herd fish. Then the orcas take turns swimming into the mass of prey and feeding. They have been observed working together to tip icebergs on which seals are perched, dumping the seals into the water where other orcas wait. In Argentina they have been watched purposely beaching themselves to capture sea lions that they have chased into shallow water.

opposite: *A diver photographs a spotted dolphin off Hawaii. Spotters and their relatives, the spinner dolphins, are being decimated by tuna fishermen in the eastern Tropical Pacific.*

Old whalers reported that when a herd of orcas attacked a large whale they would bite their quarry's lips and tongue and try to hold its head underwater. Despite the reputation of the orca as a hunter, some populations live entirely on fish. Attacks of orcas on humans are rare and seem to be largely cases of mistaken identity, since they tend to involve people in parkas standing on ice floes, where they resemble seals or sea lions.

Some orca populations are migratory. For example, those that frequent Antarctic waters from November through April apparently migrate to coastal waters in other parts of the southern hemisphere during the rest of the year. Other populations, such as the orcas of Puget Sound, do not migrate. Presumably, whether an orca population migrates is dependent upon its habitat and food resources.

Differences in behavior patterns are also based upon feeding habits in two other species, the spotted dolphin and the spinner dolphin. The spotted dolphin is found throughout tropical seas, both in coastal waters and in the open ocean far from any shore. It is smaller than the bottlenose, growing to a maximum of eight feet long and 250 pounds. Spotted dolphins are often caught in nets set by tuna fishermen, and some studies on the dolphins' behavior when trapped in large, encircling nets have revealed some aspects of their social life.

When the dolphins are trapped for the first time, they usually panic. Spotted dolphins have a reputation among aquaria personnel for being high-strung and easily excited. Their natural tendency is probably aggravated when the individuals confined in the nets are accustomed to living in open seas. However, spotters that have been netted and released tend to calm down when netted again and will often congregate near the section where experience has taught them they will be released. When netted they tend to form social groups. The nature of some of the groups is predictable—females and young together and juveniles together. But observers found one unexpected type of grouping that apparently is unique to spotted dolphins, the forming of senior-male squads. These include three to eight animals, seemingly dominant males, that would

swim slowly in tight formation, nearly touching one another and coordinating all their activities, such as breathing and diving. Some male–female pairs also would swim together with fins touching. Some evidence suggests that spotters, much like orcas, live in stable subgroups and that subgroups combine to form large herds of several thousand individuals. Also, spotters often travel with other species, particularly spinner dolphins.

Spinners are slightly smaller than spotters, weighing 120 to 135 pounds and growing to a maximum length of seven feet. They live in the warmer parts of the Pacific, Atlantic, and Indian oceans, with some populations living close to shore and others living far out to sea. Like the spotters, they live on squid and small fish. Their name comes from their habit of surging from the water in great spinning leaps, rotating as many as four times around the axes of their bodies during one leap.

A nearshore population of spinners lives around Hawaii. Its daily behavior is dictated by its feeding habits. The dolphins rest by day in bays, swimming slowly in groups of about twenty animals. At night they combine into larger aggregations that may include several hundred individuals and move offshore

to feed. Apparently the larger number helps the dolphins do a better job of searching for food. The small, daytime groups do not appear to be stable. Membership seems to change daily. However, pairs seem to stick together.

Spinners and spotters are closely related, and the mingling of the two species in the open ocean is thought to be another adaptation to the need for food and shelter. Unlike spinners, spotters feed by day and rest at night. This difference may allow the two species to benefit one another when herding together. While one rests, the other is active and alert, presumably providing a safeguard against predators and other dangers.

Spinners and spotters share another habit. In the eastern tropical Pacific—the warm sea west of Latin America—they frequently congregate with schools of yellowfin tuna, presumably because they feed on the same prey that tuna eat. This behavior has led the dolphins into the nets of tuna fishermen, resulting in the deaths of millions of spinners and spotters over the past three decades and to passage of a landmark federal law. It is a classic example of the dangers that dolphins face when they clash with the commercial interests of humankind.

Dolphins in Distress

Until the late 1950s, commercial fishermen caught tuna by *chumming*, which is the dumping of bait off a boat. The tuna would be attracted to the bait and, once in a full-pitched feeding frenzy, would bite anything, making them easy victims for the unbaited hooks used by the fishermen. But then the fishermen decided to take advantage of the spinners' and spotters' habit of swimming above schools of tuna. The fishermen developed a new technique, called *setting on dolphins*. They would look for signs of dolphins roiling the surface and for flocks of feeding seabirds. The tuna boats would then ease within close range of the dolphins and dispatch speedboats to circle the animals, working them into a milling mob in much the way that dolphins themselves herd fish. The tuna would continue to swim below the dolphins, forming an increasingly compact mass. Around this crowd of dolphins and tuna the fishermen would lower nets as much as a mile in length and 600 feet deep, trapping the mammals and the fish in a mesh corral. The net would be open at the

bottom until the dolphins and tuna were completely surrounded. Then the fishermen would close the bottom by drawing in a cable strung through the lower edge of the net, pulling it shut the way a drawstring closes a purse, and everything in the net would be hauled onto the tuna boat. Hundreds of trapped spinners and spotters would be drowned in the net or crushed by the machinery that hauled in the nets.

The death toll among dolphins during the first years of tuna purse seining are almost too incredible to believe. In 1959, one of the first years in which nets were set over dolphins, perhaps 100,000 of the animals died. The following year the number quite likely jumped to half a million. By 1972 nearly 4 million had died in tuna nets. The actual toll was doubtless higher, since the official figure accounts only for dolphins dead in the nets and not for those that died of injuries after release. Anyway, numbers alone may not tell the whole story. For example, when a single tuna boat in a single day in 1987 killed

200 to 300 Costa Rican spinner dolphins, the rarest of the spinner subspecies, it may have wiped out half the average number of individuals added to the population by birth in any given year. In this case the number was small, but the effect perhaps immense.

By the late 1960s tuna fishermen were developing techniques that were supposed to help dolphins escape from the nets. Nevertheless, the death toll hovered at half a million yearly into the early 1970s. Partly in response to public outrage over this dramatic loss of dolphins, Congress in 1972 passed the Marine Mammal Protection Act. That year an estimated 368,600 dolphins—doubtless a minimum figure—died in the nets.

The act made it illegal for U.S. citizens to take or harass marine mammals. It also outlawed most importations and sale of marine mammals or products made from them. However, the law allowed some exemptions to its restrictions. Marine mammals could be captured for scientific research and public display. And commercial fishermen could continue to kill dolphins for two years subject to regulations designed to reduce the kill. During this time Congress apparently hoped, optimistically, that the tuna-fishing industry would find some way to lower the level of kill. The act also authorized a two-year research program with a potential cost of $2 million to help improve the fishermen's technology. At the end of the two years, quotas were to be set for the number of dolphins that could be killed in tuna nets. In this way the act sought to reduce the incidental take "to insignificant levels approaching zero mortality and serious injury rate."

Since the act did not define "insignificant levels" and set no deadline on achieving the goal, the Secretary of Commerce—to whom the act gave authority over dolphins—as late as 1975 issued a general permit to the American Tunaboat Association, an organization backed by such corporate tuna boat operators as Ralston-Purina, owner of Chicken of the Sea, and H. J. Heinz, which owns Star-Kist. Conservationists sued, arguing successfully in court that the National Marine Fisheries Service, an agency of the Department of Commerce, had failed to comply with the protections required by the act. The Secretary of Commerce subsequently set a quota of 78,000 dolphins killed in 1976. When that number was reached in October of that year, fishing was stopped. The tuna-fishing industry sought to fight the closure in court, but lost. In late 1977 the Secretary of Commerce issued a new regulation that set a gradually lower kill level over a five-year period. The original intent of the law, to reduce the kill to near zero, was ignored during the Reagan administration. At the behest of the tuna-fishing industry, the allowable incidental kill was set permanently at 20,500 dolphins by 1984 amendments to the Marine Mammal Protection Act. Also during the Reagan years, funding for research on ways to reduce the kill was cut.

The overall effectiveness of the act in protecting dolphins from tuna nets has been hampered by a number of internal weaknesses. To determine how many dolphins are killed by tuna fishing, the National Marine Fisheries Service after passage of the act assigned special "observers" to accompany about a third of all fishing trips. The number of dolphin kills reported by the observers was, and still is, used as a basis for determining the total kill. Unfortunately, the veracity of the data collected by the observers has been called into serious question. According to reports from observers, tuna boat fishermen often attempted to bribe observers or intimidate them with physical threats. In many cases this worked. In 1988 two observers revealed that official figures probably represent no more than half the dolphins killed. In addition, a study by a crew member of a boat that had no observer indicated that the level of kill on his vessel was significantly higher than the average kill on boats that have observers, suggesting that data collected by the observers is skewed.

Unreliable kill figures are not the only problem. Enforcement of Marine Mammal Protection Act regulations has been lax. According to a report from the Department of Commerce, fines for violations are so low relative to income from tuna that many captains treated fines as a sort of overhead, part of the cost of setting on dolphins. Moreover, even though the law was amended in 1984 to ban the import of tuna from foreign nations that lacked programs to protect dolphins from netting, the National Marine Fisheries Service never issued the regulations needed to administer such bans. The reason for the delay suggests that the service plays into the hands of the tuna fishermen: Said one service official, a draft of regulations governing foreign fishing was dropped because the U.S. tuna industry and participating foreign nations did not like it.

In 1988 films of extensive dolphin deaths in tuna nets were released by the California-based conservation group Earth Island Institute. The sight of

The Dall's porpoise is among the fastest dolphins, reaching speeds perhaps as fast as thirty miles per hour. It swims so fast that it throws up a characteristic rooster tail of water behind it as it goes. A native of the North Pacific, its numbers are being reduced by nets set for fish.

hundreds of dolphins drowning in nets or being dismembered and crushed in the net-hauling machinery fueled renewed outrage. When the Marine Mammal Protection Act was reauthorized in 1988, dolphin protection received several boosts. Observers are now to travel on all U.S. tuna boats. Captains with poor records in dolphin protection are supposed to lose their licenses. However, many U.S. tuna fishermen have sought to escape the legal restrictions by registering their vessels under foreign flags. This approach may soon prove fruitless, since the new amendments embargo tuna from any nations that fail to reduce their dolphin kills by 1990 to a level comparable to that of the U.S. tuna fleet.

It is impossible to predict just how effective the new protections will be. Since the act was first passed in 1972, with its goal of reducing mortality to about zero, nearly a million dolphins have died in tuna nets. Future improvements will depend not just on passage of laws and amendments, but on enforcement of them.

Another species hard hit by fishermen is the Dall's porpoise. A black porpoise with a white belly and flanks and white edging on its dorsal fin and tail flukes, the Dall's is perhaps the fastest of all cetaceans. It can reach a speed of thirty miles per hour, throwing up a rooster tail of foaming water in its wake. About 900,000 Dall's live in the North Pacific as far north as the Bering Sea, from Japan to California. About 20,000 die yearly in some 2,000 miles of

nets set nightly by the Japanese, Taiwanese, and South Koreans fishing for North Pacific salmon. The number caught has declined in recent years, even though the number of drift nets being set has increased, a sign that the Dall's porpoise is probably dropping quickly in numbers.

Another 10,000 Dalls are killed deliberately each year off Japan for meat. In 1988, Japan killed at least 25 percent of the Dall's population as a backlash to an international whaling ban that ended Japanese whaling. Among developed nations, Japan takes one of the most serious tolls of dolphins. In addition to thousands yearly being killed for meat, hundreds of dolphins die annually in the Iki slaughter. Killing for meat may increase in the near future because of a worldwide ban on whale hunting. Japan has already succeeded in acclimating dolphins to life in fresh water so that the animals can be raised in lakes and slaughtered for meat. The Japanese are also planning to develop whale farms in the same way.

Though the numbers of dolphins killed in the Japanese fishery may seem low, catches of this size year after year may deplete local populations. What little is known about dolphin reproduction indicates that the animals breed slowly, probably no more than a single offspring every two years. In addition, little or nothing is known about the size of dolphin populations. The effect of any level of kill is unknown and unpredictable.

Dolphins, porpoises, and other whales may face

far more devastating problems than entrapment in fishing nets. Human activities are bringing changes to the seas that threaten the entire oceanic ecosystem. One problem is declining fish populations. For example, California fishermen destroyed their sardine fishery half a century ago, and Peruvian fishermen in the mid-1970s demolished their anchovy stocks. Since 1984 fish landings in U.S. inshore waters have dropped 25 percent. The poundage of fish caught has declined 18 percent off New England and 42 percent off the Southeast. The declines are due in part to increasingly intensive commercial fishing, but also to ocean pollution and loss of estuaries and other coastal wetlands in which many fish species breed. The occurrence of declines in various fish species throughout the globe indicates that something crucial is amiss in the ecosystem. Moreover, the harvesting of Antarctic krill—shrimp-like creatures that occur in millions of tons in the Southern Ocean—is taking away vast quantities of food vital to many species from fish to whales. Depletion of the ozone layer in the Antarctic is also contributing to declines in krill. Because krill are at the basis of the Antarctic ecosystem—feeding whales such as humpbacks and also feeding the fish that in turn feed everything from sharks and penguins to dolphins and whales—a decline in krill could convulse the entire natural community of the Southern Ocean.

But not just the food base of dolphins and other sea creatures is under assault. So too is the integrity of the dolphins' habitat, the oceans themselves. The oceans have been used for centuries as dumps for human waste, and abuse of the oceans is beginning to show. One problem is plastics pollution. About half of all human-made debris in the ocean and along the coasts is plastic items, from plastic binders for beverage six packs to plastic bags and balloons to plastic fishing nets that have drifted away or been abandoned. Small items may be ingested by animals

What to Do with a Stranded Dolphin

Several cetacean species commonly strand on coastal beaches, swimming ashore and beaching in water too shallow to support their weight. If they remain stranded for very long, they will die from lack of food, respiratory problems, and sunburn. Some species, notably pilot whales and false killer whales, strand in large groups. Others, including the bottlenose dolphin, are more likely to strand alone.

Why strandings occur is something of a mystery. One hypothesis suggested that the animals suffer from middle ear infections that cause them to become disoriented, but this idea has not been backed by any evidence. Another idea proposed that the animals were instinctively following old migratory pathways that ceased to exist thousands of years ago. This seems to raise the question of why the animals had not stranded themselves out of existence long ago. A new hypothesis suggests that the animals are responding to abnormal centers of magnetism, but this idea is groundless because it has not yet been proved that cetaceans navigate by sensing the Earth's magnetic charge.

It is quite likely that mass strandings occur because an entire pod of whales blindly follows a misguided leader onto the shore. Bob Schoelkopf, who heads the Marine Mammal Stranding Center at Brigantine, New Jersey, says that pods of whales seem sometimes to follow old or ailing leaders to shore so that they can gather around it until it dies. Once the leader is dead, the stranded animals can sometimes work their way back into the water. In some cases, they may need human help to succeed. Here is what Schoelkopf says you should do if you come upon a live, stranded dolphin or whale:

1. Call your local stranding center—a number of them are located on all coasts—or the National Marine Fisheries Service and report the stranding.

2. Keep people and pets away from the animal.

3. If the animal appears to be drying, carefully cover it with wet towels, being sure to keep the eyes and blowhole uncovered.

4. Do not try to push the animal into the sea; almost all stranded animals are ill, Schoelkopf says. They came ashore for a reason, and trying to put them back into the water may only aggravate the problem.

5. Try to keep the animal quiet and undisturbed.

If you find a dead dolphin or whale, report it to the National Marine Fisheries Service or the local police department. Do not try to remove any parts of the animal, as possession of any parts is illegal. Even dead cetaceans are protected by federal law. This is done to keep poachers from killing cetaceans for teeth or other organs and then claiming that they took the parts from animals they found dead. It is also an important part of the effort to stop trade in cetacean products.

Our Beleaguered Oceans, and How to Restore Them

The oceans are seriously threatened by pollution throughout the world. The American Oceans Campaign, an organization founded by actor Ted Danson to educate U.S. citizens about ocean problems and to promote development of a national oceans policy, has outlined the following problems involving U.S. coasts and fishery resources:

- More than 16 trillion gallons of sewage and industrial waste, much of it laden with toxins, are dumped into coastal waters and rivers every year. Every major harbor, bay, and estuary in the continental United States has been damaged, some perhaps irreparably. Human waste, plastic debris, and medical wastes foul beaches around the nation and often require the closing of beaches to public use. Pollution kills countless marine mammals and other aquatic organisms yearly, including species on the endangered list.

- Federal figures indicate that 40 percent of U.S. shellfish-producing areas are either closed or have restrictions on take because of chemical or bacterial pollution. Contaminated fish and shellfish pose dangers to the health of millions of consumers. Pollution threatens fisheries and tourism, both vital economic sources that provide tens of thousands of jobs and generate billions of dollars in income.

- Coastal barrier islands and other sensitive coastal areas are being strained to the limit by overdevelopment as the bulk of the nation's population concentrates on the coasts.

- Offshore oil and gas activities degrade air quality, threaten marine and coastal life with oil spills, and dump major quantities of contaminants into our coastal waters.

Ted Danson, National Audubon Society president Peter Berle, and the leaders of seven other conservation groups have signed a resolution calling for the following six solutions to these problems:

such as dolphins and can cause death by blocking the intestine. Free-floating nets made of monofilament plastic can survive in the ocean for years, perhaps centuries, entangling dolphins and other sea creatures, such as seals, sea lions, and sea turtles. Entangled animals can drown or suffer open wounds that lead to infection.

Perhaps more insidious, because it is invisible, is chemical pollution of the seas. Tissue samples from bottlenose dolphins living off the East Coast of the United States show twenty times the level of carcinogenic PCBs than the federal government believes safe for human health. Studies of wild-caught dolphins and whales have shown that the mercury levels of their blood decline the longer they are held in captivity, a sign that perhaps the natural environment is becoming deadly. This was perhaps most graphically illustrated by the dolphin die-off of 1987.

Bob Schoelkopf, founding director of the Marine Mammal Stranding Center at Brigantine, New Jersey, was perhaps the first to notice that something was amiss among the bottlenose dolphins of the Eastern Seaboard that year. In an average summer his staff usually finds two or three dead dolphins on the Jersey shore. But Schoelkopf had already located two or three times that number by mid-June, and the tally continued to rise. "More and more showed up," he recalls. And all had something in common—lesions on the face and body, as if the animals had swum through a caustic chemical spill.

Schoelkopf notified the National Marine Fisheries Service, which sent some of its law enforcement staff to seek evidence of a spill. A crew member of a vessel that had cruised offshore reported that he had participated in an illegal dumping of chemicals into the ocean off New Jersey, but investigation failed to turn up evidence of that spill or any other.

Meanwhile the death toll continued to mount. Three to five dead bottlenose—more than the total number for an entire average summer season—were turning up *daily* on the Jersey shore. This was particularly alarming since it could be safely presumed that every dolphin found dead might represent several that died at sea and subsequently sank into oblivion or vanished down the maws of sharks. By the end of the summer ninety bottlenose dolphins had been located by the stranding center. Only one was found alive, Schoelkopf said, and it died within three minutes of being put into the center's pool.

The die-off was not limited to New Jersey waters. The death toll seemed to move south, peaking off the Southeast in late fall. By the time the die-off

1. Enactment of a federal oceans- and coastal-protection policy to direct national legislation in a comprehensive and coordinated effort toward reducing coastal pollution and restoring estuaries, wetlands, and fisheries.

2. Strong enforcement of and adequate funding for the goals outlined in the Clean Water Act, Endangered Species Act, Toxic Substances Control Act, Coastal Zone Management Act, Federal Insecticide, Fungicide, and Rodenticide Act, and other laws relating to coastal protection.

3. Funding for coastal and oceans research, including alternative systems for sewage and waste dumping and incentives for re-

ducing the flow of industrial toxins into coastal waters, as well as creation and enforcement of regulations for handling, transporting, and disposing of toxins.

4. Enactment of new, comprehensive legislation designating and protecting ecologically sensitive and important areas of the oceans for scientific study and for the enjoyment of future generations.

5. Support of efforts by coastal states to ban offshore development in environmentally and economically sensitive areas where it would threaten beaches, coastal communities, and commercial and recreational fishing.

6. Support of congressional deferral of outer–continental shelf oil development in unexploited areas pending a complete review of existing oil-development laws and regulations coupled with creation of a national energy policy that emphasizes clean, safe, renewable, and efficient energy sources.

You can help achieve these important goals by making your feelings about ocean pollution, offshore oil development, and ocean protection known to your state and federal legislative representatives. Protecting the world's oceans will ultimately benefit all humankind by preserving valuable food resources and by limiting the toxic pollutants that eventually come back to haunt us on the waves that wash our shores.

---

came to its apparent end, nearly 750 bottlenose dolphins were known to have died. Officials at the National Marine Fisheries Service concluded that perhaps half the coastal bottlenose population had been lost.

The service undertook a study to determine the cause of the die-off. The study was released in 1988 and concluded that the cause was a red tide, which is a population explosion in a species of red algae that swells the plant's numbers so greatly that the sea turns red. The plants produce a toxin that can accumulate in the tissues of fish that ingest the plants. The federal report said that the red tide had begun in the Gulf of Mexico, where red tides are relatively normal events, and then had been carried around Florida and on north by unusual variations in ocean currents. Federal figures indicate that the die-off moved north up the coast.

Schoelkopf argues that data in the report were incomplete. Because ninety dead bottlenose dolphins had washed ashore in New Jersey before deaths reached a peak in the Southeast, Schoelkopf says that the die-off clearly began in the North and rolled south. The federal report has avoided this conclusion by listing only nine dolphin deaths off New Jersey. All other deaths recorded at the stranding center were ignored, federal officials maintain,

because Schoelkopf was not part of the team assigned to collect data on the dead dolphins. Schoelkopf scoffs at this idea, since the federal government paid the center $9,600 for data on dolphin deaths in 1987.

Schoelkopf also objects to the conclusion of the report on biological grounds. If the red tide came from the Gulf of Mexico, he asks, why did no dolphin die-off occur in the Gulf? If the bottlenose died from eating contaminated menhaden—a fish believed to carry concentrated red tide toxins in its tissues—then why did no other fish-eating species, such as gulls, pelicans, or other marine mammals, die off in unprecedented numbers?

Schoelkopf suspects that the real reason for the die-off has never been discovered and that the fisheries service is not making any effort to do so. "If someone from NMFS found heavy toxic pollution in the ocean off New Jersey, what would that do to tourism and to the fishing industry in that area?" he asks. If the government can lay the blame on a natural disaster, such as a red tide, he says, then the public will be more likely to accept the problem with equanimity. Tourism and fishing will not suffer.

Schoelkopf is convinced that the dolphin die-off is evidence of serious toxic problems in the sea. He remarked that PCBs have been dumped into the ocean in the New York Bight, 100 miles off New Jersey, for years and also reach the ocean in runoff from estuaries. PCBs and other toxins are invisible, but they are moving through the sea just as surely as are the myriad bits of floating debris that show where humanity has disposed of its wastes. They have to go somewhere, Schoelkopf says. PCBs, for example, do not break down; they accumulate. And they become increasingly concentrated in the tissues of fish that feed on contaminated foods, and in the tissues of animals that feed on contaminated fish. Thus the poisonous chemicals found in the flesh of dolphins may warn of contamination that reaches people as well, as seafood on dinner plates.

Postscript

If you were to go in June to Virginia's Eastern Shore, you might choose to sail through The Nature Conservancy's Virginia Coast Reserve, a scattering of islands within sight of the mainland that rise gently above the gun-metal sea. The islands exist in a sort of geological symbiosis with the ocean, their eastern shorelines continually eroded by waves and wind, their western sides continually building as sand is brought to them. Some islands move slowly west toward the mainland; others are spinning like stars, their shorelines spiraling around them.

If you sail among these nomadic islands you may see coursing through the waves a handful of bottlenose dolphins. They will arch above the sea, they will pause to look your way, and they will keep their distance. As they cut across the water's surface, they seem as much a part of the sea as do the waves. And there is about them something so spritely that they seem almost to be the souls of playful children given form and life.

More than just beauty is in the eye of the beholder. Those living dolphins speak to the imagination of many things—of dolphins sculpted in marble centuries ago in ancient Greece, graceful imitations of graceful living things; of the mysteries held close in the oceans; of the depths the dolphins have plumbed; of the things they have seen. Sight of them invites musings about the limits of their intelligence. If they are capable of wonder, does the world beyond the dry shores appear to them a vast mystery, as great a void as the oceans were to humans in the millennia before Columbus? Are shorelines to dolphins grim signs of hostile environments?

As you sail you might pass close by one of the islands, and on its shore you might see the rotting carcass of a dolphin lying just within reach of the waves. Sight of that sea beast warming in the sun may lead you to think about the great die-off and may give birth to a whole line of more somber musings. The animal quite likely died of some natural cause. But in a globe poisoned in so many places and so many ways by human waste, who knows? The dead dolphin conjures images of oil residue glistening on water, of toxic spills fanning out from industrial centers into dark rivers and thence into the sea. It speaks of fish populations shrunk by the hungry maws of trawl nets. It speaks of dolphins cut to pieces in blood-red seas.

We and the dolphin are at a crossroads. With the dolphin, we have a chance to protect a wild species before, rather than after, it has plunged toward perdition. With the dolphin, we have a chance to show whether, despite all the knowledge science has accrued in our lifetime, we will continue to function as if guided only by the ignorance of the past.

ANCIENT FORESTS
RAGE OVER TREES

Based on the Audubon Television Special by
James and John Lipscomb and
Narrated by Paul Newman

FROM THE Pacific Northwest to southeast Alaska lie the last great expanses of North America's finest pristine forests—forests centuries and centuries old, untouched by axe or saw. No forest elsewhere is like them. Rain-dripping ferns crowd the forest floor, and velvet mosses cover rock and fallen tree, bright green and so soft that they have to be touched to see if they can really be so soft. These mosses and the dense undergrowth hush the visitor's every footfall, so that he steps along in utter silence, moving like a ghost. This silence gives the visitor a strange sense of invisibility, the feeling of being at unity with the stillness of the woods, of being witness to a world that existed before humankind. It seems as if he stands on the threshold of eternity.

The trees all around soar so high that an observer standing at the foot of a typical giant must put his head back and back and back to see to the top. His arms flung wide apart cannot span the living trunks, and if he stands beside a fallen giant, he cannot see over it to the other side. The trees' roots—curling up out of the earth and twisting across rock and soil for twenty or thirty feet, then sinking under again—are greater in girth than a stout man.

There is a peculiar grandeur in the silence of these trees, a sort of majesty in their immense immobility. To see them is to know that they do what the human body and mind were never meant to do—live and prosper for centuries. For them, the Crusades, the Magna Carta, the witchcraft trials of old Salem, the founding of our nation, the Industrial Revolution, and the moon landing are all incidents of a single lifetime. Pre-Columbian natives, Lewis and Clark, and modern hikers may all have sought shelter beneath the same living tree. If the purpose of life is to survive, are these trees, then, the crown of creation?

Once, vast untouched forests covered large portions of North America. They were among the first of the natural wonders met 400 years ago by settlers from across the Atlantic. Today, only a few scant stands of untouched forest remain, wild fragments where the centuries abide without the scars and confusion of human progress.

Ed Abbey once wrote that our forests are holier than our churches, and that we should treat them accordingly. The first Europeans to set foot in North America thought the forests were lumberyards. And used them accordingly.

Forests, Logs, and Lumber

The woodlands to which the first European settlers came stood deep and dark across the land. They enshrouded most of the East, from New England to Florida, from the Atlantic to the Mississippi. One English settler said of the new continent, "There is too much wood; and, when on the barren peak of some rocky hill, you catch a distant view, it is generally nothing but an undulating surface of impenetrable forest."

For some colonials, the forests were eerie and ominous. An eighteenth-century physician who traveled the Northeast with German mercenaries complained, "In the eternal woods it is impossible to keep off a particularly unpleasant, anxious feeling, which is excited irresistibly by the continuing shadow and the confined outlook." But for most settlers the forest was a seemingly endless warehouse of supplies. In the forests of Maine, the British Crown laid claim to towering white pines that had grown straight and true for hundreds of years. The pines were cut and made into the masts of British ships. Forests throughout the Northeast, dominated by hardwoods such as oak, hickory, sugar maple,

and the now virtually extinct chestnut, provided settlers with construction materials, fuel, and charcoal. Thousands of acres were cut and burned just to clear the land for farming.

The forests of New England and the Northeast were the first to disappear. By the middle of the nineteenth century, commercial lumbering operations were quickly mowing down any eastern woodlands the colonials had missed and casting about for fresh timber. Late in the century they found it in the Great Lakes region, where within a few years hundreds of thousands of acres were cut wastefully: In an area called the Kingston Plain, one company made only 160,000 board feet out of a total cut that should have yielded more than a million. (A board foot is one foot square and an inch thick.) The destruction of some areas was total. On the Kingston Plain, for example, the pines never grew back. Nearly a century later, the region is marked only by the stumps of the old trees, gray as iron, tombstones of desolation, monuments to an age of excess and waste.

The loggers' interest also turned to the South,

A logging crew in Michigan in about 1900. Virtually all the big, ancient trees in the Great Lakes region were cut around the turn of the century.

Loggers pose with their ancient quarry, taken from a Washington forest in 1905. Since then, the logging industry has cut down perhaps in excess of 80 percent of the state's virgin forests.

where the first Spanish explorers had complained of woods so dense that a horse could not be ridden through them. The old trees fell throughout the early years of this century. For example, from about 1900 into the 1920s, some 700 million board feet of cypress lumber were taken from the Louisiana bottomlands yearly, and 100 million board feet were taken yearly from Florida. By the 1930s the logging industry had cut the last of the untouched forests in the South. Even the Southwest, where pine forests covered southern New Mexico and Arizona, did not escape unscathed. Loggers reached those woods at about the same time that they swept into the Great Lakes region, with similar results.

When the forests disappeared, more than trees were lost. The forests were the superstructure of a complex biological web that sheltered a tremendous quantity of life. The destruction of the woodlands therefore made certain the extinction of animals already hard pressed by uncontrolled hunting. At the start of the colonial era, the northern woods were home to millions of deer and elk. The elk were wiped out in the nineteenth century and, by 1900,

the deer were so thoroughly depleted that their eclipse seemed imminent. Moose, today largely restricted in the East to the New England states, were found as far south as Pennsylvania, and caribou roamed parts of New England and New York. Even bison were common, a dark-haired subspecies that roamed the woods in herds of several hundred animals. A group of eighteenth-century hunters in western Pennsylvania killed nearly 700 of them in two years. In the same era, near New York State's Lake Onondaga, bison were common enough that individual animals rubbing against a new log cabin destroyed it within hours after it was built. Predators, too, were plentiful. Throughout the East, the nights were punctuated by the howlings of wolves. Mountain lions were so numerous that their tracks crisscrossed winter snows in Pennsylvania, where their hides were sometimes used to line the walls of cabins.

The eastern woodlands were home to one of the greatest wildlife spectacles of all times—the great flights of the passenger pigeon. Seeing the birds in New England in the 1600s, John Josselyn wrote, "I have seen a flight of Pidgeons in the spring, and at *Michaelmas* when they returne back to the South-ward for four or five miles, that to my thinking had neither beginning nor ending, length nor breadth, and so thick I could see no Sun, [and during breed-ing season] they joyn Nest to Nest, and Tree to Tree by their Nests many miles together in the pine trees." Raphe Hamor, early in the 1600s, wrote, ". . . wilde Pigeons, in winter beyond number or imagination, my selfe haue seene three or foure houres together flockes in the aire, so thicke that euen they have shaddowed the skie from vu." William Strachey, who traveled Virginia in the early seventeenth century, said in a letter home that the flocks were "like so many thickned clowdes" and expressed the fear that he would not be believed "yf I should expresse what extended flocks, and how manie thousands in one flock, I have seene in one daie. . . ."

The pigeon's numbers were sustained for many years after settlement. As late as the mid-nineteenth century, the passenger pigeon was the most nu-merous species of bird in the world. Its numbers nearly equaled those of all other North American bird species combined. In the autumn of 1813, naturalist and artist John James Audubon, while traveling by wagon from near Henderson, Kentucky, on the Ohio River to Louisville saw a flock on the wing that darkened the sky. "The air was literally filled with Pigeons," he wrote, "the light of noon-day was obscured as by an eclipse. . . ." At sunset, he wrote, "the Pigeons were still passing in un-diminished numbers, and continued to do so for three days in succession. The people were all in arms. The banks of the Ohio were crowded with men and boys, incessantly shooting at the pilgrims. . . . Multitudes were thus destroyed. For a week or more, the population fed on no other flesh than that of Pigeons, and talked of nothing but Pigeons." Audubon estimated that a single column included more than a billion birds. A flock that flew over Ontario was estimated to include nearly 4 billion.

The passenger pigeon ranged throughout the eastern woodlands, flying at speeds of up to sixty miles an hour, finding food wherever it could be had—from the acorns of the hardwoods to the seeds of the pines. Its vast numbers show the tremendous quantity of living things the untouched forest was capable of supporting. Audubon guessed that the flock he saw consumed about 8.7 million bushels of nuts and seeds every day. Alexander Wilson, another early artist-naturalist, calculated that a single flock he observed ate some 17.5 million bushels daily of nuts and seeds.

The passenger pigeon vanished from the wild at the end of the nineteenth century. It had been hunted into extinction for the meat markets and so its feathers could be used to stuff pillows. In some places it was used to feed hogs. The last great flock, 250,000 birds, settled down to roost near Bowling Green, Ohio, in April 1896. Hunters, many sum-moned to the site by telegram, converged on the birds. No more than 5,000 pigeons escaped, only to fly off into oblivion. The last pigeon seen in the wild was killed in 1900 by a boy with a gun.

By the time the passenger pigeons died to the last bird, its entire world had changed. The wood bison was gone, and the eastern cougar and the wolves of the Pennsylvania woods, and the woods themselves. Probably less than 5 percent of the northeastern woods remained at the turn of the twentieth century.

But the destruction of woodland wildlife did not abate. The new century would see the cutting of southern forests bring about the demise of the na-tion's largest species of woodpecker, the ivory-bill. Larger than crows, ivory-bills lived in the hardwood forests that grew along southern streams. Each pair needed about 2,000 acres of forest for feeding and raising young. They fed upon insects, which they found by digging under the bark of trees with their powerful bills. Audubon reported seeing an ivory-bill detach pieces of bark eight inches long from a dead tree with a single blow of its bill. Within a few hours the bird had denuded thirty or forty feet of the trunk, starting at the top and working its way down.

The flight of the ivory-billed woodpecker, de-scribed by Audubon as "graceful in the extreme," must have been beautiful to see, a reward to anyone who braved the bird's dense woodland home. Wrote Audubon, "The transit from one tree to another, even should the distance be as much as a hundred yards, is performed by a single sweep, and the bird appears as if merely swinging itself from the tip of one tree to that of the other, forming an elegantly curved line." The bird vocalized "at al-most every leap which it makes, whilst ascending against the upper parts of the trunk of a tree, or its highest branches," filling the woods with a call that was "clear, loud, and yet rather plaintive," and audible for half a mile.

The largest woodpecker in North America, the ivory-billed was wiped out by loss of bottomland-hardwood forests throughout the South.

Grotto Falls on Roaring Forks River lies in a small, untouched section of Great Smoky Mountains National Park in eastern Tennessee. The park is one of the few places in the East where a fairly large number of ancient trees still survive, uncut through the centuries.

Probably never common, since it was restricted to a limited bottomland habitat and each pair needed a large piece of land, the ivory-bill ebbed away early in this century as the bottomlands were cut for lumber, cleared for farmland, or dammed for reservoirs. In 1939, it was estimated that perhaps fewer than two dozen ivory-bills survived. The species' fate is still uncertain. Occasional sightings are reported, but most biologists believe that the ivory-bill disappeared with the South's last untouched stands of bottomland hardwoods.

The loss of the southern long-leaf pine forests nearly wiped out another woodpecker species, the red-cockaded. Not much larger than a house sparrow, the red-cockaded woodpecker was found across the South from the Atlantic into eastern Oklahoma's forests. Today it is scarce throughout its range. It lives in colonies that begin with a breeding pair. The pair excavates a hole in a tree trunk and in it rears its young. Female offspring fly off to join another group, helping to prevent inbreeding. But at least one male offspring stays with the parents and helps peck new cavities into nearby trees until a colony is built in which each resident bird has its own cavity shelter. The colonies may be used for fifty years or more by succeeding generations of red-cockaded woodpeckers.

The colonies are easy to spot because the birds peck smaller holes just below each cavity and from these holes long columns of sap drip down the trunk of the tree, much as wax runs down the sides of a candle. Biologists believe that the sap prevents invasion of the cavities by predatory gray rat snakes. The cavities, used as shelters, nesting sites, and refuges from an important predator, are thus crucial to the survival of the red-cockaded woodpecker.

Research indicates that the birds can build cavities only in pines older than sixty years. These are trees old enough to have red-heart disease, a fungal infection that softens the inner wood of the trunk, making it easier for the woodpeckers to build cavities. The age at which trees become useful varies with species. The preferred cavity tree is the long-leaf pine, which needs to be almost a century old before it is useful to red-cockadeds.

The red-cockaded's numbers have declined throughout its range because of logging. Lumber companies, like the woodpeckers, preferred to cut the old pines first. Today, most southern pine lands are cut every eighty years or so, too soon for the forests to develop into prime red-cockaded wood-

pecker habitat. The bird was added to the endangered species list in 1970. No more than 10,000 survive.

As the forests of the Southwest were cut late in the nineteenth century and early in the twentieth, the United States lost completely another species, the thick-billed parrot, a green bird with red markings on the head that flew in flocks throughout the pine woods of New Mexico and Arizona. It was so common that its loud, raucous call was a part of daily life for anyone who lived near the southwestern pine woods.

The thick-billed was last seen in the United States in 1935. It had been one of only two parrot species native to the United States. The other was the Carolina paroquet, a yellow-headed green bird of the Southeast that was hunted into extinction around 1900. Hunting may have been a factor in the thick-billed's decline, too, though loss of the forests doubtless played a part: Pine seeds were about 80 or 90 percent of the bird's diet. Thick-billed parrots still survive in Mexico, and some Mexican birds are being released in parts of Arizona in an effort to return the species to the United States.

Doubtless some species were lost before they were ever known. Audubon's bird paintings include a few small species unknown to science. Were they mistakes of identification? Hoaxes? Or were they species dying away even in Audubon's day, ebbing into nothing as the land they lived in was changed for all time? No one can say with certainty.

Only tiny, widely scattered acreages of untouched forest remain in the East—a few hemlock stands in Virginia and Tennessee, a scattering of ancient white pines in Maine, some cypress trees hidden away in a few rugged swamps in the South. All the forest that eastern residents and visitors see today is regrown woodland, usually called *second growth*. It is impossible to measure now the changes wrought by the cutting of the forests, because second growth tells us nothing of what life was like in the pristine woodlands. The only clues are the records left by early settlers, who rarely stopped to ponder what they were doing to the land. But even they, as early as 1753, suspected that the cutting of the trees was changing the face of the continent. "Our Runs [streams] dry up apace," wrote geographer Lewis Evans about southeastern Pennsylvania, "several which formerly wou'd turn a fuling Mill, are now scarce sufficient for The Use of a Farm, the Reason of which is this, when the Country was

Pafsenger Pigeon.
COLUMBA MIGRATORIA. Linn
Male 1. Female 2.

The passenger pigeon was once the most numerous bird species in North America, if not the world. Its numbers may have exceeded 5 billion. Dependent in part on hardwood forests, the birds were driven to extinction in the wild by hunting and habitat loss before the end of the nineteenth century. Painting by John James Audubon.

*The red-cocked woodpecker was more common early in the nineteenth century, when
John James Audubon painted this picture, than it is today. Dependent on ancient pine
trees for building its nesting colonies, the bird's range and numbers have shrunk with
the spread of logging in the South.*

137

cover'd with Woods & the Swamps with Brush, the Rain that fell was detain'd by These Interruptions."

It was not for another five generations, however, that anyone would stop to consider that perhaps the cutting of the forests should be arrested, that perhaps a living tree was more valuable than its timber.

The U.S. Forest Service

Although concern for the survival of North American forests was being expressed as early as 1868, when the commissioner of the federal government's General Land Office predicted that the nation's forests would be gone within half a century, it was 1876 before the first bill calling for protection of public forests was introduced in Congress. That same year, a rider was attached to a federal appropriations bill that authorized the Secretary of Agriculture to conduct a study of future timber needs and of methods for forest preservation and regrowth. The Agriculture Department subsequently established a forestry division and, in 1878, issued a report calling for forest protection. Eight years after that, Congress gave official recognition to the Agriculture Department's Division of Forestry, which was primarily a research agency, since the national forest system had yet to be created. Nevertheless, from this small beginning sprang the U.S. Forest Service, the federal agency in charge of the national forest system.

The Forest Service now has a staff of 39,000 full-time personnel who manage nearly 200 million acres at an annual cost of about $2 billion. It is in charge of some of the largest pristine areas in the United States, including the majority of designated federal wilderness areas in the lower forty-eight states. Its domain includes the habitat of some 3,000 fish and wildlife species, and it is crucial to the survival of such threatened and endangered species as the gray wolf, grizzly bear, and red-cockaded woodpecker. Lands managed by the Forest Service also produce about 15 percent of the timber harvested yearly in the United States and about 23 percent of the softwoods, such as white pine. The role of the Forest Service in protecting untouched forests is particularly important, since most of the remaining ancient forests are on the national forest system. On state and private lands they largely have been cut.

Like many of the trees it manages, the Forest Service took decades to grow to its current immense size. In 1886, when the Division of Forestry was created, the federal government did not even have the legal authority to create national forests. However, support of a forest reserve system grew through the 1870s and 1880s and culminated in 1891 in the enactment of the Forest Reserve Act. This law allowed the president to create forest reserves—federally protected woodlands—out of any public lands covered with timber or undergrowth. During the next two years, presidents William Henry Harrison and Grover Cleveland established more than 17 million acres of forest reserves. By the time he left office in 1897, Cleveland had more than doubled the existing reserve system by creating thirteen more reserves encompassing 21 million acres.

The next landmark in Forest Service history was enactment of the Forest Service Organic Administration Act in 1897. This law declared that the purpose of the reserves was to improve and protect the forests, secure favorable water flows, and furnish a continuous supply of timber. It also put the federal government into the logging business by putting the reserves under the control of the Secretary of the Interior and authorizing him to sell reserve timber. The Interior Department moved quickly to assume its new responsibilities. It received its first funding for forest reserves in 1898 and established a forestry division within the General Land Office in 1901.

Interior was not, however, the only agency with a stake in the new forest reserve system. The Department of Agriculture's forestry department was growing rapidly under the enthusiastic leadership of Gifford Pinchot. Coveting the reserves administered by Interior, Pinchot began campaigning to put all forest reserves under his control. He had some powerful help, since one of his closest friends and supporters was Theodore Roosevelt, who had succeeded to the presidency after the assassination of William McKinley in 1901. The exposure of land frauds in Interior's General Land Office gave the coup de grace to Interior's role as an administrator of forest reserves: In 1905 Congress transferred the reserves to Agriculture. Also that year, the Bureau of Forestry was renamed the Forest Service.

Pinchot had been trained as a forester in Europe, where limited forest resources and a dense population dictated that foresters treat wood as a scarce commodity that must be harvested carefully, with the land replanted for future logging as soon as it was cut. Because of his training, Pinchot believed that the national forests should be used for practical purposes, such as timber production and grazing. His European approach, which views forests as wood factories, set the pattern for the Forest Service's managerial role and still tends to dominate the outlook of federal foresters today. This traditional interest in maximizing the amount of wood a forest produces is a big impetus for the cutting of ancient forests, where the old slow-growing trees have ceased to add large quantities of wood annually.

Roosevelt and Pinchot worked tenaciously to expand the forest reserve system. By the time Roosevelt left office he had created 132 million acres of park and forest reserves. In 1909, William Howard Taft stepped into the presidency, and the ascent of the Forest Service stalled. Pinchot was dismissed in 1910, and the forest reserve system lost several million acres to homesteading plans and boundary adjustments. In 1911, however, the service was permitted to take a new approach to forest preservation. This began with passage of the Weeks Act, which authorized funding for the purchase of forest reserves in the East, though it did so with certain limitations. The Forest Service could buy only lands located on the headwaters of navigable streams out of concern that the law would be declared unconstitutional if not limited to areas related to interstate commerce. Moreover, the service could buy land only with the consent of the legislature of the state in which the lands were located. In 1924, however, the Clarke–McNary Act expanded the authority of the Weeks Act, permitting the Forest Service to establish national forests anywhere within the watershed of navigable streams. In this way, the federal forest system grew nationwide.

During its early years, the Forest Service concentrated primarily on the cutting of the national forests for timber. However, after World War I, the increased mobility of the American public because of the automobile gave birth to a new interest in outdoor recreation. This led in the 1920s to a push to ban logging in the national forest system's best recreation lands, those that lacked roads and permanent structures. These lands were interchangeably called primitive, wilderness, or roadless areas. The first

official primitive area—set aside from all development—was designated in 1924 in the Gila National Forest in New Mexico.

During the 1930s pressure built for designation of more wilderness areas. A leader in this movement was Bob Marshall, who became head of the service's new Recreation and Lands Division in 1937. Under his guidance, the service established tough regulations that banned roads, timber harvesting, motorized transportation, and permanent occupancy in designated wilderness areas. After World War II, however, increased demand for timber because of the housing boom put new pressures on the forests. When the Forest Service proposed to open the Three Sisters Primitive Area in Oregon to logging, wilderness enthusiasts pushed for a law that would protect roadless areas for all time. In 1956 the first wilderness bill was introduced to Congress and failed. The National Wilderness Preservation Act, which gives roadless areas strong protection from all forms of permanent human encroachment, was not passed until 1964. In 1975 the Eastern Wilderness Act was passed to protect smaller, less pristine areas in eastern forests. Although any large federal roadless area can be declared wilderness by Congress, most designated wildernesses are on national forest roadless areas.

Within the past three decades, two important laws were enacted that gave legal shape to the Forest Service's management of the national forests. One of these was the 1960 Multiple-Use Sustained-Yield Act, which declared that the forests would be administered for outdoor recreation, grazing, timber, watershed protection, and fish and wildlife management. Until this law was passed, it was not clear where the service's responsibilities lay. However, although this law says that the forests are to be used for more than the production of wood, it does not give priority to any one use. Consequently, a great deal of contention centers on Forest Service logging plans, with timber interests seeking larger cuts and conservationists seeking more protection for wildlife and greater emphasis on other uses.

The second significant law is the National Forest Management Act, passed in 1976. Under this law, no cuts are to be scheduled on stands of trees that have not reached the end of their mean annual increment of growth, which is the age at which the trees' growth rate ceases to increase yearly. Exceptions are permitted with public input. This approach ensures that trees are not cut before they have stopped adding significant amounts of wood each year, but it does not protect ancient trees whose growth has slowed. In the eyes of many conservationists, the Forest Service thus has continued to view the national forests primarily as sources of timber and has forced other considerations, such as wildlife protection, to take a back seat to logging. For example, to many traditional foresters the last of our ancient, untouched forests are only decadent old growth, woodlands long past their prime and well past the age at which the dominant trees are growing significant amounts of new wood each year. Interested in maximizing the amount of lumber produced on every acre, foresters would cut down the untouched forests to permit younger, more rapidly growing trees to sprout. However, this approach overlooks the biological fact that forests are more than trees and lumber, that second growth differs so much from old growth that many wildlife species that live in ancient forests do not do as well in second growth. For these creatures, the cutting of the last stands of the nation's unprotected, untouched forests may be a harbinger of doom, as surely as the logging practices of an earlier age contributed to the end of the ivory-billed woodpecker and the thick-billed parrot.

The Tongass: A Troubled National Forest

Some of the oldest remnants of untouched forest in North America lie along the mountainous coast of southeast Alaska. Many of the spruce and hemlocks there were already old when Alaska was known only to Native Americans. They were ancient and lofty 300 years ago, when Russian ships for the first time came to Alaskan waters. They were a living part of the land when the land was sold to the United States more than a century ago. Now they are a part of the nation's largest national forest, the Tongass, some 17 million acres spread along rugged coastline and across myriad islands that rise steeply from the chill sea, like broken pieces of a fragmented shore.

In many places the Tongass is still a wild land. On one forested island alone, researchers have counted more grizzlies than survive in all the lower forty-eight states. Bald eagles nest in the crowns of spruce and hemlock 200 feet tall. In winter the forest offers both deer and wolf a refuge from deep snow. And yet, much of the ancient forest is gone now. The first commercial logging began in 1833. As local economies grew in the nineteenth century, so did the logging industry. By 1926, six sawmills were cutting timber for local use and export. By 1930, most of the easily accessible timber had been cut. The giant trees survived primarily in the steepest, most rugged areas. But even these trees soon were threatened, beginning in the 1950s when the Forest Service successfully concluded a long campaign to develop a wood pulp industry in southeastern Alaska.

The pulp industry was an essential factor in federal plans to sell timber from the Tongass. The cutting of sawlogs—those suitable for milling into lumber—was not by itself profitable because of the high costs of processing and shipping in Alaska. But if a pulp industry—which reduces trees into pulp for making such products as paper—could be developed, loggers could clearcut large areas, removing not only the large-diameter sawlogs, but also the small-diameter and low-grade pulp trees. Clearcutting was the cheapest logging method and, because it would feed both lumber and pulp industries, the most profitable.

However, offering the prospect of cutting pulp-grade trees in addition to sawlogs was not enough to encourage lumber companies to risk the great expenditures required to build pulp mills in southeast Alaska. The Forest Service had to sweeten the deal further by offering fifty-year logging contracts, rather than the usual three-to-five-year contracts. In addition, the price for this long, ensured supply of timber was set low enough to enable the companies to compete with mills in Washington State and, furthermore, could be lowered during any five-year operating period, but not raised.

The largest purchasers were Ketchikan Pulp Company, now called Louisiana Pacific–Ketchikan, and the Alaska Lumber and Pulp Company, owned by a Japanese corporation. Ketchikan Pulp signed its contract in 1951 and opened its mill in 1954. That year the level of logging jumped from less than 100

A farflung view of the fjords and islands of the Tongass National Forest, which encompasses the largest expanses of untouched forest left in the United States. Under the mandate of a 1980 congressional act, the forest is being cut with a tremendous loss of wildlife and of federal dollars under an act of Congress passed in 1980.

million board feet yearly to more than 200 million. Alaska Pulp signed its contract in 1956. Logging continued to climb. In 1984 the southeast Alaska harvest totaled 443 million board feet.

About 50 to 60 percent of the trees in southeast Alaska are pulp grade. Most of the pulp produced in Alaska is shipped to Japan, where it is used to make products such as rayon, acetate, and cellophane. Some 40 to 50 percent of southeast Alaska's trees are larger-diameter sawlogs, suitable for processing into lumber. In order to protect employment at local mills, federal law and Forest Service regulations prohibit the export of unprocessed cut trees, called round logs, from national forests. This protection is called the "primary processing rule." Because of it, round logs are processed by Alaskan mills into cants, which are rough slabs about eight and a half inches thick that are exported for cutting into lumber in other nations. Lumber is not made in Alaska because of prohibitive economic conditions, including the high cost of building the mills that would do the

job and, ironically, the lack of a significant local market for finished lumber, since most houses in Alaska are constructed of lumber from the Pacific Northwest.

During the past decade a new market in round logs also has developed. It is fed by Native Alaskan corporations, which are not subject to the primary processing rule. The Natives entered the market in 1978, and in 1983 began exporting in excess of 200 million board feet of round logs yearly. Little can be done to halt the cutting of untouched forests on Native and other private lands. So it is in the Tongass that any hope for the untouched forest must be found.

The logging of the Tongass will have far-reaching, harmful effects on wildlife. In many ways, this was not entirely anticipated. Traditional ecological wisdom taught that mature forests are poor wildlife habitat. The crowns of the trees, according to this belief, grow together and close like a lid over the earth below, shutting out the sunlight that stimulates the growth of shrubs and other plants eaten by animals such as deer. As the forest ages, overshadowed ground plants decline and so do the animals that feed upon them. This in turn causes predators to dwindle. By contrast, again according to this belief, life teems after a forest is cut. Ground cover grows and deer and other herbivores move in and prosper.

The idea that untouched forests are biologically destitute is based on studies of second-growth woodlands. The biologists who studied mature second-growth forests presumed that what they saw there also was true for untouched forests, traditionally called old growth or overmature, decadent forests by the logging industry. However, studies conducted during the past fifteen years in the pristine portions of the Tongass and in other pristine forests in the Douglas fir region suggest that what may be true for second-growth forests is not true for untouched forests.

One of the most important differences between second-growth and untouched forests is the canopy formed by the crowns of the trees. In virgin forests, where trees live out their full lives—practically every acre in prime old-growth forests has several trees at least 300 or 400 years old—the canopy is uneven, with many open spots left when old trees die and fall. Also, the tops of many old living trees are broken and shattered with age or by high winds or lightning or some other natural accident, which adds to the unevenness of the canopy. This unevenness allows sunlight to reach large portions of the forest floor, stimulating the growth of dense undergrowth. This is evident in pristine parts of the Tongass and in the fragments of untouched forest throughout the Northwest and British Columbia, where the forest floor is crowded with ferns and other undergrowth and seemingly every rock and fallen tree is carpeted with moss and crusted with lichens.

Second-growth forests—those that grow in the wake of logging—because they are dominated by young trees have relatively few fallen trees and standing dead trees. They tend to be clean forests. Old growth is characterized by large numbers of dead trees. The many fallen trees that encumber human travel through old growth are storehouses of nutrients for the forests. A single tree might take up to 500 years to decompose, slowly feeding its nutrients into the soil. As it decays, it feeds and shelters generations of small creatures—from beetles to

salamanders to rodents—which in turn feed larger animals. The dead tree's nutrients, returned to the soil by bacteria and fungi, feed the new trees that come after it.

Trees that fall across streams play a special role that contributes to the health of a forest's aquatic life. They act like dams, slowing the flow of the water and holding back debris long enough for insects, bacteria, and other creatures to decompose it. Fish find shelter in the pools and feed upon the insects that live on the rotting trunks. Cutting trees along streams increases the amount of muddy runoff during rains, making clear streams turbid and killing off fish that require cool, clear waters. Moreover, the placid pools created by fallen trees disappear when streams are scoured of debris, so that fish lose the insects and other foods that accumulate in the pools.

Even the standing dead—trees that died slowly of diseases or other causes and turned into hollow upright shells called snags—are important nesting sites for birds and mammals. Depending on their size, snags might serve for years as the winter dens of black bears and as nesting sites for a variety of birds. The life of the forest thus depends not only on living trees, but on dead ones as well.

The ancient portions of the Tongass benefit wildlife in another way. During winter, when snows lie deep along the shore, deer are able to escape into the untouched forest, where the trees hold out much of the snow. Fresh clearcuts are buried too deep in snow for use by deer even in moderate winters, but in the untouched forest the buildup of snow is gradual, so that starvation conditions are shortened even in the worst winters. When clearcuts regrow, the deer usually use untouched forests six times as much as they use second growth.

The full impact of the cutting of the Tongass on forest wildlife is not fully understood. However, biologists have predicted that in some areas, logging will reduce the deer populations up to 75 percent. Wolves, too, may decline, since their fate is linked to that of the deer and other prey species. The greatest concentration of grizzly bears in the United States occurs in southeast Alaska, and the bears spend the winter in dens in the untouched forest. The Tongass also is home to 10,000 bald eagles of breeding age, and it is predicted that logging will wipe out 90 percent of their nesting and perching sites. Cavity-nesting birds, which comprise about 20 percent of the bird species in coniferous forests and include

A grizzly bear and cub feed upon fish in an Alaska stream. Grizzlies are among the animals that will be affected by the cutting of the last of the ancient trees in the Tongass National Forest.

several owl and woodpecker species, probably will decline unless special provisions are made to protect snags. Furbearers, such as martens, will probably avoid clearcut areas and may decline. Fishermen, both sport and commercial, surely will see declines in the catch of fish such as salmon.

Despite their importance to wildlife and their increasing importance as the last fragments of a vanishing ecosystem, the untouched forests in the Tongass are not slated by the Forest Service for more than token protection. Of the 17 million acres encompassed by the Tongass National Forest, nearly 11 million are unforested rock and ice or are too poorly forested for logging. Of the remaining 6 million acres, about 4.6 million are categorized as good commercial forest. About 1.6 million of these acres are protected from cutting, 1.75 million are slated

for logging, and the rest are available for cutting in the future. Most of the finest dense, untouched forest—classified by the Forest Service as *high-volume timber*—is available for cutting. Of the 100,000 acres of high-volume land, only 9,000 have been designated as wilderness by Congress; the other 91 percent is scheduled for cutting, as is fully 77 percent of the forest's good commercial timber lands. Most of the sites protected as wilderness lie in the areas of rock and ice. Only 22 percent of the 8 million acres slated for protection from cutting is rated as intermediate or better habitat for deer, while 86 percent of the area to be cut is considered important for the animals. The Forest Service and the timber industry do not much lament the loss of the old trees. After all, they say, cutting down the old giants rids the land of "decadent" trees and replaces them with

143

A Sitka black-tailed deer gazes from the edge of an untouched portion of the Tongass National Forest. Logging of the forest's ancient trees may reduce black-tailed deer populations in some areas by as much as 75 percent.

faster growing youngsters. The trees, they say, are a renewable resource.

But the untouched forests are not renewable. Only centuries of growth free of humankind can create a pristine forest such as the Tongass, but the Forest Service plans to cut each logged site again within 100 to 125 years. Thus, the trees may return, but the forest will not. Within the next two centuries, as much as 80 percent of the deer habitat will be lost. And over the life of a cut, predicted one Forest Service biologist, habitat loss "could add up

to 35 to 40 percent for those species, such as deer, that are closely related to old-growth forest."

The Forest Service, despite its long history of treating the national forests as wood factories, is not entirely to blame for this destructive management of an irreplaceable resource. The Alaska National Interest Lands Conservation Act of 1980, which determined which lands would be administered by which federal, state, and native agencies and how they would be managed, includes provisions that require a high level of logging on the Tongass. Specifically, the act declared, "The Congress authorizes and directs that the Secretary of the Treasury shall make available to the Secretary of Agriculture the sum of at least $40,000,000 annually or as much as the Secretary of Agriculture finds is necessary to maintain the timber supply from the Tongass National Forest to dependent industry at the rate of four billion five hundred million board feet measure per decade." Furthermore, Congress ordered that the $40 million, or more if it became necessary, would not be subject to reduction by the administration nor subject to the annual appropriations process through which virtually all other federal expenditures must pass. The money was to be made available automatically.

Given that in the 1950s the Forest Service, in its attempt to encourage the development of southeast Alaska's pulp industry, had already sold Tongass timber at rock-bottom prices, the Alaska Lands Act provision was a blatant giveaway. It was done at the behest of Alaska Senator Ted Stevens, who in turn was working in behalf of the timber industry. Writer George Laycock, in *Audubon* magazine, explained the background for the Tongass provision.

> Where did Stevens get his $40 million figure and the annual quota of 450 million board feet? "The timber industry wrote those provisions," says veteran wildlife biologist Jack W. Lentfer, retired Southeast Division supervisor of the Alaska Department of Fish and Game.
>
> Lentfer also recalls the logging industry's political intimidation. "Our department," he says, "was not even allowed to provide information on how this timbering would affect fish and wildlife habitat."

Initially, the Alaska Lands Act supported the pulp mills at tremendous loss to the federal government, which has earned as little as two cents for every dollar it has invested in the Tongass logging operation. From 1982, when the $40 million yearly started flowing from Congress, to 1987 the Tongass received $386 million. The total income credited to the forest by the Forest Service in those years was $32 million. Since only $4 million of that was produced by timber harvest, the gap between expenses and income was in excess of $380 million. Much of this money was spent building roads into the forest to give timber companies easier access for logging. The Forest Service's enthusiasm for road building is doubly destructive. It not only wastes funds, it also makes areas that were previously roadless unsuitable for wilderness designation.

In addition, the timber companies themselves have been involved in schemes that cut into federal timber receipts. After the Alaska Lumber and Pulp Company and the Louisiana Pacific–Ketchikan Pulp Company lost a $1.5 million lawsuit brought in 1975 by a small local pulp mill that charged the companies with price-fixing violations of the Sherman Anti-Trust Act, the Forest Service reviewed its sales record to see if the price fixing had reduced federal income. It was discovered that the pulp companies' finagling may have cost the government as much as $81.5 million. The money has not been recovered.

It is sadly ironic that in some areas the cutting of the Tongass is threatening local economies. For example, the Forest Service wants to cut the trees that grow along the Lisianski River on Chichagof Island, a prime area for deer, bear, and waterfowl that earns nearly a half-million dollars yearly from its salmon fishery alone. The salmon industry may decline, along with other wildlife values, if the Forest Service

Lumberjacks move a log on the Tongass National Forest. The federal government has spent $40 million yearly since 1980 to subsidize the logging companies that are cutting the ancient trees of the Tongass.

A logging town in Washington state, around 1905, sits perched along a river among the rubble created by its workers.

goes through with plans to spend some $3 million on roads and timber-sale administration along the Lisianski so that trees in the area can be sold to the Sitka mills for $40,000.

It seems incongruous at best, and irrational at worst, that while the United States is using its politi-cal and economic power in an attempt to halt the cutting of Latin America's tropical rainforests, the nation is, under its own laws and at great financial cost, cutting down most of the few remaining pieces of temperate rainforest within its own boundaries. And not in Alaska alone.

The Pacific Northwest

Commercial logging came to Oregon, Washington, and northern California in the nineteenth century and has claimed 90 percent of the forests that grew there. Today, a battle rages over the fate of the remaining 10 percent with the logging industry clashing with biologists, conservationists, and out-door extremists.

Like the Tongass, the woodlands of the Pacific Northwest are temperate rainforests, characterized by a high level of annual precipitation. These forests are dominated by a large diversity of conifers. Along a narrow strip that lies between the ocean and the coastal mountains from southern Oregon to Alaska is the sitka spruce/western hemlock forest. The oldest of these trees have lived for as long as 800 years, growing to 300 feet tall and 14 feet in diameter. In the lower elevations of the coastal mountains grow the Douglas fir/western hemlock forests, where the oldest Douglas firs may reach 1,000 years in age and stand 350 feet tall, with thick bark to resist the frequent fires that sweep through this region. Douglas firs also dominate the mixed-conifer

opposite: *Ancient trees silhouetted in autumn mist along French Creek valley in the Willamette National Forest. Trees such as these are the target of loggers seeking to cut the last of Oregon's unprotected, untouched forests, which lie almost entirely on public lands.*

Fallen trees are characteristic of untouched forests. This dead giant in Olympic National Park in Washington sprouts plants and gives the spark of life to mushrooms and mosses, which continue to support the health and growth of the forest.

forests in the drier parts of southern Oregon and northern California. Higher up the coastal mountains of Oregon and Washington are fir forests, dominated by trees ten centuries old but less than 200 feet high, such as silver and noble firs. Higher still is the mountain hemlock forest, trees of a cold and rugged land that grow slowly—a 500-year-old mountain hemlock is less than 100 feet tall.

Both the Forest Service and the federal Bureau of Land Management administer public forests in the Pacific Northwest. A quarter of the gross revenues from the national forests go to local county governments in lieu of real estate taxes that the Forest Service would owe were it a private landowner. Half the gross revenues from Bureau of Land Management forests in western Oregon go to local counties for roads and schools. These financial arrangements give local residents an important stake in the timber industry and the cutting of pristine forests. The sums involved are considerable. Unlike the Tongass, these forests make a considerable amount for the federal government. Oregon's Willamette National

Forest, for example, is the top timber producer in the national forest system.

Wildlife, too, has a stake in the forests. More than 200 species of vertebrates live in Pacific Northwest forests, and about 25 percent of them are most abundant in the untouched woods. These include martens, fishers, a variety of bats, the northern goshawk, northern spotted owl, and pileated woodpecker. The forests are also home for several endangered and threatened species, including American peregrine falcons, northern bald eagles, and a remnant grizzly population. The extent to which these species depend on pristine forests is unknown. Says Jerry Franklin, a Forest Service plantologist, "No one, I think, can seriously deny that there are old-growth species that just really aren't going to be able to exist outside of old growth. I think it's highly probable that there are such species." Indeed, cur-

opposite: *A tree in the Willamette National Forest begins its journey to a lumber mill with a crashing fall amidst the growl of a chainsaw.*

149

The Northern Spotted Owl

Much of the heated controversy that has characterized timber harvest on federal lands in recent years has centered on the northern spotted owl, which is confined primarily to the coastal mountains and Cascade Range of Washington and Oregon and to northern California's coastal mountains. People concerned with the bird's survival have clashed again and again with loggers because the cutting of the ancient forests in the Pacific Northwest in all likelihood will lead to the owl's extinction. Northern spotted owl populations are declining at about 0.8 percent yearly in Oregon and at about 0.45 percent in California, primarily because of the cutting of ancient, untouched forests.

Biologists have found that although northern spotted owls will occasionally use cutover and second-growth forests, they are much more likely to occur in untouched forests. Biologists such as Eric Forsman, who has studied the owl for

A northern spotted owl.

years, believe that the bird cannot survive without untouched forests. Why the owl needs ancient forests is not entirely clear, but it seems likely that it finds proper perching and nesting sites and/or primary

food sources only among the old trees.

The fate of the spotted owl has varied slightly from state to state. In national forests in northern California, up to 550 pairs of owls are being protected, and each pair is being provided with a minimum of 1,000 acres of untouched forests. Some national forests are experimenting with selective cutting of trees in areas used by the birds. The Bureau of Land Management, which has some holdings in northern California, is planning to protect about a dozen sites used by owls. California has no plans for owl management.

The Bureau of Land Management has no plans for managing spotted owls in western Washington, where it administers little land. The Forest Service plans to protect 112 pairs. The state government has no plan for protecting habitat for the owl.

The front line of battle in the spotted owl war is Oregon, where the Forest Service and the Bureau of Land Management control most of the ancient forests left in the state. The Bureau has tended to oppose any effort to protect the birds. When, in the mid-1980s, a panel of

rent research suggests that in the future biologists will compile an increasingly longer list of old-growth dependent species. For example, until the past year or two, it was not known that three amphibian species—the tailed frog and the Olympic and Del Norte salamanders—were old-growth dependent; or that a shorebird—the marbled murrelet—was old-growth dependent; or that red-backed voles, red tree voles, hermit warblers, and golden-crowned kinglets seem to do best in pristine forests. These discoveries suggest that information on untouched woodlands is simply too rudimentary to make sweeping statements about the needs of wildlife for untouched forests. Similarly, it is too rudimentary to provide sound guidance for the cutting of the last pristine stands.

Lack of knowledge about the ecological roles played by pristine forests extends into areas of direct economic interest to local residents. For example, in the Six Rivers and Shasta-Trinity national forests in California, the clouding of streams by erosion after

logging led to an 88 percent decline in valuable chinook salmon populations and cut the steelhead population by 60 percent. Some researchers tie the decline of the Pacific Northwest salmon industry after World War I to the logging of pristine forests and the clearing of fallen logs from streams. Urban water supplies may also be affected by logging. Mt. Hood National Forest alone produces $24 million worth of domestic water annually. Clearcutting of the old forests may also lead to outbreaks of insect pests, since clearcuts tend to have higher densities of pest insects than do pristine forests.

Even when the Forest Service has attempted to preserve fragments of untouched forest, the efforts often have been crippled by lack of knowledge about how the forests function ecologically. Since World War II, logging on Pacific Northwest national forests has turned mountainsides and river valleys into checkerboards of 25- to 50-acre clearcuts interspersed with uncut patches of forest of about the same size. The Forest Service believed that this pat-

biologists appointed to study the owl question concluded that the Bureau and the Forest Service combined should provide a minimum of 1,000 acres of untouched forest for each of 400 pairs of owls—figures the panel considered essential to saving the *bare minimum* number of owls needed to ensure the subspecies' survival—the Bureau agreed to protect only 300 acres per pair. The Forest Service, which the panel said would need to protect 290 pairs, agreed to protect only 263.

Since the mid-1980s, biologists have learned that the estimated amount of untouched forests needed by each owl pair varies from place to place. In some areas the birds need nearly 4,500 acres per pair. The federal agencies have persisted, however, in keeping maximum protected areas to less than 3,000 acres.

Conservationists have become so concerned about the owl's survival that in 1988 an Oregon chapter of the National Audubon Society requested that the northern spotted owl be added to the endangered-species list. This was an action that the timber industry was loathe to see happen. If the owl were listed, the Bureau of Land Management, the Forest Service, and the Oregon Department of Forestry would find it legally impossible to ignore the owl's needs when planning timber-harvest levels on public lands. In 1989 the U.S. Fish and Wildlife Service approved the listing proposal, but only after being ordered to do so by a federal court.

The obstacles that the various state and federal agencies have posed to protecting the 2,700 pairs of owls thought to live in the Pacific Northwest reflect the logging industry's political power. Within each agency are biologists committed to wildlife protection, but their voices tend to be stifled by the cries of the timber industry. The loggers' view is perhaps best summed up by a bumper sticker, popular with the saw-timber crowd, that reads, "Save a logger, kill the spotted owl." Loggers put tremendous pressure on the agencies whenever a portion of their cut is threatened, regardless of how small that portion is. For example, in Washington, where 80 percent of the old forests already have fallen before the loggers' saws, the Forest Service's owl-protection plan would reduce the annual cut by only 5 percent, but it still is aggressively opposed by loggers.

In 1988, another species entered the limelight that glows on the spotted owl when the National Audubon Society proposed that the marbled murrelet, a shorebird that nests almost exclusively in untouched forests, should be federally listed as endangered. If the Fish and Wildlife Service agrees, the murrelet may further highlight the importance of ancient forests to wildlife and intensify the controversy. Meanwhile, for the owl the future is dim. In the 1986 *Audubon Wildlife Report*, biologists Eric Forsman and E. Charles Meslow said that current management plans will cause large reductions in owl numbers and that barred owls—close relatives of the spotted—are forcing spotted owls off their range in some areas. The biologists concluded, "These factors do not bode well for the future of the spotted owl. About the best that can be expected is that management for the species will result in a greatly reduced, but viable, population of owls."

Meanwhile, the timber industry continues to cut 170 acres of ancient trees daily, 62,000 acres a year.

tern would help protect the integrity of the forest. Instead, it has created vulnerable fragments that quickly succumb to environmental pressures. Deer and elk tend to overuse the ancient, untouched remnants, destroying the remnants' value for animals that depend on old-growth forest. Moreover, the small patches, open to the full brunt of powerful winds, are easily blown down. In 1983 windstorms knocked down 3,400 acres of Mt. Hood National Forest that had been heavily roaded and cut into patches. The minimum size needed to maintain the stability of old-growth stands is still not clear, but research suggests that the fragments should be ten times the size of those created by traditional Forest Service checkerboard clearcutting.

Current Forest Service logging plans offer little promise that the loss of untouched forests will be stemmed. More than half the remaining untouched areas on Olympic National Forest in Washington State are slated for cutting during the next fifty years, along with half the remaining untouched forest on California's Shasta-Trinity national forests and 69 percent of the old growth on Oregon's Siuslaw National Forest. Current plans call eventually for saving no more than 5 percent of the ancient trees on the Shasta-Trinity.

Congress in 1989 gave its approval to continued and extensive logging of the Pacific Northwest's last stands of unprotected, untouched forests. In a rider to the appropriations bill for fiscal year 1990, Congress voided all court injunctions brought to stop the cutting of ancient trees on lands administered in Washington and Oregon by the Bureau of Land Management and the Forest Service and took away the right of citizens and conservation groups to seek further injunctions in any future cuts planned in the two states. However, the rider specified that if a suit is brought to stop a cut, the Forest Service must put off logging in the disputed area for 45 days, giving the courts a limited time to reach a decision. The rider also ordered the logging of 7.7 billion board feet of timber by October 1990. This is such a large

A clearcut atop a mountain peak in the Willamette National Forest in Oregon. The red gash is a road cut into the forest to facilitate logging. Roads provide access into pristine areas, making forests and their wildlife vulnerable to a variety of human intrusions.

Protecting the Biggest Trees

Perhaps the largest living things ever were the monkey-thorn trees of South Africa's Transvaal. They grew to 400 feet tall, with trunks 150 feet around. The last of those giants fell to saw and ax long ago. Only diminutive young monkey-thorn trees remain.

We have done a better job—though just barely—of saving North America's titan, the California redwood, which can tower more than 300 feet tall. About 12 percent of the redwood's original acreage still remains uncut, roughly a quarter of a million acres out of an original 2 million. About 150,000 acres of redwoods, including 60,000 acres of virgin, pure-stand redwoods, are protected in thirty-two California state parks. Redwood National Park protects another 78,000 acres, but less than 2,000 acres are pure-stand virgin redwood forest. Cities and counties protect another 22,000 acres.

Despite the trees' rarity after years of logging, they are still being cut on private land. Most of the approximately 20,000 acres of virgin redwoods left on private lands lie in Humboldt County, and for them time is running out. A holding company called Maxxam Group has taken over the Pacific Lumber Company, which was selectively logging its 16,000 acres of Humboldt County redwoods. Maxxam plans to clearcut the holding, presumably to help retire the $800 million debt they built up when they bought Pacific Lumber. The cut will destroy not only timber, but jobs, because when the cut is over, the company will be out of business. The logging of the redwoods is strictly a scheme to make a quick buck. Many residents in the area oppose the cut, but there is little that can be done to control logging on private lands.

A stream in an untouched portion of the Willamette National Forest lies deeply shadowed in ancient trees.

cut, says Jim Pissot, the National Audubon Society's specialist on wildlife issues, that survival of the northern spotted owl will be jeopardized.

Although the rider ordered the Forest Service to avoid fragmenting large stands of ancient trees and to stay out of areas used by owl pairs, it required these protections only to the "maximum extent practicable," giving the Forest Service broad discretionary control of logging. Citizen advisory committees were formed for each national forest to help set the agenda on cutting. However, the committees are required by the rider to meet such a high level of logging production that under any circumstances they will be required to approve more than 80 percent of all logging plans slated by the Forest Service. Moreover, each committee is supposed to include seven members with an equal balance of environmentalists and representatives of the logging community. However, in appointing each committee, the Forest Service is choosing two environmentalists, two loggers, and three people from the community at large. Since the communities from which the at-large members are drawn are financially dependent on logging, the committees tend to be stacked in favor of cutting trees.

The congressional approach, says Pissot, included some good intentions and shows that Congress at least recognizes that untouched forests are important enough to warrant special consideration when slated for logging. However, the results stemming from the rider do not appear promising. "As far as what will happen this year, on the ground," says Pissot, "it will be a disaster."

As the untouched forests of the Pacific Northwest have dwindled, many local residents have become increasingly militant in their defense. In many cases, organized groups have staged sit-ins on logging roads, blocking logging trucks moving into and out of the national forests. Some individuals have attempted to stop cuts by spiking trees in sales areas. This involves driving nails up to a foot long deep into trees. The spikes are nearly invisible once driven in and pose a serious hazard to loggers. A chainsaw can break if it hits a spike, causing the chain to fly loose and injure a logger. Some militant groups have urged spikers to avoid spiking trees so low to the ground that a logger would hit them. Instead, the groups say the spikes should be hammered in higher up, where their presence would not be detected until they jam expensive equipment when the logs are run through a mill.

Of course, the object of spiking is to keep the trees from ever getting to the mills. Militants hope to achieve this by reporting their spiking activities to logging companies and the Forest Service, since logging companies refuse to cut spiked areas for fear of damaging equipment or injuring personnel. However, spiking also polarizes opposing viewpoints and sometimes backfires. One Oregon logging company quickly clearcut a pristine forest, taking more acreage than the Forest Service sale plan called for, when a militant threatened to spike the area. The owner of the logging company said if the spikers were willing to risk the health of his personnel, then he was not going to help save trees.

Much of the anger that burns around the logging issue is an emotional reaction to the loss of scenic beauty as lush forests are replaced with barren clearcuts. But the anger is also a reflection of the forest's value as something other than timber. Tourism is a major industry in the Pacific Northwest, and it is based on the presence of splendid natural vistas.

Aesthetics and the desire to protect trees as part of the tourist economy lie at the heart of a logging battle that has raged for nearly thirty years. The battleground is Opal Creek, which rushes clear and foaming over the mossy rocks of Oregon's last uncut watershed. The creek is located deep in an untouched wooded valley on the Willamette National Forest. The Forest Service decided to cut that valley in 1962. At the forefront of the fight to save Opal Creek and its ancient trees is George Atiyeh. Now in his forties, Atiyeh says that he fell in love with Opal Creek when he hiked up to it, fly rod in hand, as a boy of eleven. "I was just awed even at 11 years old by the beauty of the place and the size of the trees and the whole thing," he recalls.

The adults in Atiyeh's family knew Opal Creek well. One of Atiyeh's uncles owned a mine on Battle Ax Creek just above the point at which Battle Ax joined Opal to form the Little North Fork River. When eleven-year-old Atiyeh reported his fascination for Opal Creek to his relatives, he was told that the Forest Service had slated the area for logging. "I made up my mind then that I wasn't going to let it happen," he recalls. "It really kind of tears me up when I think this is the last . . . the only valley that hasn't totally been fragmented and destroyed. God's pocket."

In the early 1960s, when the cut was first announced, the Atiyehs opposed it. Atiyeh engaged in some guerrilla activism himself as a teenager, pulling

Forest advocate George Atiyeh flies his airplane over clearcuts in the Willamette National Forest, Oregon. Atiyeh is continuing a long-time family struggle to stop the logging of Opal Creek valley, one of the few remaining Oregon stream valleys that have never been logged.

up Forest Service survey stakes and sabotaging equipment. But the real fight in Atiyeh's life began when his uncle died and Atiyeh later became manager of the mine. "Originally I thought when my uncle died, what [the Forest Service] would do is, they'd just go ahead and they'd take over the camp and do what they wanted." But then Atiyeh started to carry on the struggle his grandfather had pioneered. The loggers, he says, "really started ripping out their hair because they figured, well, here we go again."

Atiyeh is not alone in his quest to stop the sale of Opal Creek timber. He estimates that about 800 hikers visit the creek yearly. Said one woman,

> I've taken my grandchildren backpacking up here. My granddaughter was six and a half, and her little brother was two and a half. And we came backpacking up here, and we've done it ever since. My granddaughter will be a senior in college next year. So you know how important a place this is to us. This is one place where I could lay down in front of a logging truck and feel okay. I don't approve of that sort of activism usually, but for this place I could.

In 1984, the supporters of Opal Creek lost one attempt to protect the area when Congress turned down a proposal to designate the creek and surrounding valleys as a wilderness. But they have continued their efforts, opposing the cuts in the press and at public hearings held by the Forest Service as part of its planning process. They fear not only the loss of beautiful scenery, but other values as well. The rare northern spotted owl lives in the Opal Creek drainage, and biologists believe its survival depends on the rapidly disappearing untouched forests. The city of Salem takes about 25 percent of its drinking water from the Little North Fork River. Atiyeh predicts that logging around the Opal Creek and Battle Ax Creek headwaters will add large amounts of mud to the stream.

On the other side of the argument are people such as Robert Freres, whose family has been in the lumber mill business since 1922. He owns four mills in Oregon, turning at least a million board feet of timber weekly into chips and plywood, and employs about 250 people. He says that seventy Oregon

Opal Creek rushes through an untouched forested valley in the Willamette National Forest in Oregon. The trees help keep the stream clear by holding back erosion.

towns are dependent for their existence on the mills—towns such as Lyons, with a total population of perhaps 900, and Mill City, population 1,500. In the area are six or seven other mills about the same size as his, Freres says, indicating that the mills employ nearly 2,000 workers in an area where that number is a sizable segment of the population. The towns depend on the timber industry. "Take away the mills, and you would turn them into ghost towns," says Freres.

Freres' lumber company, and most others except for the giant Weyerhaeuser firm, are dependent on public lands for timber. Freres, for example, owns no timber lands of his own. Companies that do own forest lands had cut down most of their big, ancient trees by the 1950s. Most have replanted their land,

Conservation activist George Atiyeh walks along a path in Opal Creek, an untouched, forested valley in Willamette National Forest in Oregon. He hopes to save the valley from Forest Service logging plans.

Fallen trees lie in silence in the valley of Opal Creek. An ancient tree in an untouched forest may influence its environment for nearly 2,000 years: as a living creature for up to 1,200 years and as a decaying source of nutrients for up to 500 years more.

but the new trees will not be old enough to cut for several decades. During the interim, the logging companies expect national forest lands to fill their need for big trees. Freres readily admits that without the national forests and Bureau of Land Management woodlands he would be out of business. He believes that Atiyeh and others like him should be satisfied with forest lands already set aside as national parks or wilderness areas. "We have 2 million acres of wilderness set aside in Oregon," he argues in the Audubon television film. "We have almost 50 percent of the land base set aside in the Willamette, and [forest preservationists] say why not just this area? We've got 40 percent, and how about this much more? What is enough? I feel enough is enough."

Concern about lack of timber and mill closings is rampant in the Pacific Northwest, where in recent years many mills have closed and many jobs have vanished. However, many closings, Atiyeh suggests, were unrelated to wilderness designations. In the early 1980s mills in the Pacific Northwest were outdated and inefficient, and their unionized workers were highly paid. The mills consequently were unable to beat competitors in Canada and the South. Many lumber companies closed down and sold their mills to other companies, which reopened them as nonunion shops. New equipment automated the mills, cutting back the number of employees needed to turn out 1 million board feet of timber by 35 percent. By 1986 the mills had increased their output and decreased the number of workers by 13 percent. A mill that in 1978 produced 2,000 board feet of plywood veneer per employee now has each worker turning out 10,000 board feet. Between 1979 and 1986, jobs in the Oregon-Washington wood products industry decreased from 133,400 to scarcely 100,000 even though timber production increased from 11.2 billion board feet to 12.3 billion.

Some experts predict that the situation will grow worse in the years ahead. New technology may extinguish another 26,500 Washington and Oregon jobs within the next half-century. However, the picture is not entirely black. One study indicates that 13,400 jobs will open up during the next fifty years if Oregon and Washington stop the export of round logs cut on state and private lands and require that the logs have to be processed into lumber and furniture by local companies.

Atiyeh, himself a former logger and timber broker, voices another concern about the future. Most of the private lands are completely cutover, making the untouched forests on public lands the last of

An independent agent at the Freres Lumber Company mill near Lyons, Oregon, measures a log to help determine the price that logger and mill owner will set as its value. Like many mills in the Northwest Pacific, this one is equipped only for processing the big, ancient trees to which it has tied itself economically.

An 800-year-old tree meets a modern motto at the Freres Lumber Company mill near Lyons, Oregon.

Down this path at Freres Lumber Company have traveled many ancient trees. After the bark is removed and the ends cut off, the logs are sent by conveyor belt to a lathe that cuts them into the thin veneer from which plywood is made.

their kind. If the mills, which have already cut 90 percent of the forests in Oregon, need the last 10 percent on public forests in order to survive, what, Atiyeh asks, will they do when they have cut all that? "Our communities are going to dry up and blow away," he says.

"I'm not opposed to logging," Atiyeh says.

"It's what made Oregon Oregon." He thinks that logging of the second-growth forests can continue to supply the lumber mills if it is done wisely. He even thinks that small stands of old growth—some are no more than forty acres—also could be cut because they are too small to provide good wildlife habitat or to attract tourists. But he sees a different use for the

The ship Aqua Garden *at Coos Bay, Oregon, loaded with 5 million board feet of lumber cut from Northwest Pacific forests and ready for shipment to Japan.*

big stands, such as the 11,000 acres of Opal Creek, which he believes will be more profitable than turning them into plywood. This is tourism.

Tourism and recreation already add more than $6 billion yearly to the economies of Washington and Oregon. Recreational use of the national forests in Washington, Oregon, and California accounted for more than 92 million visitor days in 1987. "These beautiful old trees, we can sell them a thousand times over to people who want to come and see them," says Atiyeh. "If we throw away this lumber and leave it a wasteland, what's going to happen to Oregon?"

That is a question with which recreation planners are already attempting to grapple. Studies show that within the near future, the forests will not be able to meet the demand for roadless-area recreation. A federal study of five Pacific Northwest national forests that the Forest Service identified as key to meeting future recreational demand indicates that within the next fifty years, the forests will be able to accommodate only 22 percent of the people coming to them for roadless-area recreation. And yet, the Forest Service is moving ahead with plans to build roads into many of the finest remaining old-growth roadless areas and log them.

Lumbermen argue that old-growth areas will survive for many years because they are being cut at the rate of only 1 percent yearly. Forest Service plantologist Jerry Franklin says, however, that we are eliminating unprotected old growth by reducing it to small fragments, that there is less of it than anyone thought, and that it is being cut at a faster rate than anyone suspected. Also, it takes more than 200 years for the old growth to replace itself, Franklin says, but the Forest Service is planning to cut it every

80 years. As in the Tongass, the trees return, but the old-growth forest does not. Of particular concern, Franklin indicated, was the lack of protected untouched forests. The 3 million acres set aside as wilderness in Washington, he says, include very little old growth. Says Franklin in the Audubon television program, "There's almost no significant old-growth Douglas fir/hemlock forest preserved in the state of Oregon. For all of its interest in conservation, Oregon has almost none of its legacy preserved." Forest Service officials disagree with Franklin, countering that some 4 million acres of old growth remain in Oregon. This illustrates a vexing problem for anyone investigating the old-growth question. Everyone, it seems, has a different definition for what constitutes old-growth forests. For the Forest Service, old growth is any stand of old trees. But in most cases in Oregon, conservationists are talking about the premium stands of old growth, the sort the service calls high-volume timber land. Estimates of old-growth acreage shrink abruptly when high-volume lands are measured. And even the Forest Service admits that only 300,000 acres of the 4 million they label as old growth are permanently protected from logging in Oregon. Again, as in the Tongass, wilderness areas are sited on marginal lands, not on prime untouched forests.

Particularly alarming is the lack of success that foresters have had in regrowing cut forests. Foresters often seek to plant trees on cutover land, creating timber plantations by using seedlings of species that produce desirable wood. The long-term future of this practice is increasingly in question. In the South, the amount of wood coming from second- and third-growth forests is declining. The cause is unknown, but it may have something to do with the

Canada's Pacific Forests

"If you go down to the woods today, you're in for a big surprise." That was the catch phrase, in big letters, on a full-page advertisement in a Canadian hunting and fishing magazine. The phrase appeared at the bottom of a photo in which deer lurked among the tall ferns and huge trees of an ancient forest. The ad was supposed to bring tourists to British Columbia by promising unexpected sights of outdoor splendor. But in reality, the big surprise is more likely to be that the forests are gone.

About 94 percent of British Columbia's untouched forests are on public lands, but 93 percent of that land has been turned over to four major lumber companies in perpetual leases that virtually give the loggers all rights to the forests. The rate of cutting is so fast— more than 5 billion board feet yearly— that probably all commercial forest lands, which are those with the biggest, oldest trees, will be cut within the next seventeen years. Canadian conservationists fear that the cutting will destroy valuable salmon streams, wipe out bald eagle nesting habitat and send the birds into decline, and reduce elk and deer populations. Even orcas, also called killer whales, may be affected. Siltation as a result of deforestation may ruin Vancouver Island's Tsitka River, driving away the orcas that gather every summer in the shallow waters at the mouth of the river.

Although the ancient, untouched forests of British Columbia, which include the tallest sitka spruce trees in North America, are being cut at a tremendous rate, local conservationists are hard pressed to save them. Only 2 percent of British Columbia's forests are protected, compared to 12 percent in Washington State and 4 percent in Oregon. The total amount of protected untouched forest in all British Columbia is only 460,000 acres, roughly two-thirds the amount cut by British Columbian loggers every year. About 95 percent of the timber comes from virgin forests. Conservationists struggling to protect the forest face a particularly daunting challenge because, unlike their U.S. counterparts, they have no legal standing that allows them to sue in court to stop clearcuts. Also, public lands are leased to loggers without public hearings, and no environmental-impact statements are required for potential logging sites. On top of all that, British Columbia lacks a Wilderness Act that would help win protected status for roadless areas, and there are no national forests.

The current state of affairs in regard to the destruction of untouched forests in British Columbia is perhaps best symbolized by what is happening along Carmanah Creek, an untouched river valley on Vancouver Island. Carmanah is on public lands, but when conservationists tried to enter the area in the late 1980s MacMillan Bloedel, the timber company that leases the valley, tried to block them. When a court ruled that private citizens could enter the lands even if they are leased, the conservationists initiated a survey of the river valley. They found that it is one of the finest sitka spruce forests in Canada. One spruce over 300 feet tall is the tallest tree in Canada and may be the tallest sitka spruce in the world. Bloedel had planned to cut the valley in the year 2003, but when company officials heard that conservationists wanted to protect the Carmanah, logging was started in 1989.

opposite: *These trees on the Olympic National Park in Washington are safe from cutting, but they represent only a small portion of the untouched forests that once dominated the Northwest Pacific. Forest ecologists believe that too few large acreages of untouched forest have been protected from logging.*

loss of soil nutrients that occurs when trees are removed for lumber instead being left to decay into the earth. This may be a warning for the Pacific Northwest. Says independent forestry consultant Chris Maser,

If we remove all of the wood from the forest floor we will eventually greatly impair the ability of the trees to grow. This is the way nature reinvests into the system. . . . There will never be a forest here again because we are insisting on one plantation after another plantation after another plantation. We don't ever plan to allow these trees to recycle. We don't ever plan to allow nature to heal the processes below ground and to recapitalize the soil nutrients. In Germany, for example, they've learned that after two rotations [each cut and regrowth is called a rotation] such practices cause a decline in productivity. But it isn't our problem, it's the future's problem. . . . You can always cut old growth, but once it's cut we can't grow it back. No one has ever done it.

No One Has Ever Done It

A great many things have never been done where untouched forest is concerned. The pristine forest's importance to wildlife has barely been studied. Its importance to the purity of urban water supplies and to the integrity of the fishing industry has barely been studied. That old growth is a renewable resource has always been taken for granted, but it has been neither studied nor demonstrated. No one has answers on any of these subjects. But current research is turning up information so startling that it should give pause to anyone who believes that log-gers can move ahead with their chainsaws secure in the belief that the forest will simply grow back.

One of these studies concerns roots. The roots of a mature tree may encompass 300 tons of soil—roughly the equivalent in weight of more than 150 automobiles—even though the roots of most trees lie no deeper than three feet underground. The roots course for yards through the subsoil, reaching out far from the trunk of the tree. And, biologists are discovering, they may reach out for one another.

A Douglas fir forest, for example, seems to grow

From Tiny Rodents Mighty Evergreens Grow

The California red-backed vole is an inconspicuous little rodent, a drab, grayish creature that scurries among the leaf refuse of the ancient forests. But it has evolved over the millennia to fill an important niche that shows something of the hidden intricacy of untouched forests.

The vole eats almost nothing but mushrooms, including the truffles that grow beneath the soil. The truffles and other mushrooms are vital to the health of the forest ecosystem. As they grow, the fungi wrap themselves tightly around the root tips of the big trees. They also send tiny feelers into the outer layers of the roots. This connection allows the trees to draw nitrogen, minerals, and water from the fungi, which in turn take these substance from the soil. Without the fungi, the trees by themselves would not be able to absorb these nutrients. The fungi also produce chemicals that stimulate root growth in the trees. The process is not all work and no play for the fungi, since they absorb sugars from the trees.

Truffles reproduce by producing spores from which new plants grow. However, the fungus grows entirely underground. It cannot disperse its spores without help. The help comes from the voles. When the truffles are ready to give off spores, they emit a strong odor that allows the voles to locate them. The voles dig up the truffles and eat the parts that hold the spores. When the voles excrete the spores after moving around in the forest, they help to spread the truffles to new areas. Thus trees, truffles, and tiny rodents are linked together in a vital chain critical to the integrity of the entire forest.

more successfully if alder trees are mixed into it. The reason is in the roots. Among the roots of alders live bacteria that convert nitrogen in the atmosphere into a form that the alders can use and store. The Douglas fir roots, which lack nitrogen-fixing bacteria, mingle with the roots of the alders and take advantage of the alders' nitrogen system. In other cases trees become even more intimately involved with one another. More than 100 different types of trees have been found to form massive living networks by interlocking their roots with those of nearby trees of the same type. The roots of different individual trees graft together, and water and nutrients actually pass from tree to tree. In some cases a tree trunk may die and rot, but its root system, grafted to nearby living trees, survives. Writes biologist and journalist Roger B. Swain, "Root grafts are now forcing us to reconsider our notions of individuality when looking at trees. . . . "

Even more amazing are connections between trees of different species. Botanists have discovered that subterranean fungi are part of a process that passes nutrients around among trees of *different* species. Swain writes, "How direct the transfer of nutrients, and whether there is net flow between species, is still being studied, but the notion that plants are always independent self-serving organisms has been knocked into a cocked hat."

Clearly, the forests are vastly complex, and so little is known about them that no one can predict what the cutting of them portends. "It is entirely possible we are creating a future 'wet desert' in the Pacific Northwest," writes journalist David Kelly in his book, *Secrets of the Old-Growth Forest*. "Nobody knows what that would do to the annual rainfall levels in the region where more than half the hydroelectric power consumed in the United States is now generated. Jerry Franklin suggests only half-jokingly that this new ecology might consist almost entirely of blackberry bushes. In that case spring runoffs might be so massive as to destroy our existing dam system."

We and our forebears have cut in excess of 90 percent of the 850 million acres of forest that once covered much of North America. Some figures indicate that as little as 2 percent of the original forests remain. They have become rare ecosystems, ecosystems in danger of extinction.

More than two decades ago Congress passed the first Endangered Species Act in recognition of the need to protect vanishing species. It was a landmark law that catapulted wildlife conservation into a new era. The same foresight that saw the development of endangered-species protection is now needed to provide wiser conservation and management of our endangered ecosystems. The languishing of our untouched forests clearly shows our need for an endangered-ecosystems law that will protect not just individual vanishing species, but whole complexes of species, vast numbers and varieties of plants and animals whose survival is now jeopardized. Such far-reaching protection would be far more effective than our present piecemeal policy of trying to manage the conservation of one species at a time. Without such protection, we will soon trade all our rich and irreplaceable untouched forests for a few more truck-loads of lumber. All the mysteries of the pristine forests will be forever unreachable and unexplored, and the old, old trees replaced with more of the ruin that humankind so often leaves behind.

ARCTIC REFUGE

A VANISHING WILDERNESS?

Based on the Audubon Television Special by
Wolfgang and Sharon Obst and
Narrated by Meryl Streep

ALASKA'S ARCTIC COASTAL PLAIN is a harsh and peculiar land. In summer the sun does not set, and in winter it does not rise. The growing season is short, giving plants no more than ninety days of growth yearly. A tree 300 years old may stand little taller than a man.

In winter, temperatures may sink below −70°. Precipitation, in the form of snow and rain, is about equal to that of the Mojave Desert. In summer, only the top few inches of soil thaw, giving vegetation a shallow foothold. The earth below is ever-frozen permafrost.

And yet, Alaska's arctic coastal plain and its offshore waters are rich in wildlife. Nearly a quarter of a million walruses live there, and innumerable seals and hundreds of polar bears. Thousands upon thousands of caribou, uncounted wolves, and several hundred muskoxen roam the plain at certain times of year. Migratory birds breed there—tens of thousands of snow geese and sandhill cranes, a million shorebirds of various species, ducks, terns, black guillemots. Some birds merely pass through—half a million oldsquaw ducks, a million king eiders.

Despite its abundant wildlife, the plain is not pristine. About 90 percent of the 1,100 miles of arctic coast lying within the United States has undergone some form of development. Only 125 miles, all within the Arctic National Wildlife Refuge, remains untouched, and now even this remnant is coveted by the oil and gas industry. If it is lost, the wilderness of the arctic coastal plain will have been sacrificed for the last time to human development. Nothing will be left to take.

Settlers in a Land of Ice

Human settlement of the Alaskan arctic began perhaps 20,000 years ago, though the stage had been set for it some 100,000 years before when, for still-unknown reasons, the Earth had begun to cool. As the global climate chilled, summer in northern regions was neither long enough nor warm enough to melt away all the snow that fell in winter. Year after year the snow piled higher and higher, the immense weight of it crushing bottom layers into glacial ice. In some parts of the north, the height of the glaciers

An arctic fox, one of the small predators of the North Slope. Before winter it will shed its dark hair and become completely white.

exceeded the height of the tallest of the Rocky Mountains, sheer walls of ice fully three miles high, moving slowly out of the north, reaching across Canada and into the northern United States.

The glaciers held within them about 17 million cubic miles of water, much of it robbed from the sea. The oceans ebbed from many shores and, 400 feet lower than they are now, subsided from land masses that had lain under shallow waters. And so, at the peak of the most recent ice age, Alaska was joined to Siberia by a plain that stretched 1,000 miles from its northern border to its southern. Into North America across this ample bridge came a wide variety of Asian wildlife—moose, bison, lions, beavers, musk-oxen, even chipmunks. And people.

The people came from the Old World tundra, where they had hunted vast herds of ice age mammals. They wore furs and fashioned tools from bone. Their weapons were spears and knives, with points and blades chipped from stone. They probably lived in tents like teepees, made of animal hides stretched over a wooden frame. They probably believed in an afterlife and may have practiced religious rituals that centered on the bear, an outgrowth perhaps of a cult that dated back tens of thousands of years to the Neanderthals. Their foods were bison and woolly rhino, horse, reindeer, and woolly mammoth. And food was plentiful. Mammoths alone were so abundant that in recent years the frozen remains of nearly 120,000 of them have been found in the Soviet

Union, so abundant that their ancient tusks, with those of the extinct mastodons, have supplied half the world's ivory.

The hunting people crossed the land bridge into Alaska 15,000 to 20,000 years ago, entering a world where mammoths and other game animals, and saber-toothed cats and dire wolves and cave bears, had never known humankind. When the glaciers began to retreat, about 15,000 years ago, the people found their way into southern Canada and the United States. Then, as the world warmed, the huge ice age mammals vanished. Perhaps the human hunters contributed to the extinctions, pressing too hard upon creatures already stricken by climate change and habitat loss.

Seven thousand years passed, the Earth warmed, and the glaciers retreated to about their present positions. As the glaciers had fallen back, the northern forests had spread in their wake, and as the forests had expanded, so had the ranges of the animals that dwelled in them. The people, too, moved north, following the game. The northernmost peoples were nomadic, moving onto the treeless tundra in the warm months and retreating south to the forests when the cold set in. They hunted caribou and

moose, fished with baited hooks, traveled by canoe, and lived during summer in tents and during winter in log houses.

Not until about 4,000 years ago did a people arrive who could live year-round in the arctic. These were the Paleoeskimos. They came from Siberia, crossing the sea ice and spreading during the next 3,000 years all across the New World arctic to Greenland. Their culture developed in virtual isolation from the rest of humanity. They lived year-round in skin tents that probably were divided inside into sleeping and working areas. In winter they clustered around fires fueled with driftwood, willow, bones, and fat. They were the first in North America to use the bow and arrow, and they fed primarily on caribou and muskoxen but also ate fish and seals. Though they lacked boats, some groups hunted a variety of sea mammals that they found along the edge of the sea ice or killed from shore. They left behind camps littered with the tiny stone tools that characterized their culture. Rings of rocks arranged thousands of years ago to hold down the edges of Paleoeskimo tents are still found today by arctic travelers.

About six centuries before Christ, Paleoeskimos

A red-throated loon mounts its nest on the arctic coastal plain.

dwelling along the arctic shores of the Bering Sea began a major cultural change by turning increasingly to the hunting of sea mammals—seals, walruses, and whales. New materials and ideas reached them from distant lands—from across the Bering Sea, where trade routes reached into China, and from Native Americans as far off as Washington state. By the year 500 they had boats—single-man kayaks and the larger umiaks that required rowing crews. They had iron and pottery, they had recurved bows—a weapon that must have reached them from Asia—and they wore armor of bone. They lived in permanent villages in log houses covered with turf. In summer they killed a bountiful supply of meat, mostly from sea mammals, including the bowhead whale. They fed well throughout the winter in houses lighted with soapstone lamps fueled by the oil of sea mammals.

About 1,000 years ago the Earth warmed slightly, reducing the sea ice all across the arctic. This was ideal for travel by boat, and the arctic dwellers suddenly expanded their territory, pushing south and dispossessing the inhabitants of Kodiak Island and pushing east to Greenland. Everywhere they went their technology allowed them to overwhelm the remaining Paleoeskimos. And then nature played a cruel trick on them.

It started in the seventeenth century. The climate cooled markedly. The hunting of whales and other sea mammals became more difficult as arctic seas froze for longer periods of time. Unable to lay in large supplies of meat over the summer, these people—their lives culturally linked to the sea—were forced to spend winter in houses made of ice and snow. For subsistence they hunted seals, sitting by holes in the sea ice and stabbing the seals with spears when they came up to breathe. Their life became impoverished and marginal.

It was in this condition that they first met the Europeans, and it was this culture that came to be associated in European society with the name "Eskimo," based on an Algonquin Indian word meaning "they who eat raw meat." The Eskimos prefer their own appellation—Inuit—which means simply "the people" or "the real people."

Europeans first met the Inuit of the Canadian arctic in the late 1500s, when the English and the Dutch were searching for a Northwest Passage to the Orient. During the next century, European whalers nearly wiped out the whales of the eastern Canadian arctic, and the Inuit in parts of the region were slowly reduced by European diseases and alcohol. The Alaskan arctic, however, still lay beyond the reach of European ships and became one of the last strongholds of the Inuit and the animals they hunted.

Two Centuries of Plunder

At the start of the nineteenth century, the Alaskan arctic was still unspoiled and largely unexplored. Its seas had been traveled primarily by British ships trying to wend a path to the Orient through floating ice and frozen seas. Only some twenty years had passed since British explorer and sea captain James Cook had proved beyond the shadow of all doubt that Alaska and Siberia were not joined.

Intense exploitation began in 1848, when Yankee whalers sailed through the Bering Strait and discovered the seas teeming with thousands of bowhead whales. The bowhead was a favored quarry of the whalers because it was relatively slow swimming and floated when dead. European whalers had already wiped out the bowhead in the Canadian arctic, just as Yankee whalers had demolished the nearshore whale stocks off New England. The whalers needed new hunting grounds. After bowheads were located in the Alaskan arctic, fleets of whaling ships arrived each summer. Some even stayed the winter, locked in the sea ice until spring opened the water and brought back whales, seals, and walruses. The whalers hunted all these creatures, and their activities quickly cut into the sustenance of the local Natives, who were already sinking as the alcohol and disease imported by the foreign seamen took their toll. In some cases, whalers stole slaughtered bowheads from the Inuit, depriving the Inuit of crucial food supplies. As the whales, walruses, and seals declined, so did the Inuit.

Two arctic species were lost entirely in Alaska—the muskox and the Steller's sea cow. The muskox,

Thoughts of the arctic may call to mind images of snow and ice, but in fact the coastal plain in summer is awash in beautiful flora.

shaggy survivors of the Ice Ages, were distant relatives of sheep. They traveled in herds and, when threatened, stood shoulder to shoulder in tight circles, their heavy, curved horns outermost. A good defense against wolves and bears, the defensive circles made them easy victims of any hunter equipped with firearms. Whalers and trappers helped wipe out the animals completely. The muskoxen that roam Alaska today come from animals imported from elsewhere and released.

The Steller's sea cow lived in the coastal arctic waters of the Bering Sea. It was a massive seal-like creature related to the Florida manatee. Adults were up to thirty feet long and weighed as much as seven tons. The only larger sea mammals were the whales. Sailors found sea cows easy to take for meat, since the animals scarcely put up a defense when they were impaled with hooks attached to ropes, dragged ashore, and butchered alive. The sea cow was first discovered by science in 1741. It was wiped out by 1768, less than three decades later.

Other wildlife waned as the arctic took the brunt of civilized exploitation. At the start of the nineteenth century, perhaps 20,000 bowhead whales roamed Alaska's arctic seas. By 1900 scarcely 1,000 remained. In the Bering and Chukchi seas, late nineteenth-century whalers and hunters killed nearly a quarter million walruses in two decades. By 1914 the walrus population had been cut more than 85 percent. Millions of seals had been killed, and thousands of polar bears were shot for fur and fun. The Inuit collapsed, too. Their numbers were halved within a single generation—victims of new diseases, a loss of game, and a clash of cultures.

When the wildlife ran out, the exploiters left. The Inuit returned to a semblance of their old life. Then, after World War II, the U.S. military built a string of defensive bases in the arctic and located thousands of troops there. By the time Alaska became a state in 1959, many Inuit had picked up new technologies from the military, replacing harpoons and spears with guns, and boat oars with motors. The old ways were starting to ebb.

But much of the arctic coastal plain was still pristine, a place where tens of thousands of caribou arrived with the spring, where grizzlies and wolves still led lives for the most part unhampered by the machinations of modern humankind. And then oil was discovered on the frozen arctic coast and beneath the seas beyond. A new rush began.

Black Gold, Midnight Sun

Explorers early in this century knew that oil could be found in the Alaskan arctic. They saw it oozing out of the earth along river banks. They heard tales of it from the Inuit, who spoke of a lake of pitch on the arctic coast that poisoned any animal that drank from its waters. Formal exploration for this oil did not begin until decades later, a search that proved fruitful on July 18, 1968, when Atlantic Richfield (a U.S. oil company) and British Petroleum drilled an exploratory hole on the stretch of Alaska's arctic

---

Oil, Gas, and the North Slope

Alaska's North Slope, 250 miles above the Arctic Circle, extends for 600 miles along Alaska's north coast, from the Canadian border to the Chukchi Sea. The conduct of oil and gas development at the North Slope's Prudhoe Bay stands as an alarming omen of what will doubtless occur in the Slope's last pristine stretch, the Arctic National Wildlife Refuge, if the oil industry conducts business as usual.

Development begins with exploratory drilling. Most exploratory wells are dry and have to be plugged and abandoned, but successful exploratory wells are replaced with many, similar, development wells.

Development wells generate a great deal of waste. They require that a water- or oil-based fluid, called "mud" because of its appearance, be pumped into the shaft created by the oil-well drill. The mud lubricates the drillbit and removes soil and other cuttings when it is pumped back to the surface. Cuttings are removed from the mud at the surface and dumped into "reserve pits" dug next to the drilling rig. Leftover mud also has to be dumped, for example when excess mud is collected, or a new type of mud is needed, or a well is abandoned. Usually leftover mud goes into the reserve pit, too, though it may be simply dumped into a well shaft if a well proves dry. When oil and gas in productive wells are not under enough pressure to drive them into the well, oil companies force fluids into the well to increase pressure. These fluids may require disposal, too. In addition, the mud and other fluids used at a well site arrive in barrels, usually fifty-five-gallon drums, which also have to be dumped. The problem is compounded because the drums may contain toxic substances that leak if the drums rust.

Wastes at Prudhoe Bay have been disposed of in the following ways:

- Injection into the Earth: wastewater from drilling operations is commonly disposed of this way, either by running it down the open space between the well shaft tubing and the casing that surrounds it or by pumping it into wells created specifically to inject the water into deep layers of the Earth.
- Discharge of reserve pit fluids to the tundra: prior to the summer of 1988, when the practice was banned, waste fluids could be simply poured onto the tundra; in 1986, 64.6 million gallons of waste were dumped on the tundra in this way.
- Discharge of reserve pit fluids by road watering: until 1988, fluids could be sprayed on roads to harden the surface; in 1987, 36.9 million gallons were dumped this way. The Alaska Department of Environmental Conservation has stopped issuing permits for discharges onto tundra and roads.
- Stored at drum-cleaning facilities where empty drums are rinsed and crushed.
- Stored at hazardous-waste disposal sites.
- Recycled for use in certain types of testing.
- Dumped into an oily-waste landfill or into a solid-waste landfill.
- Burned at a municipal incinerator that accepts domestic garbage and some industrial waste.
- Destroyed at small waste-oil burners.
- Shipped to the lower forty-eight states for treatment and disposal—this involves limited quantities of hazardous wastes.

A recent Environmental Protection Agency study of the North Slope oilfields scarcely inspires confidence in what the oil companies would do at the Arctic National Wildlife Refuge were it opened to development. EPA found that it is "scientifically difficult to document the effects of discharges of oil and gas wastes to the environment on the North Slope. . . . Similarly, information on the success of restoration techniques such as reseeding of tundra appears to be limited." In other words, after a decade and a half of drilling at Prudhoe Bay, we still do not know what is going on up there. Although the EPA report cites some cases of improvements in waste disposal, it admits that the improvements were not done at the initiative of the oil and gas industry, but because of lawsuits brought against the companies for violating the federal Clean Water Act or because of new, stricter state regulations.

In the measured language of an EPA

coast known as the North Slope, at a place called Prudhoe Bay. This was the fifty-first hole the companies had sunk and was to be the last if unsuccessful. But it struck oil. Further exploration indicated that a huge reserve lay under the arctic, triggering another invasion of Alaska and starting a heated environmental battle that in many ways is not over even now.

It began within weeks after the discovery of oil. The state of Alaska moved quickly to auction drilling rights around Prudhoe Bay, making nearly $1 billion in a single morning's auction. Oil companies started planning a pipeline to carry oil from the North Slope to southern refineries. And then all the planning and money ran into a stone wall. The Inuit.

The Inuit had been overlooked in all of Alaska's

dominated by a pro-development administration, the report concluded that it had "observed or documented several operating or waste management practices that are, at best, questionable in terms of their ability to prevent environmental damage. EPA's observations can be grouped along a continuum ranging from accidental and quickly corrected violations of permit requirements, to neglect of regulatory requirements, to indifference toward potentially inappropriate practices that may not be covered by permit requirements."

EPA also reported that "violations of State and Federal environmental regulations and laws are occurring at an unacceptable rate" and that "industry's responsiveness to requests for corrective action were sometimes not timely." To back its claim, EPA noted that Atlantic-Richfield, after receiving three requests in two years to clean up a spill at one of its pads, still failed to respond to the satisfaction of the Alaska Department of Environmental Conservation. During the EPA study, many spills were discovered that had not been reported to the state by oil industry operators, but had been left untended without cleanup.

Drilling mud is dumped onto the tundra at ARCO's West Kuparuk Production Pad.

An Alaskan Native fishing in the Arctic National Wildlife Refuge. Changes in game distribution and pollution of streams caused by oil development threaten the livelihood of Natives still dependent on wild game for food.

previous get-rich-quick schemes. But in the matter of North Slope oil they could not be ignored. They had an organization of their own to represent them, and they were laying claim to virtually the entire realm of the North Slope, some 60 million acres.

The Inuit organization and its claims were relatively new developments. They had come to life only a few years before, when the U.S. Atomic Energy Commission announced plans to build a deep-water port at Cape Thompson by blasting away the bedrock with an atomic bomb. In making its plan the commission overlooked a nearby Inuit village that, along with about 50,000 surrounding acres, would be contaminated by nuclear fallout that also threatened the survival of the wildlife upon which the Inuit depended. The Inuit held meetings to discuss the plan, and one of them—Charles Edwardsen, Jr., also called Etok—used the forum to bring up the

history of Inuit repression by foreign profiteers. Eventually Inuit outrage stifled the Energy Commission's plans. But Etok did not let the matter drop. When he heard about natural gas deposits in the North Slope, he organized both Inuit and nearby Indian community associations into a group called the Alaska Federation of Natives. The Inuit and the Indians had never surrendered their land rights to the United States, and now each of the federation's participating associations outlined North Slope land claims based on historic hunting traditions. They presented the claims to the state of Alaska and the federal government.

The Alaska Native Federation's claims alarmed the oil companies. The companies wanted to be sure that they owned the oil rights for which they had paid, and the word from Washington was not making them feel very comfortable. Secretary of the

Interior Stewart Udall said all federal land transfers and oil and gas leases along the North Slope should be held up until ownership of the land was resolved.

The native federation turned down all offers of a cash settlement, holding out for legal ownership of the land and for control of its development. Eventually they won. Congress, in the Alaska Native Claims Settlement Act of 1971, turned over ownership of nearly 69,000 square miles of Alaskan lands to the state's 85,000 native peoples. For the rest of the land—which comprised nearly 90 percent of Alaska—they were given nearly $1 billion in cash.

The Inuit quickly showed a certain degree of business acumen. In 1973 they held a referendum and voted to hit the oil companies with $7 million in taxes, a vote later upheld by the Alaska Supreme Court when the oil industry contested it. Turmoil soon arose within Inuit circles, however. Most of the billion dollars from the land settlement was used to develop some 200 native corporations which seek to profit from Alaska's resources. While many Inuit cling to the old hunting lifestyle, the native corporations have joined with the oil companies and other commercial interests in seeking to capitalize on Alaska's resources. This has made the Inuit culture a house divided against itself.

While the Inuits were fighting their battle, the environmentalists were fighting theirs. Concerned that uncontrolled oil development would destroy the wildlife values of the Prudhoe Bay area, the conservation community fought for safeguards that would remove the threats posed by oil spills and waste disposal. They also tried to stop construction of a pipeline that would carry oil from Prudhoe Bay to Valdez, 800 miles south, fearing that it would thaw the permafrost and block caribou migration.

A polar bear roaming the ice flows. Biologists lack the data needed to understand how oil and gas development will affect the bears, though increased losses of polar bears are expected.

In a compromise that would have avoided the caribou area, conservationists sought to route the line south through western Canada. The fight wore on for years. When the oil shortage struck the nation early in the 1970s, the oil companies took the lead. Construction on the forty-eight-inch pipeline commenced in 1975 and was completed three years later. However, some of the environmentalists' concerns were addressed, too. Heavy equipment at Prudhoe Bay is transported on vehicles with big balloon tires to minimize damage to the tundra topsoil. Use of multiple rigs is limited by special drilling techniques. All construction, but not drilling, stops when the central arctic caribou herd—about 15,000 animals—begins calving or moves to the coast to escape insects.

Since it started production, Prudhoe Bay has turned out about 2.2 million barrels of oil a day, an eighth of the nation's daily consumption. As many as 6,000 workers have been employed there at one time, making the arctic oilfield a larger population center than most midwestern farm towns. The oil industry has touted Prudhoe Bay as a prime example of how oil development and wildlife can coexist. The caribou herd, they say, has even increased by about 15 percent. However, a report on Prudhoe Bay oil development prepared by the Department of the Interior for California Representative George Miller showed another side to the story. The oilfield and its pipeline, the report said, have destroyed some 11,000 acres of vegetation used by Prudhoe Bay wildlife, including 20,000 birds. Wolves, bears, and other predators, Dall sheep, marine fishes, and most bird species in the area have declined. Some 23,000 oil spills have occurred since 1972, the two largest involving a total of nearly a million gallons. Even the smaller spills permanently damage the delicate arctic environment. And twenty of twenty-one major waste-storage pits have been cited in violation of Environmental Protection Agency standards because they were discharging toxic chemicals, heavy metals, and carcinogens into nearby wetlands. The oilfield emits such high levels of gaseous pollutants that the air over Prudhoe Bay is no better than that of several major U.S. cities. Nevertheless, the pollution level is within the standards set by the Environmental Protection Agency, so there is little or no hope for improvement. Oil companies clean up the area only when compelled to do so. When a congressional contingent visited in 1987, a single company hauled away 1,000 cubic yards of debris that had been ignored for a decade. One company that went bankrupt left behind hundreds of rusty drums filled with petroleum liquids, leaving the responsibility for cleanup to the state.

When Prudhoe Bay opened, about 11 billion barrels of oil lay under its soil. About half of that is now gone. Consequently, the oil industry is now turning its eyes to what is probably the last promising oilfield in Alaska, another section of arctic coastal plain. It lies within the Arctic National Wildlife Refuge, and it is the only stretch of the 1,100 miles of arctic coast in the United States that remains completely untouched by developments such as military bases, native towns, or oil projects.

The Arctic National Wildlife Refuge

The 19 million acres of the Arctic National Wildlife Refuge are virtually pristine. They show visitors what much of the world might still be like if humanoid apes had not long ago come slouching out of Africa and begun shaping the Earth to their own ends. On the refuge, shaggy horned beasts still run on cloven hooves from their ancient foes, the wolf and bear. In braided rivers swim fish that have never seen hook or bait. Caribou pale and gray move in myriad numbers, on and on to distant horizons, like the ghosts of the great southern bison herds extinguished by guns and hunters more than a century ago. Here in summer a mosaic of ponds reflects the briefly setting sun, shining like mirrors. Here a brilliant golden plain sweeps away and away to distant mountains, poised like jagged ocean waves against the sky. On the mountainsides wild sheep stand on thin rock ledges, ivory statues against dark earth and rock. Here twentieth-century man and woman may yet be able to look upon land never seen by human eyes or marked by human tread.

The refuge was years in the making. It began in a small airplane that carried Olaus J. Murie, president of the Wilderness Society, high over the Brooks Range and out over the coastal plain. It was 1951, and Murie had behind him many years of wildlife

The Arctic National Wildlife Refuge.

research in Alaska. As he flew he saw below him straggling herds of caribou pressing toward Canada for the winter, and wolves, bears, moose, sheep, waterfowl. And he saw something else. He saw, or imagined he saw, a vast wilderness preserve, stretching 100 miles south from the Beaufort Sea, from Canada west to the Canning River, 165 miles.

Murie joined with other wilderness advocates in trying to bring his vision to life. It was the work of a decade. Not until 1960 did Secretary of the Interior Fred Seaton issue an order designating nearly 9 mil-

lion acres in the northeast corner of Alaska as the Arctic National Wildlife Range.

More land was added in 1980, when the Alaska National Interest Lands Conservation Act designated much of the original area as wilderness, added another 10 million acres, and changed the name to the Arctic National Wildlife Refuge. The eastern quarter of the coastal plain was designated as wilderness, which meant that no development could occur there unless an act of Congress authorized it. Wilderness designation also was proposed for the rest of

A snowy owl swoops down like a whirl of living snow.

the refuge's coastal plain, all of which had been part of the original preserve. But though the area is a critical calving ground of some 200,000 caribou and an important gathering area for as many as 300,000 snow geese, no decision was made to protect it as wilderness. Instead, Section 1002 of the Lands Conservation Act ordered the Interior Department to investigate the potential for oil and gas development on the 1.5-million-acre coastal plain, which subsequently became known as the 1002 area. More than 100 miles long and 16 to 34 miles wide, this area has been the focus of nearly all the controversy that has stormed over the arctic refuge for the past decade.

The final report on the 1002 area was released in 1987. Based on geological data, it concluded that there was a 19 percent chance of finding an economically recoverable oilfield in the 1002 area, provided that oil was selling at $33 a barrel. At the time the study was released, oil was selling for less than half that, putting the economic feasibility of development into question. Moreover, the report said that if oil were found, there was only a 5 percent chance that it would be a big reserve, perhaps 9 billion barrels. Finding a smaller quantity, if any was found at all, was much more likely: Oil companies were given a 95 percent chance of coming across 600 million barrels, an amount that would not make the area worth developing.

A male and female king eider cruise the waters of the Arctic National Wildlife Refuge.

Seismic equipment grinding across the arctic. The gear is used to set off explosive blasts that permit developers to locate potential oil and gas deposits. The blasts probably will affect wildlife movements and distribution, with potentially far-reaching results. For example, if the sounds alter seal distribution, polar bear survival could be jeopardized by loss of food.

The Porcupine caribou herd sprawls across the Arctic National Wildlife Refuge. The herd includes some 200,000 animals and offers a wildlife spectacle that can be matched only in Africa. The refuge has been called an American Serengeti.

Although the odds were against finding oil and the mean estimate for recoverable oil was only about 3.2 billion barrels—enough to last the nation for about seven months—Secretary of the Interior Donald Hodel in the final report on the 1002 lands recommended opening the arctic refuge's entire coastal plain to the oil and gas industry. This report was sent to Congress, which has been deliberating ever since on whether to turn over the refuge to oil developers.

If Congress yields to the oil industry, the Arctic National Wildlife Refuge coastal plain will soon be changed profoundly by heavy equipment, buildings, and oil rigs. Because the arctic heals slowly, the changes will be long-lasting, possibly permanent. Ditches dug in the Canadian arctic by Elizabethan explorers remain after 400 years, and tracks etched into the arctic soil by hand-drawn carts 160 years ago still survive. The scars of modern industry will be

deeper and more extensive, and will disappear no faster.

The oil companies will need to build another pipeline, running it west across the land for 150 miles to hook up with the line at Prudhoe Bay. They will need roads, at least 300 miles of them. Barge ports will be needed so that supplies can be shipped in. A town will be built, made of prefabricated buildings and industrial equipment and peopled by thousands of oil workers. The industrial complex will be visible for miles across the flat plain, just as the burning glow of the Prudhoe oilfield is visible at night to Inuits living forty miles away. In the words of the 1002 report, "The wilderness value of the coastal plain of the Arctic Refuge would be eliminated, except for the area of the refuge east of the 1002 boundary between the Aichilik River and the Canadian border which is designated wilderness."

Because the great caribou herds that move across

it in most summers look much like the teeming herds of the African plain, the Arctic National Wildlife Refuge has been called the American Serengeti. Indeed, the refuge is in many ways the last patch of wilderness in the United States to have survived the colonization of North America virtually unscathed. Wolves can still be seen shadowing vast herds of hoofed prey, a sight that vanished from the lower states a century ago. Polar bears den there, the only place on U.S. lands where they do so. Eagles wheel in open skies above wide open land. Geese in crowded flocks turn the earth white, like snowfall.

The effects of oil development on refuge wildlife are hard to quantify, but studies have suggested that many species will dwindle. The area is vital to snow geese. Up to 300,000 of them may gather on the refuge at one time. They nest and feed there, fattening for the long flight south in autumn. It is not clear how industrial development will affect them, but it is known that the birds react negatively to aircraft. Flocks have been flushed by the sounds of airplanes flying nine miles distant, which has a more harmful effect on the birds than might be expected. One study determined that aircraft keep juvenile snow geese so active that they burn up about a fifth of their fat reserves, energy they need for their long fall migration. A report by the U.S. Fish and Wildlife Service concluded that the average number of geese gathering at the refuge could be cut in half by development.

Tundra swan hatchlings huddling for warmth on the Arctic National Wildlife Refuge. The arctic coastal plain is a prime breeding area for tens of thousands of swans, geese, and other birds.

Caribou from the Porcupine herd adrift in the Arctic National Wildlife Refuge.

The Fish and Wildlife Service also anticipates losses in shorebirds, golden eagles, grizzly bears, muskoxen, moose, wolves, and wolverines and possible losses among polar bears. Two of the big losers will probably be the local caribou herd and the Native peoples who have depended on them for several centuries.

The refuge caribou are nomadic animals that winter in Canada and migrate in most summers to calving grounds on 1002 lands. Called the Porcupine herd after a nearby river, they number more than 200,000, and millennia of biological adaptation have made it so that all the females drop their calves within a three-week period. Anything that affects their behavior during that period could have vital consequences on the herd.

About 7,000 Alaskan and Canadian Natives living in the refuge area take from the caribou herd each year up to 7,000 animals, making caribou a substantial part of the Natives' diet. Victor Mitander, chair-man of Canada's Porcupine Management Board, says the caribou are essential to the health of local peoples and that their lifestyles would change "drastically" were the herd reduced. In recognition of this, Canada has outlawed oil development in a refuge contiguous with the Arctic National Wildlife Refuge and has asked the United States to do the same on 1002 lands. So far, the U.S. government has refused, at least in part because no definitive conclusion has been reached about how oil development will affect the Porcupine herd.

The fate of caribou at Prudhoe Bay might be expected to foreshadow the future of the Porcupine herd. At Prudhoe Bay, caribou have increased by about a sixth since the pipeline was built. However, the reason for this increase is unknown. No biologist is likely to say that pipelines and oil development are good for caribou. Instead, some believe the herd has increased because oilfield workers have reduced local populations of wolves and bears, which often prey

The struggle for life in miniature: A short-tail weasel carries its prey, a lemming, to a safe feeding site in the Arctic National Wildlife Refuge.

The Porcupine caribou herd grazing on the Arctic National Wildlife Refuge. Plans to drill for oil on the refuge could alter the herd's yearly migrations and jeopardize the cultures of Native Americans that still hunt the caribou.

on caribou. Regardless of why they have increased, Prudhoe caribou actually may not indicate anything about what will happen on the 1002 lands. The Prudhoe herd is not even a tenth the size of the Porcupine and has a far larger area to move around in. The massive Porcupine herd is restricted on the arctic refuge to the narrow coastal strip. The *draft* report on 1002 lands, released for review in November 1986, predicted "a major population decline [in the Porcupine herd] and change in distribution of 20–40 percent." However, in the final report, issued the following April, this warning was changed to read "a major population decline or change in distribution." The changing of *and* to *or* in the final report and deletion of the magnitude by which distribution might be affected make the estimates of potential impact on the caribou seem much less

severe. Why these changes were made has not been satisfactorily explained. Interior Secretary Hodel said the change was meant to correct a typographical error. Federal biologists said they had been forbidden to discuss these or any other changes.

One important alteration concerned streams and wetlands. Oil developers will need millions of tons of gravel in order to build four or five airstrips, drilling pads, and pipeline structures and to surface roads. The 1002 draft report said the gravel would come from streambeds, creating pits up to fifty feet deep that would serve as reservoirs to provide year-round water supplies. No one knows how this will affect stream flow and surrounding wetlands, since the reservoirs were dropped from discussion in the final report. Potential damage to wetlands by waste disposal is also poorly quantified. Where the draft report said wetlands damage would be moderate, the final report said minor.

A major concern of conservationists is oil spills, particularly if the oil companies follow through with plans to drill in the shallow seas just offshore. Offshore drilling usually is done from ships or artificial islands built of gravel. Drilling ships can fall victim to collisions with massive icebergs. Tugboats are used to push icebergs away from drilling ships, but the task is not always an easy one. Some large icebergs can be five miles across and several stories deep. Even a smaller one—six feet deep and a quarter mile across—weighs about 2 million tons and is

An arctic ground squirrel, which is prey for species ranging from snowy owls to grizzly bears.

A grizzly bear on the North Slope. The Arctic National Wildlife Refuge offers the grizzly the last pristine habitat on the coastal plain. Human encroachment and development have already seriously jeopardized grizzly survival in the Lower 48 States.

not easy to stop. To abandon a drilling ship safely can take eight to ten hours, but a captain may have to make the decision within minutes if an uncontrollable iceberg looms near. To avoid this sort of incident, drilling from ships is restricted in much of the arctic to the three months that ice is scarce.

The artificial islands are safer, since the gravel used to build them acts as a buffer to approaching ice. However, even island rigs can have blowouts, which occur when subterranean pressures grow so great that oil explodes from the drillpipe. If a blowout occurred in late August or September, when ice is forming, it could not be stopped until the next May. During the delay, a moderate blowout might bubble half a million barrels of oil into the sea. A big blowout could dump 8 million barrels of oil—roughly thirty times the size of the *Exxon Valdez* oil spill that polluted hundreds of miles of Alaska shoreline in 1989—and would eventually contaminate hundreds of square miles of sea and land. The oil would coat the underside of floating ice, and the ice could carry it nearly 1,000 miles. Contamination of beaches could kill millions of birds, seals, and other animals. Polar bears could be poisoned by eating seals coated with oil. If an oil slick thick enough to block sunlight from the surface of the sea occurred during the first two weeks of summer, plankton and krill populations could be so reduced that the whales, seals, and fish that feed upon them would begin to die off. The effects of a single blowout could last half a century.

Despite the dangers and risks, the Reagan administration moved ahead vigorously in support of arctic-refuge oil development. Long before the 1002 report was out, the administration started greasing the skids for oil developers. In 1983 the Department of the Interior accepted from the Arctic Slope Regional Corporation, one of the Native business organizations, some lands in Gates of the Arctic National Park. In return, Interior gave the corporation the subsurface mineral rights to some coastal lands within the Arctic National Wildlife Refuge and adjacent to the 1002 lands. These rights were beneath some 90,000 acres of lands owned by the Kaktovik village Native corporation, a member of the Arctic Slope Regional Corporation. Because Chevron, a U.S. oil company, had a contract with the regional corporation, the land exchange permitted Chevron to drill a test well into the refuge by placing equipment on Native lands. Chevron so far has kept the results of the drilling secret.

In another case, Fish and Wildlife Service personnel met with officials of Native Alaskan corporations in 1987 to discuss which lands the Natives would like to trade in return for oil rights under 1002 lands. Oil company representatives, barred from the meetings, were nevertheless on hand outside closed doors to offer advice to the Natives.

The Reagan administration also sought the help of the oil industry in revising the draft report on 1002 lands. For example, the draft report indicated that 311,000 acres of the Alaskan and Canadian coastal plain, constituting the Porcupine caribou herd's core calving area, were most important to herd survival. About 80 percent of the calving area lay within 1002 lands. The oil industry suggested that instead of discussing a core calving area, the report should look at a "concentrated calving area"—some 2.1 million acres, of which only 37 percent lay within the 1002 lands. Though much of the area received little use by caribou, its vast size suggested that the animals had plenty of alternative calving sites. The final report thus speaks of a concentrated calving area. The smaller core area was excised, another change that federal biologists were forbidden to discuss with the public. The Reagan administration also tried to suppress California representative George Miller's report on the environmental problems caused by oil development at Prudhoe Bay. Miller said the administration feared the report would undermine efforts to open the Arctic National Wildlife Refuge to the oil industry.

The momentum given to oil development by the Reagan administration seemed likely to win congressional approval for arctic refuge drilling early in the first year of the Bush administration. And then, on the night of March 23, 1989, the oil tanker *Exxon Valdez* ran aground in Prince William Sound, 800 miles south of 1002 lands. Its hull was gouged open on a reef and 10 million gallons of oil rushed into the sea, dooming untold numbers of birds, fish, sea otters, and seals and generating tremendous public outrage at the negligence shown by Exxon in failing to move quickly to control the spill. The incident showed the inadequacy of oil industry plans for containing oil spills and challenged the veracity of the industry's claims that it could operate cleanly in the arctic. By galvanizing public concern about oil development, it made Congress reluctant to proceed with plans to open the refuge to oil developers, at least for awhile. Without doubt, the issue will soon be revived.

Refuge Oil: A National Necessity?

Throughout the debate over the arctic refuge, the oil industry maintained that 1002 oil reserves were crucial to national security. The reserves were said to be the nation's last big oil find. A Texaco vice-president said, "The nation's national and economic security is at risk." Assistant Secretary of the Interior William Horn testified in Congress that "the public interest demands that the area be made available for oil and gas leasing."

Anyone who believed this might have been seriously alarmed. After all, the chances of finding *any* oil on the refuge were small—about one in five. It sounded as if the future of the United States were leaning on a very frail reed. But observant critics soon spotted flaws in the oil industry's claims. The maximum amount of oil anyone expected to find would have supplied U.S. consumers for no more than eighteen months, and the mean estimate of 3.2 billion barrels would last less than seven. No one could seriously propose that national security depended on such a limited supply of oil. Moreover, although the arctic refuge might hold the last large reserve, many smaller reserves exist around the nation that, together, could supply as much or more oil. William L. Fisher, chairman of the Department of Geological Sciences at the University of Texas, has even argued that oil resources and reservoirs already developed in the lower forty-eight states could by themselves stablize U.S. oil production for the next fifty years.

The oil industry's interest in 1002 oil was probably driven more by price than anything else. At the time of the big push, oil prices were down to about $15 a barrel, making the purchase of large quantities highly profitable to the oil companies. Against this background, most conservationists suggested that the oil should stay in the ground until really needed, or at least until the price went up.

Conservationists also have pointed out an alternative to drilling for oil and gas on the Arctic National Wildlife Refuge: reduction in energy consumption. The National Audubon Society, for example, supported a bill to establish uniform energy standards for home appliances. The uniform standards were designed to save the equivalent of a billion barrels of oil by the year 2000. President Reagan vetoed the bill in 1986, but signed it a year later when he feared that another veto might be overridden.

Conservationists also suggested during the Reagan years that tougher fuel economies be set for automobiles. If a national oil emergency, as maintained by the oil industry, required the drilling of 1002 lands, then clearly the Reagan administration should have put a priority on establishing automobile fuel-efficiency standards to reduce petroleum use. Instead, the administration softened fuel-economy standards for 1986, 1987, and 1988

Natural gas burns off during a flare at ARCO Flow Station 1 on the North Slope. The trail of pipelines and the blackening skies seen here foreshadow the fate of the pristine Arctic National Wildlife Refuge if oil and gas development proceed.

The Solar Alternative to Fossil Fuels

Photovoltaic cells are capable of turning sunlight into electricity and offer an environmentally sound method for generating electricity without resorting to power plants run by either fossil fuels or nuclear energy.

The power-producing components of photovoltaic cells, usually called PV or solar cells, are two or more layers of a material that can absorb light and, through a process that involves the freeing of electrons, create electricity. To produce large quantities of electricity, many cells may be combined to form PV modules. There are two types of modules: flat-plate, which work with ordinary sunlight; and concentrating, which use lenses to focus sunlight onto the cells. For greater electricity production, PV modules may be combined to form arrays.

The cost of PV-generated electricity will be competitive with other forms of generation by the end of this century. By the end of the twenty-first century, PV power may replace other power sources worldwide. The present cost of PV electricity is about thirty cents per kilowatt-hour, which is about the price paid by some utility companies for power generated by traditional means during hours of peak energy use on hot summer days. But PVs promise benefits beyond economic considerations alone, since they solve the many pollution problems associated with use of fossil fuels and the hazards that accompany nuclear power. The amount of land required for PV arrays is also comparable to land requirements for coal- and nuclear-powered plants when losses to mining, transportation, and waste disposal are added.

In addition, PVs promise great economic advantages to nations on the forefront of PV development. Demand for PVs will turn PV production into a multibillion-dollar industry during the next few decades. Though Japan leads the world in producing cells, the United States is the leader in PV module shipments. PVs promise to be an excellent means not only for liberating the United States from dependency on foreign oil, but for enhancing the nation's economic base.

---

vehicles by 1.5 miles per gallon, burning up an additional 300 million barrels of oil yearly—roughly a tenth of the mean estimate for oil in the 1002 lands. In addition, the Reagan administration supported the raising of Interstate Highway System speed limits. Ironically, Audubon energy expert Jan Beyea has estimated that if fuel-efficiency standards for cars and small trucks were raised 1.7 miles per gallon, the nation would save the equivalent of 3 billion barrels of oil over the next thirty years. In the first six months of the Bush administration, efficiency standards were raised to this level, perhaps a sign that more reasonable national energy policies lie ahead.

Conservationists have long argued that improving the nation's energy efficiency offers the greatest opportunity for saving oil. With existing technology and without making any major investments, the United States could cut fossil fuel consumption in half. Since 1973, the economy has grown 40 percent while energy consumption has remained stable. As a result, 13 million barrels of oil are saved daily, the equivalent of half the entire production capacity of the OPEC nations. Technology exists for constructing buildings that use a third to a tenth as much energy as most modern structures. New types of insulation are reducing home energy consumption by 50 to 90 percent. National use of new "superwindows" that cost less than standard windows and insulate two to four times better would save more fuel each year than Alaska produces. Forty large power plants could be shut down if consumers simply switched to using more efficient light bulbs.

The reasons for cutting energy consumption go beyond saving the Arctic National Wildlife Refuge. Burning fossil fuels to transport people and cargo pumps more than 700 million tons of carbon into the atmosphere yearly. The average American passenger car adds its weight in carbon to the atmosphere each year. This carbon is acting like a glass shield over the Earth, permitting the sun's heat to come in but not allowing it to escape. This is the infamous *greenhouse effect*, and it threatens to create major shifts in crop-growing areas throughout the world over the next fifty years. Improving worldwide energy efficiency by 2 percent annually would keep global temperatures within 2 degrees of current levels.

Improving energy efficiency is only half the answer, though, since fossil fuels inevitably will run out. Energy experts say that by the turn of the century, world oil and gas production is expected to be in an irreversible decline as the Earth's reserves are used up. The opening of the Arctic National Wildlife Refuge would do little to slow the decline, since the reserves the refuge may hold even in the best-case scenario would be too small to supply more than a few months of fuel. New sources of energy

The Brooks Range aglow in the waning sun of the Arctic National Wildlife Refuge.

will have to replace fossil fuels. Fortunately, progress already is being made in developing natural sources. The cost of using photovoltaic cells, which convert sunlight into electricity, has dropped until the cells are nearly competitive with other forms of electricity generation, and the decline in price is continuing.

Wind turbines, too, have proved themselves efficient at producing electricity. California had 17,000 wind turbines producing 1,500 megawatts in 1987. Permanent solutions to the nation's energy problems lie in developments such as these, not under arctic soil.

The Arctic National Wildlife Refuge: Other Values?

The world is becoming increasingly pragmatic, or so it seems. The worth of a wild place is being calculated more and more in terms of dollars, in terms of the profits it can produce. But what dollar value do we put on the culture of the Gwich'in Indians, a Canadian group that depends on the caribou, a people that will probably be destroyed and certainly will be dramatically changed if the Porcupine caribou herd diminishes? What is the culture of the traditional Inuits, those who have not joined the new native corporations, worth in dollars and cents? The Inuits have learned to live well in an environment where exposure to winter cold can kill an unprepared man within fifteen minutes. If we should lose the Inuits' knowledge, we will know less about ourselves, and less about the human ability to strive and adapt. What is that knowledge worth in barrels of oil? What is the dollar value of being able to watch a polar bear crossing the sea ice in the blaze of a blood-red sunset? Or of seeing untracked mountains lying clean and silent beyond a vast and silent plain? Perhaps that value will not be known until the roar of heavy industry tortures the solitude of the arctic coast.

Not long after the American Civil War ended, a group of hearty travelers gathered around a campfire in the midst of a strange land, where steaming hot waters gushed from the earth. It was a remote place, surrounded by mountains and far, far from civilization. Few people had ever visited it and it did not seem terribly likely that many ever would. Getting there required a hard trip by horseback, days of travel. But the men around that campfire believed the area was worth protecting from the plans of human society, worth sparing from the rush of Manifest Destiny. Eventually they persuaded Congress to set that land aside forever as a pleasuring ground for the people. And thus was born Yellowstone National Park, the first national park in the world. Two million people a year now crowd into it, traveling in vehicles the park's creators could never have imagined, over roads they could never have conceived. What if, instead, the men who gathered around that campfire long ago had argued that few people would ever visit the place, and that Congress should open it to development for geothermal energy? What if, instead, huge mechanical structures had been built over the geysers to tap their heat until, within a few decades, the geysers ceased to spray? How would we remember those men today? What would their legacy have been?

The leaders of the oil industry say the last pristine stretch of Alaskan coastal plain is not worth saving. An official with Arco Oil & Gas Company called it "a flat crummy place." Others say it has no value for recreation, that too few people will ever go there. Is it upon visions such as these that our generation wishes to be remembered in the future? Will this be our echo of the revelations discovered around a Yellowstone campfire more than a century ago? The answers to these questions lie in the fate we choose for the Arctic National Wildlife Refuge.

CRANE RIVER

Based on the Audubon Television Special by
Wolfgang and Sharon Obst and
Narrated by Leonard Nimoy

TRAVELERS HAVE BEEN coming for centuries to Nebraska's Platte River. Most of them have come on feathered wings—generations of cranes, waterfowl, and shorebirds—millions upon millions of birds. For them the river has been vital, a place for rest and nourishment on long migrations between winters in Mexico and summers in the Far North. It has been a safe harbor and a refuge, and it has been essential to their survival.

Other travelers, some 150 years ago, came to the river in long, snaking lines of ox-drawn covered wagons, byproducts of America's Manifest Destiny. They came up from the south, from towns in Missouri, or they came down from the north, from Omaha and Council Bluffs, and they converged on the Platte. For them it was not a safe harbor. It was a roadsign and a pathway. They knew that at the river they must turn west, toward the setting sun. They knew that trails that ran beside the Platte—the Oregon Trail on the south, the Mormon or California Trail on the north—would take them nearly halfway through Wyoming to where Casper now sits, and switch to follow the course of the Sweetwater. They needed no other guide for more than 600 miles. The river showed the way.

It was a wide river—half a mile in some places, three miles in others. Despite its width, it was shallow. Travelers called it a mile wide and an inch deep, though in places it was up to six feet deep. Its waters were full of sand carried out of the Rockies. Some pioneers said the suspended sand made the river glitter like gold. The water was gritty to drink, left teeth crackling with sand. One pioneer described the Platte as ''hard to ford, destitute of fish, too dirty to bathe in, and too thick to drink.''

It was a braided river, its channel broken by bars and islands where the sand built up and then ebbed away, carried off by vagaries of the current. Its banks were nearly treeless, except at the eastern end, where cotton-woods and willows lined its course. Elsewhere, prairie grasses ran to its edges. The pioneers left accounts of how Native Americans burned the prairies, holding back the growth of trees. More recent observers suggest it was the pulsing, uncontrolled flow of the Platte during spring surges that swept away saplings and kept the banks open.

The Platte was a place of hardship for the pioneers. In 1852, wagon trains along its banks were struck by a cholera epidemic. Wrote one

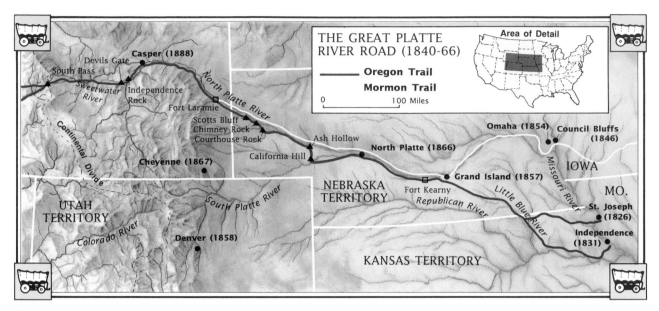

The Oregon and Mormon trails.

William Henry Jackson's painting, California Crossing, South Platte River, *gives modern observers a view of the Platte in the early 1800s. The roads of Manifest Destiny followed the river for much of its length and made it part of the lore of American settlement.*

woman who made the westward journey, "All along the Platte River was a grave yard; most any time of day you could see people burying their dead. . . . " Wrote another, "The dead lay sometimes in rows of fifties or more. . . . " Along the Platte were dug perhaps 5,000 graves.

But the river was a sign of peace and plenty, too. It was the easiest segment of the 2,400-mile journey to California and Oregon. An 1859 travel guide for those going West promised abundant wood for campfires along the eastern end of the Platte, and plenty of buffalo chips for fuel farther west. The plains around the river were often thick with game, and contemporary descriptions speak of eating pronghorn antelope during noontime stops along the banks. Herds of bison swarmed over surrounding hills and across open flats. Sometimes the pioneers would have to fire guns to keep stampeding herds from crushing down upon them.

Some 350,000 pioneers went the way West along the Platte. It began in 1841 with 100 travelers, peaked in 1850 with 55,000, and ended with 25,000 in 1866. Then the transcontinental railroad was completed and the wagon trains ebbed into obsolescence.

Now, a multitude of cities and farm towns dot prairies where pioneers succumbed to cholera and bison stampede, and the bison and pronghorn are gone. Interstate 80 rushes along the old wagon trail, abbreviating the transcontinental traveler's six months of hard travel to three days, maybe less. Even the river itself is changed. Its banks are no longer cloaked in wild grasses; they are surrounded by checkerboards of farm crops. The waters of the Platte no longer flow wide and expansive across the prairie; dams and reservoirs and irrigation systems and power projects have siphoned them away and at times even run the river dry. And yet one of the wildlife spectacles of the Platte lingers on. It occurs once yearly, cyclical and certain, one of the great mysteries of nature. It arrives on a million trembling wings; it calls from the skies in wild, trumpeting song. Its lifeblood is the river and the little water left in it, water that irrigators and developers covet.

The Sandhill Cranes

They come to the river early in the year, when March has not yet turned to spring. They pirouette from the clouds, wings outstretched, settling down on long, reed-thin legs among the shallow waters of the Platte and in the farm fields beyond. Their numbers build and build as spring arrives, thousands coming in daily until they swell to more than half a million strong, filling the sky with their endless bugling cries. They are the largest single gathering of cranes in the world and represent about 80 percent of the total sandhill crane population in North America.

Most of the cranes that come to the Platte each year are called lesser sandhill cranes, though they are among the largest bird species on the continent, standing three feet tall with a wingspan about twice that. They are drab birds, confederate gray tinged with buff, their only color the piercing amber of their eyes and a scarlet patch of bare skin above beak and eyes.

They come to the river from their wintering grounds in Texas, New Mexico, Mexico, and parts of the Gulf Coast. Their arrival starts in February and builds to a peak in late March and early April, when the full half-million are crowded into the Big Bend, an eighty-mile stretch of river that lies between the towns of Chapman and Overton in south-central Nebraska. While the cranes are in Nebraska, the river is their base of operations, and they rarely stray more than a mile from its channel.

The cranes remain on the Platte for up to six weeks, feeding and fattening for their long migration to northern nesting grounds. They spend more than half their daylight hours in the croplands that border the river. About 6 percent of the corn grown in these fields cannot be gathered by current harvesting techniques, so cattle are put into the fields in fall and winter. The cattle eat about half the corn left after harvest. In spring the cranes eat another 1,500 tons, about 15 percent of the corn left by the cattle. This corn accounts for about 90 percent of the fat the birds put on during their stay on the Platte. Farmers welcome the cranes' activities. Cattle feed on ears of corn, the cranes on loose kernels lying on the ground, so no competition exists between the animals. Farmer Dick Summers told Audubon filmmakers Sharon and Wolfgang Obst, "I think the

Cranes gliding on outstretched wings migrate from as far south as Mexico almost to the Arctic Circle. About 80 percent of the sandhill cranes in North America roost in spring along the Platte River in Nebraska, making river diversion a threat to their survival.

cranes and farmers have been living in harmony for a long time, and I don't think the cranes bother the farmers or the farmers bother the cranes a whole lot.''

The cranes also feed in native grasslands and in hayfields. Whatever proteins and minerals the corn does not give them, they get from earthworms, snails, and other invertebrates. The fat the birds put on is essential to their survival. They will use up nearly half of it on the month or two of flight that

will take them to their nesting grounds. Remaining fat reserves help sustain the birds during nesting.

In the evening, as the sun lies in a blood-red pool over the western horizon, the cranes soar up over the fields and grasslands and come back to settle for the night in the river itself. They arrive in scattered flocks and in combined masses, thousands upon thousands of winged shadows dropping from the sky. They cackle and call, filling the river valley with their staccato cries. They crowd the Big Bend,

A sandhill crane painted by John James Audubon. He mistakenly thought the sandhill cranes were juvenile whooping cranes.

Sandhill cranes feeding upon abandoned waste corn in farm fields surrounding Nebraska's Platte River. They also feed in the wet meadows that occur along the Platte.

the only stretch of the Platte that offers them the type of roosts they need: open, unvegetated channels 1,000 feet wide, across which they can see any looming danger, with water deep enough to keep away predators such as raccoons, coyotes, and dogs.

Sandhill cranes are extremely wary. They usually take wing if anyone comes within a few hundred yards of them. Nineteenth-century naturalist and artist John James Audubon, who traveled most of North America shooting a wide variety of birds so he could paint them, made special note of the sandhill crane's wariness.

> The acuteness of their sight and hearing is quite wonderful. If they perceive a man approaching, even at the distance of a quarter of a mile, they are sure to take to the wing. Should you accidentally tread on a stick and break it, or suddenly cock your gun, all the birds in the flock raise their heads and emit a cry. Shut the gate of a field after you, and from that moment they all watch your motions. To attempt to crawl towards them, even among long grass, after such an intimation, would be useless.

Despite their wariness, the cranes attract thousands of people to the Platte each year. Birders concentrate at such places as the National Audubon Society's 2,000-acre Lillian Annette Rowe Sanctuary, where guided field trips are offered and blinds have been set up for close viewing of the cranes. There, visitors can watch as the birds come and go from the river in early morning and evening, and they can observe an ages-old ritual, the dance of the cranes. The cranes dance with wings dropped, long legs flexing as they leap from the ground, sometimes fully eight feet into the air, then delicately return to earth on outstretched wings, feet barely touching the ground, the birds seemingly weightless, momentarily poised, then leaping again. The dance is part of the courtship of the cranes. Males and females dance for one another, building for themselves the intimacy that shapes them into mated pairs. Said one birder, "To me it's like one of the ten wonders of the world. There's no place else in the world that we have the privilege to see this."

Half a century ago it had seemed that the privilege would be lost altogether. In the 1930s, some of the nation's best ornithologists were predicting, as they had been since the turn of the century, that the sandhill crane soon would disappear. Though in presettlement times the crane had nested from Cuba to the islands of the arctic, from the Atlantic to the Pacific, by the middle of the nineteenth century overhunting and loss of habitat had essentially wiped out the bird east of the Mississippi, except in Florida. Drainage of wetlands, agricultural development, and continued overhunting for market and sport devastated remaining populations by the turn of the twentieth century. Nothing seemed likely to save the crane.

And then, sometime in the 1930s or 1940s, the sandhill crane's numbers started to increase. The reason for the sudden revival has not been entirely explained. Presumably it was linked to the abandonment of farms in the Dust Bowl years and to better enforcement of hunting laws. By the mid-1960s, Texas and New Mexico, which hold the largest wintering populations, were tallying nearly 150,000 cranes. Now the continent holds close to 600,000, representatives of six distinct subspecies. One of these, the Mississippi sandhill crane, numbers only about fifty birds living a nonmigratory life in swamps and woodlands near Mississippi's Gulf Coast. This subspecies is on the federal endangered-species list. Another nonmigratory subspecies, some 5,000 strong, lives and breeds in Florida and Georgia. The other subspecies, including the lesser, range over the West. Their numbers are so substantial that some states have opened hunting seasons on them. Most of these birds funnel into the Platte during spring migration.

When the cranes have fattened on the sustenance of the Platte, they take wing again, flying by day at altitudes up to 13,000 feet, until finally they come to their nesting grounds in northwestern Canada, Alaska, and parts of Siberia. By the time they reach the nesting grounds they may have spent two full months on the wing, covering as much as 6,000 miles.

Sandhill cranes moving into the Platte River in Nebraska during a springtime sunset. The river, when undrained by dams and irrigation projects, offers the birds a roost safe from predators.

A sandhill crane, one of the largest birds in North America. Adults stand about three feet tall and have a six-foot wingspan.

Sandhill cranes feeding in a millet field at Muleshoe National Wildlife Refuge in west Texas. Although sandhill cranes range over vast areas of the Southwest, most of them congregate in Nebraska on the Platte in spring. Consequently, their fate is hinged on the integrity of the Platte.

Sandhill cranes returning at dusk to their roost on Lower White Lake in Muleshoe National Wildlife Refuge.

They nest from mid-April to June in wet meadows and marshes. Though they crowd together during migration, they are quite antisocial while nesting. Pairs will stake out a territory that may encompass several hundred acres and attempt to keep out other cranes. On this territory the adults will find the food they need for themselves and their offspring.

Mated pairs usually lay two eggs several days apart in a nest that may be anything from a scattering of plant matter to a massive mound of vegetation. Chicks usually hatch within a month and grow rapidly in a northern world that bestows upon them nearly twenty-four hours of daily sunlight and an abundance of food. However, a chick's first meal is often the shell of its own egg, fed to it by its parents.

Not until both chicks hatch do they leave the nest. Adults are attentive to the chicks, feeding them mouth to mouth. The chicks have a hard task ahead of them. They must eat and grow fast, because the northern summer does not exceed three months. Within that time the tiny chicks, roughly the size of a newly hatched chicken, must reach nearly full size. They must be strong enough for the flight south.

As soon as the young can fly, usually by late July or early August, the birds leave the nesting grounds and gather with other cranes at staging sites located across Canada and in parts of the northern United States. There they fatten again and, in October, begin the great migration south.

Despite the crane's great numbers, its survival is perhaps no more certain than it was fifty years ago.

It is besieged on all sides by human encroachment. From the Canadian border to Mexico, the wide rivers and saline lakes that have served as the crane's prime roosting sites have been lost to drainage and development. Where the cranes once found a major migratory rest site on the Missouri, they now find strings of deep reservoirs that give them no shelter. Irrigation projects threaten the survival of North Dakota's saline lakes, important crane refuges during autumn migration. The playa-lake country of west Texas, where the cranes winter, also is being drained for irrigation. Most importantly, the Platte River, critical to the survival of nearly the entire crane population of North America, the one place to which almost all sandhill cranes must come in spring, is under such intensive pressure from urban and agricultural water interests that the whole river may soon disappear. With it will go not just the cranes, but much of the other wildlife that depends on the Platte. Seven to 9 million ducks and geese use the river during spring migration, and part of the Platte in central Nebraska has been designated by the U.S. Fish and Wildlife Service as unique and irreplaceable habitat for both sandhill cranes and white-fronted geese. Millions of ducks also use the river in winter, when at times it offers the only open water in the area. Some 200 bald eagles winter there, feeding on fish. Particular concern also has focused on two endangered species—the whooping crane and the least tern—and on the piping plover, whose population along the Platte is federally listed as threatened.

Platte River Water Projects

The Platte has been involved in the machinations of human commerce for more than two centuries. In 1739 two Frenchmen, Paul and Pierre Mallet, made a journey from the Missouri River to Sante Fe, New Mexico, in search of trade. They followed the Missouri to the mouth of a wide, shallow river that they followed westward. The Omaha Indians, who spoke a type of Sioux language, called the river Neb-leth-ska', which meant flat water. The Frenchmen called it La Platte, which carried much the same meaning. Further explorations would show that the great river had two origins, both born of snowmelt in the Rockies of Colorado, rushing clear and cold over boulder and stone. One of the rivers, the North Platte, arched north into Wyoming, then east to Nebraska, 665 miles long. The other, the 450-mile South Platte, tumbled north and then east through Colorado. The two forks joined in Nebraska to form the wide river that ran 300 miles east across the plains to the murky waters of the Missouri.

About a century later, Kit Carson guided a party of U.S. topographical engineers, headed by Lieutenant John C. Fremont, on a surveying and exploratory party that took them along the Platte. At that time, the Platte was traveled primarily by mountainmen taking furs to market. The Fremont party marked the beginning of a new era. The engineers surveyed the Oregon Trail's South Pass through the Rockies and helped open the roads west. Wagon trains started to follow the course of the Platte within the next two or three years.

One of the dangers that jeopardized the pioneers was the need to cross the Platte, particularly in places where the bottom was quicksand. The Mormons in 1847 staked out a claim to a ford near the present site of Casper, Wyoming. Here they built a crude boat and charged other pioneers a hefty fee for ferrying people and material across. The first bridge across the Platte went up in 1851, built by John Reshaw, or Richaud, also near Casper. Reshaw collected tolls for two years, then was put out of business when a better bridge was built by Louis Guinard at the site of the Mormon ferry.

The irrigation of lands around Fort Laramie apparently began as early as 1847, using water from the North Platte. A decade later, gold was discovered in Denver, miners flooded in, and the growing city stimulated the development of irrigation on the South Platte. By the end of the nineteenth century, at least twelve irrigation canals had been built on the South Platte. Two are still in use. Six diversion dams rechannel the flow of the South Platte today.

The main stem of the North Platte is studded with an equal number of storage dams that retain water for irrigation, flood control, and electricity production. Nearly 1.5 million acre-feet of water (an

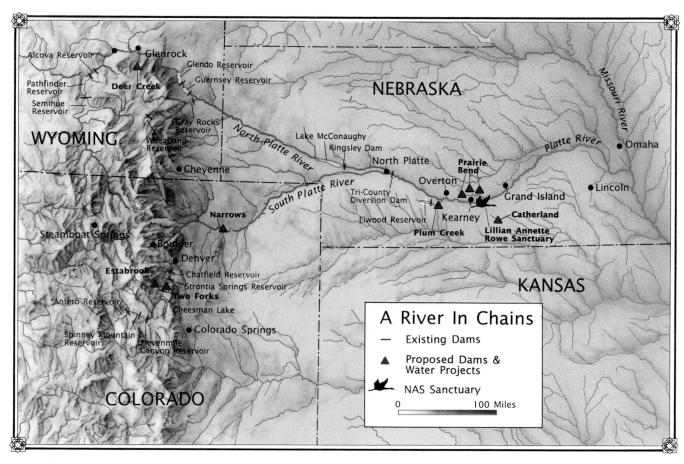

Map of dam projects on the Platte River.

acre-foot of water is enough to cover an acre with a foot of water) is tapped from the North Platte Valley yearly to irrigate 325,000 acres.

The water projects perhaps most devastating to wildlife were finished in 1941. One was the Kingsley Dam, built on the North Platte above its confluence with the South Platte. It holds back a 1.7-million-acre-foot reservoir, Lake McConaughy, and traps 70 percent of the sediment that was crucial to maintaining the broad, shallow, braided channel downstream. Some 500 miles of canals transport water from the reservoir to thirsty south-central Nebraska farmlands, some of them 200 miles away. The other devastating project was the Tri-County Diversion Dam, which lies just below the meeting point of the North and South Plattes. It is the only dam on the unified channel of the Platte, but it controls the flow of water to the east, an area that includes the Big Bend region favored by northbound sandhill cranes each spring.

The cumulative impact of all the water projects on the Platte, from the the Rockies to Missouri, has destroyed the character of the river. The flow of water and sediment that built and destroyed sandbars, swept young trees from the banks, and kept the islands clear of vegetation, has been staunched. Fully 70 percent of the Platte's historic flow is now diverted or consumed before it reaches the Big Bend. The river's channel has shrunk accordingly. In part of the Big Bend, from Kearney to North Platte, the channel was up to 2,200 yards wide in 1866, but now averages less than 100 yards. In some sections, channel width has been reduced up to 90 percent. Without the rush of sand- and gravel-laden river waters to scour them away, trees are closing in on the Big Bend, encroaching upon the once-open channels. Sand bars and shorelines are being invaded by cottonwoods and willows. The wide vistas of the Platte, required by the sandhill cranes, are being crowded and shortened, the channel choked. Where the

Dusk falls over the Platte River near Grand Island, Nebraska. Though much of the river's flow has been reduced by dams and irrigation projects, here the Platte is still wide enough and deep enough to provide spring roosting sites for sandhill and whooping cranes.

prairie river once glittered so widely beneath the sun that its banks were called the seashores of Nebraska, it now runs in narrow strands through thousands of acres of riverbed that have been converted to woodland. Analyses of annual tree rings shows that major encroachment by the trees, which started with the drought of the 1930s, became serious with the closing of the gates of Kingsley Dam.

As the river has receded, so has the extent of the sandhill crane's spring roosting sites in the river and feeding areas in surrounding wet meadows. Along the entire 300 miles of the Platte, stretches still useful to cranes are restricted primarily to the 80

miles of the Big Bend. Here, despite substantial encroachment by cottonwoods and willows over the past sixty years, the river still possesses 60 to 70 percent of its pristine width because excess irrigation water is returned to it near the town of Overton and because of maintenance activities, such as clearing of vegetation-clogged channels, by the Whooping Crane Trust and the National Audubon Society.

Within the Big Bend crowd the sandhill cranes— 10,000 birds per mile of channel, sometimes even 20,000. Confined and pressed together, the birds could fall easy victim to contagious disease or a toxic spill of, for example, agricultural chemicals transported along the river. Crowding also makes the birds more vulnerable to natural disasters, such as tornadoes. So far, enough water remains to wash away disease organisms and to protect the roosting birds from predators. But plans are in the making right now for other massive water projects. The one posing the most immediate threat is the proposed Two Forks Dam on the South Platte near Denver.

Two Forks Dam

About an hour outside of Denver, on the eastern front of the Rockies, two rivers foam over stone and gravel and come together in the shadows of mountain peaks. These are the North and South forks of the South Platte River. On trees along the South Fork and on bridges that cross it, a visitor will see small signs that declare the river a Gold Medal trout stream. This means it is a particularly good trout stream with natural reproduction, and the South Fork is in fact touted as one of the five best trout streams in the nation. Standing on a bridge overlooking the stream, it is easy to count trout six and seven at a time.

Where the North and South forks join stands the dark ruin of the old South Platte Hotel, protected in a copse of tall trees. A narrow road passes in front of the old hotel, which signs indicate might one day be a state historic site. The road crosses the

This sign tells passersby that this scenic spot on the South Platte will be inundated if the Denver Water Board succeeds in building Two Forks Dam on the river.

ENTERING ENDANGERED AREA
THIS AREA WILL BE UNDER
350 FEET OF WATER
— HELP STOP —
THE DENVER WATER BOARD'S
TWO FORKS DAM
RECREATION; NOT WRECK-CREATION

SCRAGGY VIEW

two forks at their confluence, and footpaths lead from the bridge off into the surrounding mountains. This is silent country and serene, bubbling with the sounds of the rushing mountain water. It is bighorn sheep country; it holds the last remaining herd of bighorns in the entire valley. And it is dam and reservoir country. The city of Denver wants to construct a billion-dollar dam where the two streams converge and flood thirty-six miles of valley with 1.1 million acre-feet of water. The dam would be named Two Forks, after the two rivers it would drown.

Denver first filed for the right to build the dam in 1931, at the start of an era when dam projects created thousands of jobs for the unemployed of the Great Depression. Though Denver started buying land around the North and South forks in 1941, the war and the strengthened economy after it reduced the need for the dam. Not until Denver started growing rapidly in the 1970s, its population swelling as Colorado oilfields drew in vast numbers of new residents, did pressure mount to build the dam. Water officials feared that if growth continued, the Denver region would suffer a water shortage at the start of the next century. The slowdown in oil de-velopment that began in 1985 halted Denver's growth and quelled any concerns of water shortages, but pressure to build the dam has survived. The origins of this pressure were described in an *Audubon* magazine article:

> If the water shortfall is no longer such a pressing matter, why does Denver keep pushing Two Forks? The reason is that the city badly wants the money it will get from selling Two Forks water to the suburbs. In 1974 the Colorado State Legislature passed an amendment that made it almost impossible for Denver to annex additional land—the traditional way that a city increases its tax base. The amendment was passed during the era of federally mandated desegregation, and the suburbs were fearful that if they were annexed by Denver their schools would be subject to busing. With the oil boom the city became landlocked, the upshot of which is that it now provides an array of service to the suburbs—from its art museum and pub-lic libraries to mass transit and hospital emergency assistance—for free. One way that the city could rectify this fiscal imbalance would be to make the suburbs beholden to it for water. It could sell water to the suburbs from Two Forks.

If the dam is built, 65 percent of the water it impounds will be used by single-family homes, ac-cording to U.S. Army Corps of Engineers figures.

The bumper sticker on this car parked outside the restaurant and general store at Deckers, Colorado, proclaims opposition to Two Forks Dam. Deckers and nearby homes will be deeply under water if the dam is built.

The sign on the tree designates this stretch of the South Platte River near Deckers, Colorado, as a gold medal trout stream. The trout fishery will be lost if Two Forks Dam is built.

More than half the water used in the single-family homes will go to watering lawns in a region ecologically unfit for garden grasses. In order to supply that water, the Gold Medal trout stream will have to be flooded and lost forever. The reservoir that will replace it, according to a Fish and Wildlife Service report, "is not expected to be a good fishery." Deer in the Two Forks area will lose nearly 10,000 acres of habitat. Elk will lose about 600. Up to 33 percent of the entire population of the Pawnee montane skipper butterfly, federally listed as threatened, would be lost when its habitat was inundated. According to one U.S. Fish and Wildlife Service report, "Because of past and presently proposed projects, the last remaining bighorn sheep population within the Two Forks project area would be adversely affected and probably eliminated." A second service report said that even if the City of Denver took every possible measure to protect the Two Forks area's bighorn herd both during and after construction of the dam, the herd might still be lost. "While a replacement herd could be transplanted into the area, the loss of the genes of the present low elevation herd could not be mitigated," the report declared. "It is unknown whether the replacement herd would survive."

The price of watering lawns would be even greater for the wildlife of the Platte River's Big Bend, located some 500 miles from the dam site. Two Forks Dam quite likely will draw off enough water from the South Platte to reduce flows in the Platte mainstem below the critical threshold necessary to ensure survival of sandhill cranes and other wildlife, including endangered species.

Big Bend Wildlife and Two Forks Dam

The sandhill crane's Platte River roosting and gathering sites have been ebbing for many years. In the year that Kit Carson guided the Fremont party along the river, the spring migrants probably occurred along most of the Platte in south-central Nebraska, feeding in the surrounding meadows by day and roosting in the river at night. By 1954, they were limited to a ninety-three-mile stretch between Cozad and Grand Island. Twenty-five years later, they had abandoned twenty-three miles of that area. The cranes retreat quickly from shrunken channels overgrown with brush. One Fish and Wildlife Service study found that more than 99 percent of all cranes observed roosting on the Platte and North Platte rivers in 1979 were in unobstructed stretches of river at least fifty-five yards wide. The birds—ever wary—sought areas free of vegetation, giving them a clear view for spotting potential dangers. "They avoided all segments of the river channel in which the widest available open channel was less than or equal to 50m [about 55 yards], regardless of vegetation height," said a Fish and Wildlife Service report on Platte River wildlife. Preferred roosts were always in excess of 165 yards. Such areas constituted only 26 percent of the habitat in the study area, but supported 70 percent of the study's birds.

Further compression of suitable roost sites by new dams are expected to cause shifts in crane distribution. The birds probably would crowd in ever-greater numbers into remaining wide stretches. As

In winter, the trees and shrubs that are encroaching on the Platte's sandbars stand out clearly. Because of dam projects and other water uses, the Platte no longer flows freely enough to sweep its banks and sandbars free of vegetation. Encroachment by trees and shrubs is choking the river and making it useless to sandhill cranes and other wildlife.

Sandhill cranes soaring over Goose Lake in Muleshoe National Wildlife Refuge in Texas.

water flows slow, the river would no longer help reduce the incidence of disease by washing away disease-causing organisms. Epidemics could wipe out thousands of cranes. Crane food resources could be affected, particularly in the wet meadows that are linked by water flow to the river. As water flow slows, the meadows would dry, robbing the cranes of important food supplements. If agricultural practices should ever reduce the availability of corn, in addition to these other stresses, the Fish and Wildlife Service predicts that the cranes' physical condition could deteriorate. Moreover, reproduction could be affected if the birds reach nesting habitat in poor condition.

There is no safety in numbers for the sandhill cranes. Though they number 500,000 birds, on the Platte they are only one population. If the Platte River becomes useless to them, or if it turns deadly from disease, toxic spills, or some natural disaster, that single population could be devastated or lost completely.

Despite the threat to the sandhill cranes, most federal agency and water development concerns have been directed at the Platte's endangered and threatened species, particularly the whooping crane. This species captured the public's imagination in the 1940s, when only fifteen whoopers survived, and it has held public attention ever since. The whooping

The Whooping Crane: Back from the Edge

The whooping crane is the star of one of the world's most promising conservation success stories.

According to the *Audubon Wildlife Report 1986*, whooping cranes apparently arose about 2 million years ago. They once occurred from the Arctic Sea to the high plateau of central Mexico and from Utah east to the Atlantic Coast. In the nineteenth century, the bird's principal breeding range extended from central Illinois through the northern Midwest and across Canada to the vicinity of Edmonton, Alberta. Most of the migratory whooping cranes passed through the Midwest, though one group on the Atlantic Coast used to migrate across the Appalachians into Canada. It vanished sometime before 1857. A nonmigratory population that existed in southwestern Louisiana vanished in the early 1900s.

Loss of wetlands habitat and uncontrolled hunting were probably the primary factors that drove the whooping crane almost to extinction. The nonmigratory birds in Louisiana last nested in 1939. The thirteen birds in this flock were cut to six by a hurricane in 1940. The last survivor was taken into captivity in 1948. The last nesting in southern Canada occurred in 1922. The only breeding population left after that survived in the Northwest Territories. Its nesting ground in Wood Buffalo National Park was so remote that it was not discovered until 1954 after nine years of intensive searching.

An adult whooping crane.

crane—snow white with black wing tips and crimson cheeks and crown—is the tallest bird in North America. It stands as much as five feet tall, with a seven-foot wingspan, and weighs up to sixteen pounds, about 25 percent heavier than a sandhill crane. The whooper is named for its loud call. "These cries," wrote Audubon, "which I cannot compare to any instrument known to me, I have heard at the distance of three miles, at the approach of spring, when the males were paying their addresses to the females, or fighting among themselves. They may be in some degree represented by the syllables *kewrr, kewrr, kewrooh*; and strange and uncouth as they are, they have always sounded delightful in my ear."

The birds were probably uncommon even in the 1870s. One estimate put the population at that time at no more than 800. By 1941, only fifteen survived. A study of 389 whooping crane deaths that occurred between 1722 and 1948 indicated that the heaviest losses were between 1880 and 1919 and that most of these were caused by hunters or specimen collectors.

After passage of the Migratory Bird Treaty Act early in this century, shooting of whooping cranes gradually declined. A whooping crane shot by vandals in 1988 was the first known death by shooting in twenty years. Despite the numbers lost to hunters at around the turn of the century, habitat loss was doubtless a significant cause of decline, too. Wetlands drainage, burning of nesting grounds, and conversion of prairies to cropland eliminated feeding, nesting, and roosting habitat. Grazing by livestock eliminated the habitat of insects eaten by cranes, destroyed nesting areas, and quite likely resulted in trampling of nests. As noted in the *Audubon Wildlife Report 1986*, "Settlement of the whooper's primary nesting areas by man assured the drastic population decline."

Several key events helped stop the whooper's decline. The Migratory Bird Treaty Act provided early protection, as did the creation of Wood Buffalo National Park in Canada in 1922. In 1937, Aransas National Wildlife Refuge was established to protect the whooping crane's wintering ground along the Texas coast. In the 1940s, the National Audubon Society, Canadian Wildlife Service, and U.S. Fish and Wildlife Service (FWS) started a cooperative program to protect the

birds. Passage of the Endangered Species Act and designation of critical habitat further strengthened crane protection.

In 1967, FWS initiated an ambitious experimental program designed to increase crane numbers rapidly. It had long been known that whoopers normally lay two eggs each year, but raise only one young to adulthood. The other dies. FWS officials reasoned that they could remove one egg from a number of nests, hatch the egg, and raise the young in captivity. Meanwhile, the wild cranes would rear their other offspring. This program could conceivably double the crane's reproductive rate.

From 1967 to 1974, fifty wild whooping cranes eggs were transferred from Canada to the Patuxent Wildlife Research Center in Laurel, Maryland. The chicks raised now form the nucleus of a captive flock of about forty birds. These birds act as a sort of reservoir for the species in the event that some catastrophe wipes out the wild population.

Another breeding program attempted to provide insurance against the loss of the wild birds. This program began in 1974 with the transfer of eggs from Canada to the nests of sandhill cranes at Idaho's Grays Lake. The sandhill crane eggs were replaced with a single whooper egg. The sandhill cranes then raised the whooper young as their own. Since 1974, more than 250 whooping crane eggs have been transferred to sandhill crane nests, creating a new wild whooper population of close to forty birds. These Rocky Mountain whoopers migrate with their surrogate sandhill crane parents and seem to have adapted to their foster home. So far, however, none have bred.

This may be an ominous sign, since birds often become "imprinted" on the species that rears them from hatching, refusing to mate with individuals from any species but the one on which they are imprinted. The success of the Rocky Mountain population remains uncertain as long as no breeding occurs.

The tremendous amount of work that has gone into whooping crane management has paid off. Though still on the endangered-species list, whoopers number nearly 200 birds, more than ten times the handful that survived in 1940. If the crane reaches a population size of forty nesting pairs at Wood Buffalo National Park and twenty-five pairs at each of two other sites in North America, it will be downlisted to threatened. The Wood Buffalo population should reach forty nesting pairs by 1995. Grays Lake should reach twenty-five pairs by the year 2000. Efforts to establish an eastern population may begin in the early 1990s and, because of increased egg production in Canada, should reach twenty-five pairs as early as 2015. The last two figures hinge on whether the artificial flocks breed. The Grays Lake flock should begin breeding any time now, so the answer to the question of whooping crane survival may soon be known. If they do breed, it is reasonable to expect whooping crane numbers to reach 500 to 700 birds by the year 2000, about the number that existed in the middle of the nineteenth century. At such a figure the cranes could be removed from the endangered-species list within the next thirty years, which would represent one of conservation's finest achievements in endangered-species management.

The entire whooping crane population probably numbered only a few hundred birds by the 1870s. Habitat loss and shooting dropped them to only fifteen by 1941. By then the Aransas National Wildlife Refuge had been created on the Texas coast to protect the whooper's wintering habitat, and the U.S. Fish and Wildlife Service, Canadian Wildlife Service, and National Audubon Society had started a massive effort to study and manage the species. As a result of this effort, which continues to the present, some 130 whoopers make the annual migrations between Texas and Wood Buffalo National Park in Canada, and the number is still growing.

Migrating whoopers visit the Platte River during

spring and fall migrations, roosting in its channels and feeding in surrounding fields and meadows, much as the sandhill cranes do. Only Quivira National Wildlife Refuge, a day's flight from the Platte, is used more often by whooping cranes during spring migration. The importance of the Platte to the whooping cranes was highlighted in a Fish and Wildlife Service study of the Denver water supply:

> During spring migration, wet meadows along the Platte River provide whooping cranes the opportunity to obtain food items that are essential for survival and successful reproduction. Resting and foraging during migration, whether of long or short duration, is essential in the spring to ensure that the birds arrive in a healthy condition at the breeding grounds at Wood Buffalo National Park. Healthy birds are essential for successful reproduction and, ultimately, the survival and recovery of the species. The health and survival of whooping cranes are dependent upon the condition and abundance of their habitat because, like other migratory birds with delayed sexual maturity and life-long pair bonds, whooping cranes adhere strictly to ancestral breeding areas, migratory routes, and wintering grounds, leaving little possibility of pioneering into new regions. The importance of maintaining traditional habitats such as the Platte River is especially critical given the impact of man's ongoing conversion of potholes and prairies to hay and grain production which has made nearly all of their original range unsuitable for whooping cranes.

The Fish and Wildlife Service officially recognized the importance of the Platte to the cranes when it designated the Big Bend section as critical whooping crane habitat. Studies indicate that use of the Platte by the cranes is linked to water flow. In the past, when water flows were greater and the channels were not choked with vegetation, the cranes used the Platte more frequently than other areas. In recent years, they have abandoned it when flows are low and returned when flows are high. Says the Fish and Wildlife Service report, " . . . the Platte probably would be used more frequently if higher flows of recent years continue, if habitat enhancement continues, and if suitable flow regimes can be provided and maintained."

On the contrary, if water flows decline, cranes are expected to suffer. According to a Fish and Wildlife Service analysis, "destruction or adverse modification of whooping crane critical habitat would have a direct, adverse impact on whooping crane survival and recovery." If flows drop, the cranes will lose roost sites to the encroachment of vegetation on river channels. They will lose the wet meadows in which they feed on frogs, salamanders, crayfish, in-

sects, snakes, and other animals that provide them with much of the protein and calcium they need. And they may resort to less suitable roost sites, such as the nearby Rainwater Basin south of the Platte. This again raises the specter of disease. The Fish and Wildlife Service report observes,

> Decreased use of the Platte River in recent times and associated use of the Rainwater Basin area by whooping cranes is of serious concern. . . . Whooping cranes have been reported in several Rainwater Basin wetlands where large waterfowl die-offs from avian cholera have been recorded. Three times, all in spring, in the last 11 years (spring 1975, 1979 and 1984), a total of 15 whooping cranes had to be chased from wetlands where avian cholera outbreaks were occurring. On one of these occasions, seven whooping cranes settled on the Platte River.

In addition to concerns about what Two Forks would do to whooping cranes, the Fish and Wildlife Service has examined the impact of the project on the least tern and the piping plover. The least tern is a small, colonial nesting bird found along the Atlantic, Pacific, and Gulf coasts and on major river systems in the U.S. interior. The interior population, some 4,000 birds, was listed as endangered in 1985. A little more than 10 percent of those birds nest between Kearney, Nebraska, and the mouth of the Platte. They lay their eggs on unvegetated sandbars and islands located in wide river channels. Loss of nesting habitat to water development has been cited as the cause for the interior population's decline. Encroachment by vegetation has wiped out 30 percent of the bird's Platte nesting habitat. Declines in water flow also open remaining nest sites to increased predation by coyotes and other animals and can lead to declines in the fish populations upon which the terns prey. Sudden surges in water depth caused by releases from dams during times of water excess also pose problems, inundating nests.

The piping plover is a small shorebird once found in great numbers along the upper Atlantic coast, around the Great Lakes, and across the northern Great Plains. The plover has been wiped out over much of its range, and no more than 4,200 survive. Of these, as many as 2,700 live in the Northern Plains, where the federal government has designated them as threatened. Nearly 200 nest on the Platte, one of the largest piping plover concentrations anywhere. Like the least terns, piping plovers nest on sandbars, prefer sites free of vegetation, and face the same threats from water projects.

Yet another listed species subject to concern is

The baby alligators in John James Audubon's painting of a whooping crane indicate that he observed the birds in the southern part of the nation. Whooping cranes once ranged widely over North America, but only one breeding population, which migrates between Texas and Canada, survives today.

the bald eagle. About 200 of them winter along the Big Bend, which water flow keeps ice-free longer than other stretches of the river. There the eagles feed on fish, waterfowl, and other animals. A lowering of water levels could lock eagle food resources under ice. Also, declines in waterfowl that might accompany further reductions in water flow would cut into the bald eagle's prey base and even limit hunting opportunities for human waterfowl hunters.

Two Forks and other proposed water projects on the Platte, observed a report of the Fish and Wildlife Service,

> have considerable potential to greatly alter the riparian [river] zone. The cumulative, hydrological effects would cause average annual flow decreases of 27 percent in the South Platte at Julesburg and a 21-percent decrease on the main stem Platte River at Overton. As a result, peak stages and associated scouring would be reduced, contributing to the establishment of woody and other vegetation within the open, more or less braided, channel, including existing open sandbars and islands. Over the long term, islands and higher channel areas would become attached to the flood plain, resulting in significant decrease in the width of the various active channel zones.

In a summary of the impacts that Two Forks would have on wildlife, the Fish and Wildlife Service concluded,

> The project will adversely impact the roosting habitat [of whooping cranes] available during the periods of March 23 to May 10. The project will reduce the availability and suitability of nesting and foraging habitat of least terns and piping plovers in some months and eliminate suitable least tern and piping plover nesting habitat and least tern forage fishes in 1 entire month. Bald eagles are likely to have no open water in which to forage during 17 consecutive days in 1 month.

The Endangered Species Act requires that projects, such as Two Forks, that pose a potential threat to listed species must be submitted to a study by the Fish and Wildlife Service to determine if the project will jeopardize the survival of threatened or endangered species or alter designated critical habitat. This is called a *consultation*. When the service completes its consultation, it releases a document, called a *biological opinion*, stating whether the project will jeopardize listed wildlife or critical habitat. In its opinion on the Two Forks project, the Fish and Wildlife Service said that the dam would not jeopardize the whooping cranes, the terns, and the plovers if the Denver Water Board implemented certain mitigation measures. It gave the project its seal of approval despite the many concerns for these species outlined in the service's own documents. Why it did so is a by-product of the politics surrounding western water development.

Water, Politics, and the West

In January 1825, a senator from New Jersey in an address to the U.S. Senate said that the entire plains region, from Council Bluffs to the Rockies, from Canada to the Sabine River, was "almost wholly unfit for cultivation and of course uninhabitable by a people depending upon agriculture for subsistence. . . . The whole region seems peculiarly adapted as range for buffaloes, wild goats, and other wild game." Although the region has long since become the nation's breadbox, producing surplus crops of wheat, corn, and a host of vegetables and other grains, the senator was not far off the mark. If the farmers of the plains had to depend entirely on natural rainfall to sustain their crops, the breadbasket might often be empty.

Rainfall in much of the West is a matter of extremes. In spring, snowmelt and rains swell rivers to overflowing. Before settlement, spring floods were the rule. The flows dropped off in summer, however, and the land often parched. Bernard DeVoto's description of the pristine Platte River Valley in Nebraska and what it promised for the pioneers is particularly revealing:

> This was prairie country, lush with grass that would be belly-high on your horse, or higher, by June. In May it was spongy from violent rains, in long stretches little better than a bog. The rains struck suddenly and disastrously, drowning you out of your blankets, interspersed with snow flurries or showers of hailstones as big as a fist, driven by gales that blew your possessions over the prairie and froze your bones. Continuous deafening thunder might last for hours at a time. . . . Every creek was a river, every river a sound, and every brook a morass. . . . The prairies were beautiful with flowers, waving grasses, and the song of birds . . . but not during the spring rains.

The problem for settlers was too much water at

one time of year and too little at another. In the twentieth century, the federal government in the guise of such agencies as the Bureau of Reclamation and the Army Corps of Engineers moved quickly to remedy this problem. Dams were built to hold back flood waters, which were stored in massive reservoirs. Water from the reservoirs could be used to irrigate thirsty crops.

Water and projects designed to distribute it thus became of prime importance throughout the West. State water laws give the rights to water to the first parties to use it, and water rights have assumed tremendous economic and political power and have led to serious conflicts over rights. The struggle for control of the Platte River has created a Gordian knot of shifting alliances and animosities.

One complication is the many agencies involved in water development projects. Each state has legal control over water within its boundaries. Water developers have to satisfy a wide variety of statutes, such as those governing wildlife protection, human health, and property rights. They must meet a variety of building codes. They must also nurture the support of state wildlife managers, who might try to block their plans if protected species, particularly hunted species such as waterfowl, were to be jeopardized by water development.

Before developers can begin their projects, they also have to receive permits from appropriate federal agencies. The federal bureaucratic maze is particularly convoluted. Water projects that disrupt waters within the United States must be approved by agencies such as the Army Corps of Engineers, Environmental Protection Agency, and U.S. Fish and Wildlife Service. They must be in compliance with such laws as the Clean Water Act, Endangered Species Act, Fish and Wildlife Coordination Act, Migratory Bird Treaty Act, and National Environmental Policy Act. Permits for projects that destroy wetlands are issued by the Corps of Engineers, but the Environmental Protection Agency can veto Corps permits.

The problem becomes even more complex if the waters cross state boundaries. This can create a collision of differing state statutes, officials, and objectives. The three Platte River states sought long ago to resolve competing claims for the Platte. In 1923 Nebraska and Colorado signed the South Platte Compact, in which Nebraska agreed not to intercede in any of Colorado's plans for development of the South Platte. Nebraska's disputes with Wyoming required a Supreme Court decision to bring

them to resolution in 1945. The court established the North Platte River Decree, which outlined rules governing how North Platte water would be allocated between Nebraska, Colorado, and Wyoming and the order in which reservoirs would be filled.

The decree has done little to resolve a current heated battle between Nebraska and Wyoming. The fight began when Wyoming proceeded with plans to construct a dam on Deer Creek, a tributary to the North Platte, in order to impound 66,000 acre-feet of water. Michael Jess, director of Nebraska's Department of Water Resources, filed a suit in the U.S. Supreme Court, arguing that under the North Platte River Decree, Nebraska is entitled to water from North Platte River tributaries, including Deer Creek. Wyoming countered that the decree exempted tributaries below Seminoe Dam, which is the dam farthest upstream in Wyoming. The U.S. Supreme Court now must clarify the 1945 decree. When the Fish and Wildlife Service issued a no-jeopardy decision for Deer Creek and Wyoming received a construction permit for the dam from the U.S. Army Corps of Engineers, Jess filed suit against the Corps and the Fish and Wildlife Service in federal district court on the grounds that the agencies had violated federal law in allowing the dam to go forward.

In part, the basis of Nebraska's argument is that Deer Creek Dam will jeopardize whooping cranes, least terns, and piping plovers. Jess argues that the Fish and Wildlife Service no-jeopardy decision in regard to Deer Creek is not supported by the service's own evidence. In fact, the service's decision declared that the project *would* damage whooping crane critical habitat and thus would be likely to harm listed cranes, terns, and plovers. The service approved the dam only because Deer Creek sponsors promised to use bulldozers and other equipment to remove vegetation from twenty-four acres in the Platte, widening its channel for the benefit of wildlife. To offset Deer Creek further, Wyoming has purchased 470 acres of crane habitat in Nebraska, which the U.S. Fish and Wildlife Service will maintain. Jess argues, however, that the service is derelict in accepting such mitigation in exchange for protection of the natural forces, such as water flow, that keep the channel wide and open. The Endangered Species Act, Jess says, requires the service to protect critical habitat, not trade it for artificially maintained areas. Jess is supported by conservationists, who fear that mitigation that does not depend on water flow to keep channels clear will not offset water depletions caused by Deer Creek Dam. The outcome of the court cases is pending.

Though conservationists are allied with the state of Nebraska in the matter of Deer Creek, the alliance is tenuous. Nebraska itself has large-scale plans for Platte River water. Jess has given his own seal of approval to the Catherland Project, which would transfer 120,000 acre-feet of water from the Platte River to southern Nebraska, thus removing twice as much water as Deer Creek. In granting water rights to Catherland sponsors, Jess ignored threats to whooping cranes, least terns, and piping plovers. The project is currently dead only because the Nebraska Supreme Court stopped it on the basis of a bureaucratic technicality—Jess's agency had improperly allowed the transfer of the water right from one sponsor to another.

The 1923 South Platte Compact limits Nebraska's role in opposing Colorado water projects on that river, so Nebraska is not involved in the legal dispute over Two Forks. Nevertheless, conservationists fighting the dam have once again found themselves sharing concerns with Nebraska. As with Deer Creek, the Fish and Wildlife Service issued a no-jeopardy decision for Two Forks because the dam's sponsors promised to undertake measures to keep the Platte mainstem channel open. These measures are nearly identical to those outlined for Deer Creek, though on a scale commensurate with Two Forks' larger size. However, in the case of Two Forks the no-jeopardy decision revealed clearly the corrupt power of western water politics. The press obtained internal Fish and Wildlife Service documents that cast doubt on the entire consultation process. FWS administrators had ordered their biologists to make a no-jeopardy decision *before* studies of Two Forks' biological impacts were finished. Critics of the Two

Forks project believe that in doing this the service bowed to pressure from the Denver Water Board.

The entire approval process by the Fish and Wildlife Service may reflect a growing decline in endangered-species protection under presidential administrations with little interest in conservation. The consultation process was intended to stimulate the redesign of projects harmful to listed species. Instead, under the Reagan administration, sponsors of harmful projects in Colorado and elsewhere across the nation were given no-jeopardy decisions if they simply promised to implement mitigation measures agreed upon by FWS officials and themselves. In the case of Two Forks, the negotiated mitigation does not benefit wildlife habitat because it fails to offset the water-flow depletions with the equal amount of water needed to provide wildlife with the roosting, nesting, and feeding flows they require.

Despite the lack of sound mitigation, the U.S. Army Corps of Engineers announced that it intended to issue a permit in January 1989. However, Audubon president Peter A. A. Berle and the leaders of other national organizations, using provisions of the Clean Water Act that require the Environmental Protection Agency to review Corps permits, successfully prevailed upon EPA administrator William Reilly for a review of Two Forks. Regional EPA officials then investigated the project and vetoed its permits because of its potentially heavy environmental toll. After two months of subsequent public hearings, it seemed likely that the EPA office in Washington, D.C., would kill the project. However, as these events were taking place late in 1989, water-development interests were marshaling their forces to try to revive Two Forks. But even if Two Forks were dead for good, the safety of the Platte and its wildlife would not be assured.

An Endless Parade of Water Projects

Two Forks and Deer Creek are not the only new water projects proposed for the Platte. A grand total of fourteen projects have been proposed in Colorado, Wyoming, and Nebraska. In an era of crop surpluses, they would put 369,000 new acres of land under irrigation. Total cost for all projects would be at least $3 billion. Current water flow in the Platte would be cut to near zero. In the Big Bend area near

Overton, flow would be cut 60 percent, to less than 400,000 acre-feet a year. This is 85 percent below the pristine flow of 2.6 million acre-feet yearly.

The building of dams and reservoirs has been rampant in this nation since the Depression. Folk wisdom maintains that land-locked Oklahoma, because of all its dam projects, has more coastline than the Eastern Seaboard. In 1986, when the Reagan

The chill waters of the North Fork of the South Platte River foam through the Rocky Mountains near the proposed site of Two Forks Dam, which will drown much of the stream in its own water. Because so many water projects have already reduced the flow of the Platte River, cutting off this source threatens to drain the Platte dry in parts of Nebraska hundreds of miles downstream.

administration was trying to cut back on federal funding of dams, Congress authorized nearly 300 new water projects, including dams and drainage schemes. These represent serious and widespread destruction of wildlife and natural habitat. In many cases, vanishing bottomland hardwoods, valuable to a wide range of bird species and other animals, are lost. Stream habitat is turned into lake habitat, wiping out fish and other creatures adapted to shallow, flowing waters. Dams have threatened a wide array of endangered and threatened species, from freshwater clams to fish and turtles, from aquatic insects to whooping cranes.

Many proposed water projects are unnecessary. For example, 100 square miles of seasonal Mississippi wetlands important to waterfowl are slated

Mitigation: What's Real and What Is Not

About half of U.S. wetlands have been destroyed, mostly by land development for agriculture. Loss of wetlands continues at about half a million acres yearly. Wetlands, such as the wet meadows that surround parts of the Platte, are important because they provide sustenance for a variety of wildlife. Also, because water tends to flow slowly through them, wetlands serve as a sort of filter, preventing various pollutants from entering rivers and streams and making the waterways more suitable for use by people.

The loss of wetlands and even of natural river channels, such as the wide, shallow riverbed of the Platte, to various types of land development is often allowed to occur if developers agree to "mitigate" the loss. Mitigation refers to methods for reducing or repairing wetlands damage.

Mitigation would not be a bad idea if it worked. Unfortunately, it often fails. For example, in one type of mitigation a developer buys an existing wetland that matches in size the wetland slated for development. The second wetland is donated to a state or federal agency that will preserve it. Of course, in this case, even if the second wetland is saved, the wetland that is developed is still destroyed, resulting in a net loss of wet-

lands. Moreover, the second wetland may not even be of the same type as the destroyed wetland. For example, a grassland marsh may be exchanged for a wooded swamp. These wetlands are not comparable, and protecting one while destroying the other can hardly be considered mitigation.

Even in cases in which developers try to restore wetlands or create wetlands that match destroyed areas in size, the mitigation is still of uncertain value. Little expertise exists for administering wetlands replacement of this sort. Wetlands functions and characteristics are complex and poorly understood. It is impossible to be sure that a created or recreated wetland embodies all the characteristics of a natural wetland. In addition, it is almost impossible to replace certain types of wetlands by any means. But government agencies assigned to protect wetlands have tended to ignore this. Writes Jon Kusler, chairman of the Association of State Wetland Managers, and Hazel Gorman, of the Environmental Law Institute, in the *National Wetlands Newsletter*, "Despite these uncertainties, government agencies have authorized hundreds and perhaps thousands of mitigation projects over the past decade. Unfortunately, there has been little monitoring to determine whether the projects were actually carried out and, if they were, whether they were 'successful.' The few follow-up studies which exist suggest that many mit-

igation projects are not achieving their purported purpose."

To help ensure that mitigation programs are performing as well as possible in the protection of wetlands, the following measures should be taken:

- Mitigation should be allowed only in cases in which development of a wetland is unavoidable. In every case, an effort should be made to develop upland areas, rather than wetlands. However, developers often resist this because wetlands tend to be cheaper than uplands.

- If mitigation is necessary, it should be used first to restore damaged, ecologically equivalent wetlands equal to or greater in size than the wetlands to be developed. One wetland should not be given protection in exchange for destroying another wetland, since this practice results in a net wetlands loss.

- Mitigation must be carried out successfully—and it may take years to ascertain that mitigation of a wetland has been a success—*before* any development begins.

- Mitigation should replace the same type of wetland that development is destroying. For example, a wooded swamp lost to development should be replaced with a wooded swamp, not a grassland marsh.

for drainage by the Army Corps of Engineers. The drained land is to be used for growing crops such as cotton, soybeans, and wheat, all marginally profitable and already grown in surplus. Other projects are necessary only because so little is done to conserve water. Present law even encourages waste because those with water rights must use their water or lose the rights to it. Farmers who conserve irrigation water and return it to the rivers from which it came therefore lose it to other users. According to the *Audubon Wildlife Report 1987*, a 7 to 10 percent reduction in western agricultural water use would

eliminate the need for any new water sources even if all other uses doubled.

Unfortunately for sandhill cranes and other Platte River wildlife, people do not see the problems that waste and habitat destruction are causing as time passes. Says John VanDerwalker, executive director of the Platte River Whooping Crane Trust,

> They look at the river today and see something that they think is nice. They recognize over their lifetime that a little bit of it has been lost, but so what? The problem is that you stack up two or three lifetimes and what you have is a river that's severely degraded, and

that's what we have today. . . . Now we just have a remnant of that habitat and it's disappearing very rapidly. If we don't do something about it quickly, it'll be gone in about 10 years.

For many years now, conservationists have tried to compromise with water developers in efforts to protect wildlife and still supply water for other uses. VanDerwalker has even joined with Nebraska dam developers in support of one project in the hope that Nebraska will be more likely to provide water for its Platte River wildlife than Wyoming would be. Nevertheless, on the Platte the time for compromise may be at an end. The Platte has been so thoroughly tapped for water that it is approaching a point of doom for the sandhill cranes, the whooping cranes, the least terns, the piping plovers, and millions of ducks and geese. They cannot hope to adapt to the river's loss. Says Ken Strom, manager of Audubon's Lillian Annette Rowe Sanctuary,

> After a century of compromising the integrity of the river, we're down to only 30 percent of what used to be here, and in some cases only 10 percent of the habitat. The cranes can't compromise. The waterfowl can't compromise. They have no place else to go. And it's a very little concession for us to simply leave what's here in the river intact so that those who follow will still be able to enjoy the spectacle of the cranes.

Ken Strom, manager of the National Audubon Society's Lillian Annette Rowe Sanctuary, visits one of the sandhill crane observation blinds set up along the Platte. Thousands of birders come to the sanctuary each spring to watch the hundreds of thousands of cranes that gather there during migration.

GREED AND WILDLIFE
POACHING IN AMERICA

Based on the Audubon Television Special by
Mark Shwartz and
Narrated by Richard Chamberlain

IN MAY 1988, three men climbed into two pirogues and poled into a cypress swamp near Vacherie, Louisiana. Their objective was a large nesting area used by yellow-crowned night herons, long-legged wading birds that the men, like their Cajun forebears, called "gros becs," meaning "big beaks." Though once hunted for meat and still considered a delicacy by some Louisiana natives, the birds have been protected by law since 1918.

When the three reached the heron rookery, they took out .22 rifles and commenced a slaughter so huge that it would later have law enforcement officers poring over arrest records to see if they could find anything in the books to match it. When the shooting stopped, the three Cajuns had killed at least 468 yellow-crowned night herons, most of them so young they could not fly. The men collected the birds, gutted them, and put them into ice chests before push-poling back out of the swamp.

Meanwhile, conservation officers with the Louisiana Department of Wildlife and Fisheries received a phone call telling them about the hunt. Consequently, they were at the landing dock when the pirogues arrived. Two of the gunmen spotted the officers and bolted, leaving the other with four ice chests and two sacks full of young birds. The man they caught "sang like a bird," said James Bartee, a U.S. Fish and Wildlife Service special agent. The officers learned that the men had held another hunt only two days before during which they killed nearly 200 birds more.

The evidence and testimony eventually led agents from the state wildlife department and the U.S. Fish and Wildlife Service to arrest four men for planning and conducting the kill. The purpose of the hunt remains unknown, but law enforcement agents believe the men killed the birds to provide a main course for a large political fund-raising banquet. In Louisiana gros bec is traditional and still popular, though illegal, fare at these events. The birds also may have been destined for the black market, where they sell for up to $5 each.

Killing wildlife for profit has a long history in America. It is a way of life that dates back to the first years of settlement. It is also a way of life that in the past nearly wiped out most of the game animals in the United States and that even now, in its modern incarnation, threatens wildlife throughout the continent.

Living on the Fat of the Land

When European settlers first came to North America, the continent's bounty of wildlife was a smorgasbord for survival. The colonists depended on deer and elk and bison, on waterfowl and grouse and turkeys, for sustenance and clothing, and even for tools carved from antler, horn, and bone. No laws protected North American wildlife from hunters, and wildlife was slaughtered extensively not just for food but also for commerce. Deer hides, for example, were exported to Europe by the hundreds of thousands. Virginia and the Carolinas exported at least 1.1 million hides between 1698 and 1715. During roughly the first half of the eighteenth century, 4 million white-tailed deer hides passed through the port of Charleston, South Carolina. Wild turkeys, a grouse called the heath hen, passenger pigeons, waterfowl, and a large number of other animals were hunted for market. Cod and other fish caught in American waters were shipped to Europe. Pelts from beavers, otters, mink, and other furbearers supplied the European and Oriental fur markets.

Hunters with their morning kill of waterfowl on a Minnesota lake at the turn of the century. Overkilling contributed to the decline of waterfowl late in the nineteenth century.

Egrets roosting for the night in a cottonwood tree on the Mississippi Delta in Lousiana.
The killing of tens of thousands of egrets by poachers at the turn of the century was one
of the factors that led to the first federal bird-protection laws.

Late in the 1800s, two hunters of the northern Great Plains pose with more than a dozen mule deer they have shot. Excessive killing of deer and other wildlife to supply urban meat markets nearly wiped out much of North America's game animals.

Uncontrolled hunting for pot and profit soon took its toll. Deer numbers had been noticeably reduced in New England within twenty-five years after the settling of Plymouth. In 1646, Rhode Island passed the New World's first closed season on wildlife. Other colonies soon followed the example. At first, game laws were enforced by local peace officers. Special game-law enforcement officers did not exist until 1739, when Massachusetts appointed the first deer wardens. New Hampshire was the next to follow the Bay State's example, appointing deer wardens in 1764.

The early attempts at game protection that followed during the next 100 years did little for most species and hardly stemmed the impact of sport and market hunting. Hunting seasons, when they existed at all, were generally long, lasting for months. Bag limits were liberal or nonexistent. Consequently, the nineteenth century hosted one of the worst wildlife slaughters known to history. Hunters prided themselves on the amount of game they

could kill—lone hunters would shoot hundreds of ducks, geese, wild turkeys, and heath hens in a single day. Armed with a shotgun, a market hunter might shoot 1,500 passenger pigeons in a single morning. Clubs were used to kill roosting pigeons at night. Pots of sulfur commonly were burned beneath pigeon roosts, so that tens of thousands of pigeons were suffocated at a time. The hides and meat of millions of bison were shipped east from the Great Plains, packed into trains along with the meat of wild sheep, deer, and pronghorn antelope. Even songbirds were not safe. Hunters killed hundreds of thousands of them for the meat markets that prospered in most major American cities.

By the closing years of the nineteenth century, it seemed apparent that most game species would not long survive. Of the 30 million to 50 million bison that once thundered over the plains, perhaps 500 remained. The beavers that once populated North American streams were nearly extirpated by trapping for the hat industry. River otters and sea otters nearly disappeared, destroyed for their furs. The sea mink, a large species that inhabited coastal New England, was completely wiped out. The ducks and geese whose flocks once clouded the skies were withering away beneath the twin onslaught of uncontrolled hunting and loss of the wetlands where the birds found food and shelter. One species, the Labrador duck, was common in meat markets in the 1860s and extinct by the 1870s. The pronghorn teetered on the edge of extinction, and the passenger pigeon, in all its billions, vanished from the wild, the last of them aging away and dying in an Ohio zoo. The heath hen, never able to recover from the slaughter, faded into extinction early in the twentieth century. The nation's best-informed conservationists thought the continent would soon lose its

A snow goose takes flight on Chincoteague National Wildlife Refuge in Virginia. Geese and ducks are among the most heavily poached species.

whooping cranes, sandhill cranes, ducks, geese, wild turkeys, deer—virtually all animals useful as meat or fur.

Finally, as the nineteenth century drew to a close, the alarming number of imminent extinctions stirred hunters, private citizens, and legislators to seek strong laws for the protection of wildlife. Much of the impetus for this new movement came from two camps—the hunters and the bird enthusiasts. Hunters feared that if uncontrolled slaughter were not stopped, soon there would be no game to hunt. Bird conservationists feared that the endless killing of birds to supply the millinery trade with plumes, and even with entire bird corpses, to adorn women's hats would leave woodland, field, and marsh devoid of song and living beauty. From this concern came the National Audubon Society, which has remained in the vanguard of bird-protection efforts ever since.

Bird enthusiasts and sport hunters pushed through state legislatures and through Congress the nation's first strong wildlife-protection laws and triggered a fresh concern for wildlife. Consequently, the number of game wardens employed to enforce the laws grew steadily in the early years of this century. Moreover, the increasing commitment to wildlife protection gave birth to a new field of science, wildlife management, which sought to understand the needs of wild animals and to discover ways to increase wild populations.

The new system had many faults. The laws the wardens were assigned to enforce were limited in scope, since most protected only game animals, and were often opposed by hunters who wanted to retain the liberal seasons and bag limits to which they were accustomed. Moreover, the effectiveness of early wildlife managers was hampered by lack of training and by a poor understanding of the needs of wildlife. Many of the first managers, trained as foresters or rangeland managers, knew more about trees and grass than about animals. It is not surprising, then, that the first professional wildlife managers mistakenly urged the slaughter of predators such as wolves, mountain lions, and grizzlies in the name of game protection. Even in Yellowstone National Park, wolves and mountain lions were wiped out in a misguided effort to protect elk and deer.

Over the years, however, knowledge about wildlife increased and soon helped put wildlife management on a more intelligent foundation. Hunters also became more sophisticated about their responsibilities toward wildlife, which helped quash much of the opposition to new laws. Strictly enforced closed seasons and bag limits, in addition to better law enforcement, staunched the decline of America's wildlife. Many populations began to increase, particularly as management also improved. By the 1930s, wildlife managers were initiating successful programs to move animals such as wild turkeys, deer, and pronghorn antelope from areas where they were abundant to areas where they had been wiped out. Today, white-tailed deer number about 12 million and the western mule deer about 5.5 million. Because of relocation programs, wild turkeys now occur in states in which they were never found before. Beaver populations are stable or increasing. The pronghorn antelope, though far below its pristine number of perhaps 50 million animals, is prospering at more than a million.

The old days of uncontrolled hunting are gone. Today, wildlife managers set specific hunting seasons and limits for various species. Animals such as rabbits and quail, which breed rapidly, generally have longer seasons and larger bag limits than do species that breed more slowly, such as deer and elk. Wildlife managers believe that under this system hunters kill only "surplus" animals. Put simply, the manager's concept of surplus wildlife is based on the fact that most species each year produce far more offspring than will ever survive. In the United States, Canada, and other northern regions the number of animals born in spring, when plant foods and other necessities are increasing toward an annual peak, are greater than the number that can survive the winter, when food, water, and warmth ebb to a low. A certain proportion of the animals will die, with the size of the proportion dictated by such factors as climate and the condition of the habitat. Animals that cannot hope to survive are called "surplus" by wildlife managers because the animals will not be part of the breeding population in spring and therefore are not needed to maintain the population through reproduction. Wildlife managers try to set limits and seasons in such a way that the kill by hunters does not exceed the surplus. This way, it is presumed, hunting will not damage the hunted population.

In setting hunting restrictions, wildlife managers take into consideration a number of factors. These include population data on the hunted species, the number of animals killed by hunters in past seasons, weather, and habitat condition. For example, when in the 1980s prolonged drought combined with drainage of wetlands for agricultural development to cause waterfowl numbers to sink, wildlife managers tightened hunting restrictions on some species of ducks and geese.

This system does not work like a well-oiled machine. For example, in parts of some states, white-tailed deer populations, despite hunting seasons, are too dense for the available land to support them. In some cases this has happened at least in part because wildlife managers simply did not recognize the need for bigger bag limits and longer seasons until a population explosion had occurred.

But another factor adding to the problem is hunters themselves. Hunters have often opposed measures designed to protect hunted species. For example, in the early days of game management, many hunters opposed the new bag limits and shorter hunting seasons. Hunter opposition to the hunting of doe (female) deer, which is badly needed to lower deer numbers in some crowded areas, has

A forlorn child waits for his father, who stands with federal and Louisiana state conservation officers looking over a field where the father and some friends had been dove hunting. The hunters were subsequently charged with illegally baiting doves by putting out seeds to attract the birds. Baiting for doves and waterfowl is a widespread but illegal practice that gives lawbreakers an unfair advantage over ethical hunters.

A flock of snow geese gathers on the Sacramento National Wildlife Refuge in northern California, a prime waterfowl wintering area. Illegal use of bait to attract waterfowl to hunters' blinds is a major enforcement problem in California.

been so constant over the years that it is almost a tradition. Hunters, according to opinion polls, are happiest when they see a lot of game, even if they are seeing mainly protected does. Many hunters fail to understand that dense populations of animals can be a sign of trouble. Wildlife managers often must launch extensive educational and public relations campaigns to garner hunter support for changes in regulations.

Since the development of wildlife management as a profession and the institution of good wildlife conservation laws, not a single species in the United States has been threatened with extinction by sport hunting. Nevertheless, data show that many hunters break the laws that protect the game. Breaking the laws is such a common thing that hunters and wildlife managers have even given a special name to those who routinely break game laws—they are called *slob hunters*.

Slob hunters worry wildlife managers not only because they kill wildlife illegally, but also because they give hunting a bad image and raise children in the slob tradition. By doing so, slob hunters fuel the opposition of anti-hunters who would like to see hunting ended. Although to the objective observer it seems highly unlikely—even impossible—that hunting will ever be banned in the United States, within the hunting community the possibility of a ban is a source of constant fear. Hunters fear anti-hunters because they do not want to lose their sport. Wildlife managers fear them because revenue raised from the sale of hunting licenses and from taxes on hunting equipment is wildlife management's primary source of funds.

On another level, the hunter who violates game laws is stealing money and recreational opportunity from the law-abiding hunter. The money spent to manage wildlife for sport hunting is lost if the animals are killed illegally.

Figures indicate that poaching—the taking of game illegally—is perhaps more widespread and common than wildlife managers ever thought. In Texas, forty-one of forty-two duck-hunting clubs investigated by federal agents were caught violating waterfowl-hunting laws in 1988. A recent study found that in some areas more than 70 percent of waterfowl hunters kill more ducks and geese than the laws allow. An estimated 3 million to 4 million white-tailed deer are killed illegally each year. The illegal kill of black bears in the southern Appalachian Mountains, one of the largest populations in the Southeast, equaled or exceeded the legal kill throughout the 1980s. Poaching rings in Yellowstone National Park, where all hunting is forbidden, killed elk, wild sheep, deer, and even grizzly bears, which are federally listed as threatened. The animals were sold mainly for trophies.

In California, where about 80 percent of the waterfowl that migrate along the Pacific spend winter, it is common for hunters to put out corn and other foods to attract ducks within shooting range.

This is called *baiting*. It occurs throughout the United States at various levels of intensity, and it is illegal because it concentrates ducks in one place and tends to bring them back to the site repeatedly, making them easy prey for hunters. Baiting, says federal agent Scott Pearson, "goes back to the old, old, old, old days," when market hunters baited ducks and geese to maximize their kill. Much of the baiting is done at duck-hunting clubs, which are ponds and fields rented or owned by hunters who have exclusive use of them. "Where you have a lot of duck clubs in one area, members figure they can get a leg up by baiting," Pearson says.

Some of the most serious waterfowl violations have occurred in Louisiana. The problem de-

This sign near Roger's Pass, Montana, warns hunters that they must stop for an examination of any game they possess during hunting season. Hunters that ignore the sign are quickly pursued by state conservation officers and pulled over. Officers at a similar roadblock in Idaho discovered that 40 percent of the hunters had violated game laws.

Conservation officers at a roadblock at Roger's Pass, Montana, check the tags on a mountain goat killed by a hunter. In this case, everything was in order. However, in a single night the officers collected several illegally killed deer and elk.

veloped, says federal agent James Bartee, because many rural Louisianians are subsistence hunters, relying on waterfowl for food, and because both rural and urban Louisianians are deeply entrenched in the hunting tradition. In addition, the people of Louisiana have access to tremendous numbers of birds. Says Dave Hall, a U.S. Fish and Wildlife Service agent who has been stationed in the state for more than twenty years,

> The impact of illegal hunting in the Bayou state is a result of the huge concentrations of waterfowl that winter in Louisiana's vast swamps and marshes, which represent 46 percent of the nation's coastal wetlands. The opportunity to violate wildlife laws is also an important factor. A survey we conducted among federal agents stationed in Louisiana during the 1980s indicated that hunters apprehended violating the reg-

ulations had killed four times as many ducks as legal hunters. The magnitude of some violations is spectacular. In one case, three men killed 168 ducks over a baited pond in one day, about 150 over the limit. In another case, eight Louisiana hunters—who were videotaped by federal undercover agents who posed as hunters in order to join the hunt—killed 246 geese in one day, more than 200 over the limit.

Exposure of such flagrant violations aroused legal hunters and the general public. A study of duck hunters, convicted violators, and wildlife officers conducted by Hall and Robert Jackson of the University of Wisconsin in Louisiana, Minnesota, and Wisconsin during the 1988–89 hunting season indicates that compliance with regulations is increasing among waterfowl hunters in those states. The study concluded that strong public opposition to poaching, better law enforcement, and strict punishment of violators by federal courts have helped to reduce the number of violations significantly. For example, duck-baiting cases in Louisiana declined 98 percent during the 1988–89 season, compared to the previous year.

The number of hunters who violate game laws is astounding. When conservation officers with the Utah Department of Natural Resources set up roadblocks so they could stop hunters and inspect their permits and kills, they found that 25 percent of the people who had game or fish in their possession were in violation of the law. In Idaho, 40 percent of the hunters checked at one blockade were violators. In many cases, the violations were unintentional—for example, a hunter may have failed to attach to his or her deer a special tag issued by the state and required by law. Or a waterfowl hunter who did not know ducks well may have shot one too many of the wrong species. However, even inadvertent violations can take a toll. As Scott Pearson said about California, "There are about 80,000 duck stamps sold in the state. If every one of the licensed hunters took just one bird over the limit, that would be a significant number."

Sometimes neither sport nor profit enters into the poacher's motives. Billionaire John Werner Kluge, cited by *Forbes* magazine as the second richest man in the United States, acquired some 6,000 acres in Albemarle County, Virginia, and turned them into a private estate that included a hunting area stocked with 10,000 pheasants and 3,500 ducks. Kluge's visitors were permitted to shoot the birds without limit. In one day, eight guests killed 800, and many of the dead birds were merely buried in pits. This was legal, since Kluge bought and stocked the birds, which were captive bred. However, the efforts made by his staff to keep predatory animals out of the hunting area were not legal. When federal and state wildlife agents and police raided the estate on suspicions of wildlife-law violations, they found the bodies of more than 100 protected hawks and owls buried in pits with the carcasses of a dozen dogs and the bodies of other protected birds, such as killdeer, vultures, and snipe. The staff who managed the hunting reserve, all British, were taken to court and fined $15,000, which Kluge paid. Agents from the Immigration and Naturalization Service seized the Britons as soon as the fine was paid and began deportation proceedings. The men left the country the next day.

In a similar case, a man who owned a fish hatchery in California hired college students to shoot birds that he thought would feed on his fish. Over a period of years, the shooters killed thousands of herons, avocets, hawks, and even ducks. One California officer said the toll could be some 20,000 birds, all protected species.

Protecting Game Animals Today

The enforcement of wildlife-protection laws lies in the hands of some 7,800 state officers and 205 federal agents. Federal agents are concerned with the enforcement of such national laws as the Migratory Bird Treaty Act, the Endangered Species Act, and the Lacey Act. However, the bulk of wildlife enforcement work belongs to the state officers, since wildlife management is largely the legal domain of the states. Although in Alaska and Oregon wildlife protection is administered by state police, in all other states it is handled by a special law enforcement unit within the state wildlife or natural resources agencies. About a third of all state wildlife department employees are conservation officers. Their operations consume an average of about 30 percent of departmental budgets, while the federal law enforcement program absorbs less than 5 percent of the Fish and Wildlife Service budget.

All states require their conservation officers to pass a civil service exam or complete some equivalent screening process. About a third of all states require college degrees, and nearly all require new officers to attend a police academy. The time when former poachers were made game wardens by political cronies is long past, and the conservation-officer position has become increasingly sophisticated and demanding over the past decade and a half.

Conservation officers deal with a wide variety of violations, including the killing of wildlife out of season or in illegal places, improper licenses, and illegal hunting and fishing methods, as well as cases involving drugs, stolen property, theft, murder, and

Loren Ellison: The Longest Jail Term

One night in October 1984, Loren Ellison, wanted by U.S. Fish and Wildlife Service (FWS) law enforcement agents for alleged poaching crimes, was sharing a few drinks with a friend, Pete Nylander, in a bar in a small Montana town. Late that night, Ellison and Nylander went to Ellison's house for a nightcap. At about 2 A.M., Ellison went to bed.

Nylander, however, did not go home and do the same. The night was a busy one for him, full of plans. For Nylander was an FWS undercover agent, and he and several other agents were closing in on Ellison after three years of investigation, during which they made several purchases of illegal game that Ellison had killed. Nylander called his cohorts and told them that Ellison was safely at home. This was precisely what the agents wanted, because they intended to show up at Ellison's home the next morning and arrest him.

One of the agents involved, John Cooper, remembers the final hours before the arrest. He and other agents spent part of the night studying a floor plan of Ellison's house. They were also taking into consideration the various possible complications that could occur. They knew Ellison had weapons in the house, Cooper recalls, and that his police record indicated several violent crimes, including rape, attempted homicide, and assault. They also knew that his common-law wife would probably be home with him. They made plans to avoid a violent confrontation and to protect the wife.

With all this in mind, they arrived at Ellison's home at about 6 A.M. After posting guards at the front and rear of the house, they knocked on the front door. Ellison's wife answered, and they told her they had a warrant for Loren's arrest and asked if he was at home. Apparently still bleary from sleep, she responded only by looking toward the rear of the house. The agents, knowing the floor plan, immediately moved toward the bedrooms.

Loren Ellison in Montana.

They left Ellison's wife with a woman ranger from the National Park Service.

Ellison was caught asleep and slightly hung over. When awakened he indicated that he thought the charges against him were ridiculous, but did not protest when the agents said they had to handcuff him and, according to the terms of the warrant, seize his car and some other items. "He gave us no problem," Cooper recalls. "He never cursed. He was completely docile."

Thus began the legal process that, in the end, netted Ellison the longest jail sentence ever handed down in a poaching case—twenty-three years in federal prison, with eight of the years suspended.

Loren Ellison does not fit the image of a wanton killer of game animals. He is average in height and build, with blond hair, blue eyes, and a tan that perhaps denotes his years in the outdoors. He is not, Cooper says, the sort of "Neanderthal types" that the agents often find themselves arresting in poaching operations. "Loren is not a dumb person," Cooper says. "He has a lot of things going for him. He was a good athlete and is in good physical shape. The only thing he had going against him was he was drinking a bit for a while. He had a lot of skills in the outdoors. He could have done anything he wanted."

Joel Scrafford, a senior FWS special agent in Billings, Montana, who was in on the operation that netted Ellison, echoes

Cooper's comments. "He had the intelligence and personality to be a success in any legal venture he wanted to try," Scrafford says. "The word 'charisma' has been used in connection with him many times." Women, Scrafford says, seemed to find him irresistible, and even the courtroom where Ellison was tried would fall silent when he walked in.

"He has a tremendous amount of charisma," says John Gavitt, the man perhaps most responsible for bringing Ellison to bay and now head of FWS covert operations. "If you want to look at it this way, he really portrayed the last of the American cowboys." Ellison is, in fact, descended from a long line of true westerners. His family arrived in Montana in the 1870s, early in the state's settlement. "He comes from a fine, hard-working family," says Scrafford. "His father and brother are good ranchers."

Ellison says he has hunted all his life, which was spent entirely in Montana. He sees nothing wrong with killing an animal for meat out of season. For as long as he can remember, he says, "if people in Montana needed a deer to eat, they'd get a deer to eat, or an elk." As he talks, Ellison is sitting in an office at Boron Federal Prison Camp outside Barstow, California. The country that surrounds the prison is a far cry from the cool, rugged mountain ranges of Montana, where snow-fed streams rush glass-clear over mossy rock. The prison is a tiny conglomerate of characterless government buildings that until 1979 were part of an Air Force base. The prison houses some 535 inmates, all minimum security, locked up for white-collar crimes or for probation violations. The inmates even get occasional leaves to visit their families.

No fences separate the prison grounds from the almost-featureless surrounding terrain. This is desert country, the earth cracked and dry, the vegetation a tangle of low brush, gray and lifeless looking. It is easy country to get lost in. A lone saddleback hill is the only major landmark nearby, and even if you keep it in sight, a short hike can leave you disoriented and in search of your car.

Ellison's hunting habits are what ultimately brought him to this bleak land. Gavitt says that Ellison's downfall began when Gavitt was conducting an investigation into poaching operations around Yellowstone National Park. Scrafford supplied Gavitt with some information that indicated that Ellison was involved in illegal trade in wildlife, particularly the sale of antlers from elk in Yellowstone. Gavitt, working undercover, was introduced to Ellison by Larry Myers a middleman in the antler trade. Myers had asked Gavitt if he would be interested in buying a grizzly hide. Sensing a connection to poachers, since grizzlies are completely protected in the Yellowstone area, Gavitt had said he was interested. Myers had told him that Ellison had a hide for sale and had given Gavitt Ellison's phone number.

Ellison was immediately suspicious when Gavitt called him, the agent recalls. He even asked Gavitt if he were a federal agent. But, despite his apparent doubts, Ellison met Gavitt in a bar.

Ellison never admitted having a grizzly pelt and no charge involving grizzlies was ever brought against him. However, he did agree to lead some of Gavitt's friends on big-game hunts, even though the hunters had no licenses. The "friends," of course, were FWS undercover agents.

Gavitt also mentioned to Ellison that he would like to buy some eagle carcasses. Ellison told Gavitt that he knew of a rancher who was killing eagles—which are protected from all hunting by federal law—and agreed to deliver the carcasses to Gavitt. Gavitt later learned that Ellison was the "rancher" who was killing the birds.

During this time, Ellison made a threat that has left lingering images in Scrafford's mind. Ellison, says Scrafford, used to carry a sawed-off 12-gauge shotgun under his coat and once pulled it out and cut loose with it on a tree. Then he said, "That's what'll happen to you if you turn out to be a warden."

The story Ellison tells of his contacts with federal agents varies in some particulars from that related by the agents. He

admits that, long before meeting the federal agents, he had poached game "for the subsistence of my family." But, he says, he never poached for money until Gavitt asked him to do so. "In my case, it was with the coercion and insistence of the government that I went into it," he says.

He believes that it was his involvement in the antler trade that drew him to the attention of the federal agents. He got into the antler trade in 1979 when a Korean dealer came into Gardiner, Montana, asking locals to supply him with elk antlers for shipment to Korea, where they are used in traditional oriental medicine. FWS began Operation Trophy Kill, a major investigation of poaching around Yellowstone, two years later. Ellison believes Scrafford targeted him for investigation at that time.

Ellison maintains that he collected only antlers that had been shed naturally at the end of the breeding season, though he does admit that he collected shed antlers in Yellowstone, where it is illegal. He also admits leading illegal hunts for animals such as elk, deer, and bighorn sheep and confesses to killing eagles, but he denies ever hunting in Yellowstone National Park. The area in which he guided the illegal hunts, he says, was forty miles from the park and did not involve animals from Yellowstone herds. Ellison says that he initially turned down Gavitt's request that he guide some hunters interested in getting trophy elk antlers because he did not want to kill the animals just for trophies. "To people in Montana, the primary purpose of an elk or a sheep is to eat," Ellison told Gavitt.

Gavitt responded that his friends would let Ellison keep the meat as long as they got the heads. Ellison says that he figured Gavitt was being "honest enough" in taking that approach, and adds that "the meat was good for me," so he agreed to lead the hunt. When Ellison pointed out that he no longer had a guide's license, Gavitt, who was posing as a taxidermist, told him that he would cover that for him. And that, Ellison says, led to the first hunt in January 1983. He guided the hunt without a license, which made it illegal even though elk were in season, and Gavitt subsequently had him ship the hides to an address in the East, which made the crime federal because it involved interstate commerce. In following hunts, Ellison continued to function as an unlicensed guide leading unlicensed hunters, which made the activity illegal even though the animals killed were taken in season.

In February or March 1984, Ellison says, Gavitt asked him to supply some eagles. Ellison says he did nothing to initiate the eagle killing. "It was what Gavitt wanted and when he wanted it," Ellison maintains. "Everything was initiated by the government." Eventually, Ellison killed a dozen golden eagles and sold them to Gavitt, believing Gavitt was going to mount them for friends. The arrest was made the following fall.

Ellison believes that he got his long prison sentence because he tried to fight his case in court. When offered a five-year sentence in a plea bargain, he refused. He says he realizes now that if you fight a case, you risk a sentence two or three times as long. "The first time you go through this," he says, "you don't know that. You say, I don't think this is right, I'm going to fight it."

Gavitt, however, believes that Ellison got what he deserved and is pleased with the sentence. He says that he is not surprised that Ellison was so heavily penalized. Instead, he is dismayed that so many other poachers get off so lightly.

Remembering the day he was sentenced to fifteen years in prison, Ellison says, "It's hard to describe how you feel at first. It might have taken a year to sink in." He started his sentence in a federal prison in Arizona, then was sent to Boron in April 1987.

He carries some bitterness about the circumstances surrounding his arrest and conviction. "Any way you look at it," he says, "the government was more culpable for crime than I was." He argues that the federal agents should have stopped the eagle killing after no more than two birds were killed. "I think the whole undercover operation was out of hand," he says. He believes that Gavitt asked him to kill eagles because Ellison refused to kill a grizzly and sell the hide. The point of the entire operation, Ellison argues, was to "make the charges more appalling to the public. It was purely a case of getting the public on your side without being aware of all the facts surrounding it, and that's exactly what occurred. And since I still have that attitude,

I guess I haven't learned a thing in these four years." He says, however, that he will not get involved in poaching again. If someone approached him to lead an illegal hunt now, he says, he would just take the hunter "out into the woods and rob him."

Ellison proved to be a model prisoner. As Scrafford put it, he "played the game, he jumped through the hoops." And so, partly as a side effect of an overcrowded prison system, Ellison was paroled in October 1989. Gavitt, Scrafford, and some of the former poachers with whom they are in contact have kept in mind a threat they say Ellison made before going off to jail. He had told them that his memory was long, and he would be back.

He is back now. And, Scrafford says, as a result, security has been beefed up around some of the figures involved in Ellison's arrest, including the judge who sentenced him. One agent says he doesn't think Ellison will be at large for long. Too many people are afraid of him or have grudges against him. The individual the agents describe as intelligent, charismatic, and capable of succeeding at anything will, the agent suspects, either murder or be murdered within a year of his release.

---

other charges. One violation of increasing concern is the illegal killing of fish and game so that meat and other products can be sold. This is market hunting in its newest incarnation, and for many wild populations beleaguered by development and burgeoning human numbers, it is a harbinger of doom.

Because it is often impossible to determine if a poacher caught with illegal game intended to sell the animals, no data exist to show whether poaching for profit is increasing. Nevertheless, many state and federal conservation officers suspect that it is, and they are supported by persuasive, indirect evidence. The market value of wildlife has risen greatly in recent years—enough, presumably, to increase the number of poachers willing to risk prosecution. Some big-game trophy hunters will pay thousands of dollars for guaranteed hunts conducted out of season by unlicensed guides. Some buyers will pay as much as $20,000 for a record-book elk head. The

claws from a single Yellowstone grizzly are worth about $3,000. An eagle carcass fetches up to $500, a bison skull about $400. The Oriental medical market pays about $12 a pound for elk antlers, which are sliced and even powdered for use in various treatments. Since antlers are shed each year after the breeding season, many antlers are legally collected and sold. However, a premium is paid for antlers in velvet, those still growing and covered with a soft fur. Practitioners of traditional Oriental medicine freeze-dry the antlers and cut them into wafers from which a medicinal tea is made, or grind them into flakes for use as an aphrodisiac. Velvet antlers must be cut from the heads of animals killed out of season. A pair of velvet elk antlers weighing about fifteen pounds will sell for more than $1,000.

Even the fish stocked in reservoirs and lakes by state wildlife agencies are not safe. Poachers put out illegal gill nets and catch tons of fish, which are sold to restaurants. In some states the trade in illegal fish is worth hundreds of thousands of dollars yearly. Deer also are heavily poached, with the illegal kill at least equal to the legal. The carcasses are sold for as little as $30 to restaurants, which use the cheap meat to "stretch" the more expensive beef used in chili and hamburgers. In Alaska, guides who use airplanes to hunt illegally on national wildlife refuges and national parks for animals such as bears and mountain sheep can earn up to $60,000 weekly from unscrupulous clients. A poaching ring in Washington State that sold twenty-five bald eagles and hundreds of elk, deer, cougars, hawks, and other animals made $600,000 in three years.

Poaching can make the development of sound wildlife-management plans impossible since biologists have to guess at the number of animals killed by poachers. For example, Alaskan guides who lead illegal grizzly bear hunts try to conceal their activities by falsifying documents when they report their kills. Since kill data are used by wildlife managers to set hunting limits, the false information can lead to poor management decisions. John Gavitt, head of the U.S. Fish and Wildlife Service's covert operations, told Audubon television filmmaker Mark Shwartz, "When managers believe 50 bears are being killed in a certain area, and three times that many are being killed, we have a situation where it becomes biologically impossible to manage the population."

Conservation officers have found that the best way to stop illegal commercial hunting operations is to infiltrate organized groups of poachers, but the process is expensive and time consuming. Officers chosen for infiltration must make contact with the poachers and make the poachers trust them enough to sell them illegal wildlife products. To do this, agents often set up fake business fronts, posing as real estate agents, jewelers, and hunters shopping for an illegal hunt.

Because some state wildlife agencies lack the facilities and expertise needed to infiltrate poaching operations, state conservation officers often turn to the federal government for aid. Since 1980, state and federal cooperation has cracked several major poaching rings. Illegal catching and selling of some 60,000 pounds of Great Lakes fish yearly was stopped by an eighteen-month covert investigation called Operation Gillnet. Nearly 100 violators were convicted and fined more than $120,000. Operation Trophy Kill was a three-year undercover program that sought to stop poachers who were killing elk, deer, pronghorn antelope, mountain goats, bobcats, and bighorn sheep in the Yellowstone area, including the park itself. In addition to selling trophy heads, meat, and even eagle feathers, the poachers guided hunters on illegal hunts for protected animals. Eventually, fifty poachers were arrested. Fines totaled more than $120,000, and one convicted poacher received a twenty-three-year prison sentence, the longest ever handed down to a wildlife-law violator.

A federal and state covert operation broke up an international ring of poachers dealing in live hawks and other birds of prey, including gyrfalcons sold to Arab falconers for as much as $100,000 each. The operation took three years to complete, resulted in more than sixty arrests and as many as convictions, and netted more than $500,000 in fines. An East Coast undercover operation crushed an illegal market in Chesapeake Bay striped bass that covered at least five states. More than 100 poachers were arrested and fined nearly $385,000. A covert operation completed in 1985 brought charges against nearly 300 people involved in the illegal sale of furbearers such as lynx, bobcats, and fishers.

One covert operation helped stop poachers who were attacking one of the largest black bear populations in the East. It resulted in the arrest of nearly fifty people on some 130 charges of game-law violations. It was known as Operation Smoky.

Operation Smoky: Saving Southern Appalachia's Black Bears

The black bear is an American native. Unlike the grizzly, which originated in the Old World and migrated into North America from Siberia, the black bear evolved in the New World. It is a smaller animal than the grizzly. A very big specimen might exceed 500 pounds, about half the size of a large grizzly. In parts of the South, female black bears, smaller than males, scarcely outweigh Saint Bernard dogs. The average female in southern Appalachia weighs 90 to 125 pounds in spring, when the animals are thin after hibernation.

Not all black bears are black. The nearly white

Kermode bears of British Columbia and the bluish-gray glacier bears of Alaska and British Columbia are both subspecies of black bear. Black bears throughout the United States and Canada may be glossy black or brown. Brown individuals are sometimes called cinnamon bears, though both brown and black cubs may be born in the same litter.

The black bear once ranged over most of North America, wherever forests grew. Its range was reduced during European settlement by the clearing of woodlands for agriculture. About 200,000 black bears inhabit the lower forty-eight states, though in many areas local populations are at a low ebb and may soon vanish. In the Southeast, the black bear occupies only about 10 percent of its former range. Southeastern black bear populations are limited to small zones of rugged wilderness surrounded by human development. Some of these islands of black bear habitat are so small that survival of the bears living in them is uncertain. One of the largest populations in the Southeast is in the southern Appalachian Mountains, where the rolling peaks ramble through Tennessee and into North Carolina. It includes perhaps 2,000 bears. About a quarter of the animals are in Great Smoky Mountains National Park, which lies north of Georgia on the Tennessee–North Carolina border. No hunting is permitted in Great Smoky, but for many poachers the 500-square-mile park, with its rugged wilderness area, is a focal point.

The hunting of black bears is a 300-year-old tradition in southern Appalachia, says George Jessie, a law enforcement officer with the Tennessee Wildlife Resources Agency. In the colonial period, bear hunting was vital to the Appalachian settler's livelihood. Bear meat was food, bear hides were clothing, bear grease was used to soften moccasins and was fashioned into candles. The hunting of bears long ago ceased to be a necessity, but for many people living around the park, bear hunting is one of the pleasures that makes life worth living. Said one local hunter who reputedly bludgeoned a bear to death with an ax, "To me, ain't no way nobody's going to take my bear hunting away from me. No way. I've been at it too long, and I enjoy it too much." The southern Appalachian's enthusiasm for hunting black bears may be hard for an outsider to understand. It is a matter of a long and revered history, of personal identity with a lifestyle whose roots are grounded in the early eighteenth century. As Jessie says, "Any time you're dealing with bear hunting, you're dealing with tradition."

In Appalachia, black bears usually are hunted with dogs, a practice outlawed in some other states because it is considered unfair chase. Hunters used to train the dogs by turning them loose on captive bears, a practice that is now illegal. Young dogs were turned loose with old, experienced dogs and allowed to harass and attack a bear chained in place with a collar. This was thought to teach young dogs to be aggressive with black bears. To make the practice safer for the dogs, the bear's teeth were usually broken off with an ax, or its jaw was broken, or it was shot through its paws with a small-caliber gun.

The dogs used for bear hunting are special breeds with a natural talent for tracking. They chase down a bear while their human partners run behind, straining to keep up. Eventually the bear seeks refuge in a tree, and the hunters shoot it. Said one bear hunter, "The dogs do all the work, basically. The dogs have the natural ability to hunt." To make the task easier, hunters have begun putting radio collars on their dogs so they can track the dogs with radio receivers.

As long as hunting was done for sport with traditional methods, it posed little real threat to the bears. But in recent years, the hunt in southern Appalachia took an ominous turn: The dogs were being left at home, and baits were being put out to attract bears so they could be shot by a hunter hidden in a nearby tree. Says Tennessee conservation officer Steve Nifong, "Baiting is completely contrary to what these people did traditionally." The shift by many hunters from working with dogs to using bait was an alarming sign that the killing of bears was becoming a commercial proposition.

What drove the hunters to poach was money. A whole black bear carcass has an estimated black market value to the poacher of several hundred dollars. Hides sell for about $100 each, claws for at least $1.50, or about $30 per bear. The paws, considered a delicacy, sell for no less than $20 each. Even live bears are taken by poachers. A bear that can be used to train dogs will sell for as much as $2,000.

The main commercial force driving the market for black bears is gall bladders, or *galls*, as they are called by conservation officers. The demand for bear gall bladders came from a completely unexpected source—Asia, where practitioners of Oriental folk medicine use products from the galls to treat a wide range of diseases. The bile, said Bill Cook, a wildlife biologist assigned for several years to the Great Smoky Mountains National Park, is dried to a form that resembles hardened molasses and chewed. The

After feeding on acorns high in an oak tree in the Cades Cove section of Great Smoky Mountains National Park, this female black bear withdrew to a wooded hillside for a snooze. She is from the population of bears that were being decimated by poachers who sold the bears' gall bladders to practitioners of traditional oriental medicine.

bladders are cut into wafers and chewed or ground into powder and added to food or beverages. Users believe bear galls will cure blood and liver ailments, nausea, swelling, hemorrhoids, and a variety of other ills. In some countries, such as Korea, American bear galls are in such demand that hundreds are smuggled in yearly. A gall that sells in Tennessee or North Carolina for $100 may fetch as much as $5,000 in Korea, and that is considered a bargain. In Seoul, the capital of South Korea, a gall bladder from an endangered Korean bear is worth three times as much.

The sale of wildlife is illegal in Tennessee, North Carolina, and Georgia. However, in the heart of black bear country and adjacent to Great Smoky Park is a Cherokee Indian reservation, where the sale of wildlife products is not affected by state and federal laws. Also, the sale of claws and other parts is legal in some other states, such as Idaho and Mon-

tana. Claws from the Smokies often end up in western states where they are sold in gift shops, usually incorporated into expensive silver and gold jewelry. "The claws go all over the country, wherever there's a market," says Cook. Adds Idaho hunter Steve Galles, "There's a lot of people in this world that are going to do anything for the buck. You shouldn't be able to sell parts of animals and things like that. If you couldn't sell those, then you'd take the commercialization out of it, and you'd stop a lot of the poaching that goes on right now."

Cook believes that poachers killed about 300 black bears in the Smoky Mountains park area between 1985 and 1988. A third of all bear deaths in southern Appalachia was attributed to poaching. And the problem was becoming regional as poaching rings started operating in Shenandoah National Park, some 250 miles northeast of the Smokies. Products from the bears in some cases were shipped

Willard Lambert, owner of Sissy, commands the bear to stand on her hind legs, then rewards her with Doritos. Most such exhibits have been outlawed in Tennessee, where it was thought the bears were being captured illegally as cubs to supply the roadside market.

Joe the Bear and his stuffed predecessor are exhibited for the amusement of tourists passing through Sevierville, Tennessee, about twelve miles north of Great Smoky Mountains National Park. Roadside exhibits such as this were once common around the park, but state law has banned them. Only bears caged before the law was passed remain on exhibit.

through Canada before going to the Orient. One man who paid federal agents $2,740 for fifty-one galls had traveled to the Smokies from Livonia, Michigan. A Korean, he used his seventy-eight-year-old mother as a "mule," a person who delivers illegal goods, to get the galls to Korea.

Black bear poaching was having widespread effects. From 1981 to 1987, bear researcher Roger Powell of North Carolina State University radio-collared about fifty bears in the Pisgah National Forest, adjacent to Great Smoky Mountains National Park. Powell found that about a dozen of the collared bears were killed by poachers. He became especially alarmed when poachers killed a collared bear while it was hibernating. The bear was sleeping in a hollow tree about five feet in diameter located only 200 yards off the Blue Ridge Parkway. The poachers cut down the tree in order to kill the bear. When two of Powell's assistants visited the den, they found the bear's skull with a bullet hole between the eyes. Powell says the poachers could have located the bear only by tuning in on its radio collar. He immediately cut back on his collaring program because, he said, "I feel it's unethical for us to contribute to any negative impact on these bears." In 1988 he had only two bears collared, but could have had as many as twenty. "Those major chunks of data that come in from radio telemetry have been stopped," he says. "We're doing things that have the potential to benefit the bears, and yet we have to close down because somebody is doing something illegal." The loss of data is especially unfortunate, he says, because his study area offered a better opportunity to locate collared bears than did other sites. He and his team were able to locate some individual bears 400 times within a year, about 10 times more frequently than most studies would be able to do. He says he will not resume his collaring project until he can obtain some newly developed collars whose signals cannot be received by poachers.

By 1985 it was becoming increasingly clear that state game rangers alone could not stop the poaching. Steve Nifong, who started working in the Great Smoky Mountains National Park area in 1979, said he was unable to make an arrest for illegal bear hunting during his first ten years in the area. Many times he failed to stop illegal hunts because of legal loopholes or because the hunters communicated efficiently among themselves, warning one another of Nifong's presence in time to escape. Several times he let hunters go because he was afraid that he did not have cases strong enough to hold up in court. He feared that if he arrested a poacher and a court let the poacher off, others would conclude that wildlife laws could be flouted. "I laid in bed at night trying to figure out how to do something to break it up," he said.

As the situation became increasingly serious—biologist Bill Cook believed that the survival of the black bears was threatened—Tennessee, North Carolina, and Georgia joined with federal agents to carry out Operation Smoky, a covert investigation designed to infiltrate the local market in bears. The operation was conducted in the utmost secrecy.

Poachers sell bear claws for as little as a dollar apiece. Jewelers transform the claws into silver-mounted jewelry. Demand for such jewelry by the public fuels the poacher's interest in killing game illegally.

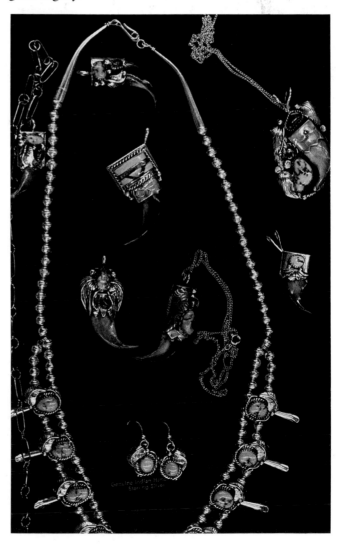

Fewer than a dozen people in the state agencies even knew it was being conducted. Says Gary T. Myers, executive director of the Tennessee Wildlife Resources Agency, an opening for a conservation officer in the Smokies area was filled so discreetly and the officer assigned to Operation Smoky with such complete secrecy that the other state officers did not even know the new man had been hired. The intense secrecy caused many southern Appalachia residents to believe that the states were ignoring the bear problem, and the wildlife agencies often were roundly chastised for their apparent apathy. Myers recalled that North Carolina, ready to make arrests before Tennessee had completed its work, delayed action despite increasing public criticism because officials knew that any arrests could ruin the big covert project.

The operation was slow because the undercover agents had to make contact with the poachers and work their way into the poachers' confidence. To do this, the agents set up a variety of front businesses. In one case, when the agents set up a front company that made hunting videos, the poachers unwittingly played into the agents' hands. The poachers' egos often led them to make flagrant displays of poached animals, even driving around their hometowns with poached bears tied to the hoods of their vehicles. Playing on this ego-driven bravado, the agents persuaded the poachers to have themselves videotaped during illegal hunts. The tapes were later used as evidence in court. The agents also assumed the roles of real estate agents and marine-supplies salesmen. Bill Cook, working undercover, posed as a jeweler in search of bear claws.

Biologist Bill Cook at his home near Knoxville, Tennessee, worked as an undercover agent and forensics expert during Operation Smoky, which broke up a poaching ring that Cook believed was on the verge of wiping out the black bears of Great Smoky Mountains National Park.

A shop advertising bear-claw jewelry in Hungry Horse, Montana. Claws taken from illegally killed Tennessee bears may be sold in gift shops as far away as New Mexico and Montana, the store owners unaware of the claws' criminal origins.

The agents soon found that the poachers did not limit their criminal activities to killing bears. Some also were involved in drug dealing and stolen property. Some were guilty of arson on federal park lands, burning woodlands to clear areas for growing marijuana. They also burned woodlands in retaliation for speeding tickets, fines for illegal fishing, and other punishments. Cook believes that two men apprehended with stolen cubs torched 2,100 acres of woodland at the scene of their crime in retaliation for being caught.

Not all of those involved in the poaching ring had criminal records. Some were lawyers, furniture makers, broom makers, and doctors. Gwang Soo Han, a Korean who lived in North Carolina, trafficked in gall bladders though he himself was a doctor and did not believe in the medicinal qualities ascribed to galls.

Many of the illegal hunts that the agents joined took place in Great Smoky Mountains National Park, which the poachers called "the big world." Once deep inside the park, the poachers felt safe and did not worry about being caught. Usually, they hunted with only one gun among them, so that if they *were* caught only one firearm would be confiscated. They hunted mostly by night, traveling in four-wheel-drive vehicles, communicating by two-way radio, and using good dogs fitted with radio collars. Hounds were usually used to track the bears, backed up by strike dogs—animals such as pit bulls that would attack the bear once it was cornered. A "rig dog" was sometimes used to locate bears along roads. The rig dog rode on the front of a vehicle, where it could scent bear tracks. To increase the odds of finding a bear, poachers sometimes baited fields with honey and other sweets. Hunters paid as much as $500 to join these illegal hunts, shooting anything the dogs chased, including wild boars and raccoons in addition to bears.

The agents who infiltrated the poaching groups

Cade's Cove in Great Smoky Mountains National Park is a haven for black bears. The animals often cause "bear jams," traffic tie-ups that occur when park visitors stop to watch as the animals feed along roads. Gates into the area from the outside are locked at night, but some poachers reportedly had keys to the locks and often slipped in at night to kill bears illegally.

were in constant danger whenever they were afield. A forty-four-year-old car dealer, said to be one of the top salesmen in his district, frequently threatened agents posing as hunters. He told two agents that he hoped they would not turn out to be law officers, because he would hate to have to dig two graves in one night. He also told agents about arson he had committed in Tennessee and North Carolina. Eventually he sold the agents $2,700 worth of bear galls and paws along with a stolen vehicle.

The agents routinely resold bear parts bought from poachers, so that the same set of claws or the same collection of gall bladders might have been used in several transactions to catch several different illegal traffickers. For example, galls purchased from poachers were sold to Dr. Han. The money Han paid was then used to help finance the undercover operation. In order to be sure that the sales involved illegal products, the agents had to determine scientifically that the materials being bought and sold really were from bears. This task fell to Cook, who spent hours in a laboratory running tests to find out which poachers had sold the agents bear parts, and which had sold them pig bladders and chicken parts.

Operation Smoky came to an end in August 1988, when conservation officers in Tennessee, North Carolina, and Georgia joined federal agents in a series of surprise morning raids that led to more than forty arrests. When the cases went to court, some poachers received prison sentences. Six members of one family were fined a total of $24,000. Dennis Russell, the car salesman who had threatened the lives of undercover agents, was held for trial without bail because a judge thought he was a danger to the agents. Russell broke down and cried uncontrollably in court.

Some local residents resented the arrests. Creation of Smoky Mountains Park in 1934 forced many long-time residents off of land that became federally protected. These evictions helped to unify opposition to the park among some families. In the Audubon television special, Leonard Williams, who was not arrested but whose relatives were fined the $24,000, declared, "Blood's always thicker than water. So when you do something to one, you just about do it to 50 percent of the county. . . . And you're not going to stop the poaching in Graham County, nor on the national park, nor nowhere's else." Nevertheless, the operation had many local supporters. Cook said he was surprised at the number of people who expressed their appreciation for the effort. Newspapers throughout the park region editorialized in favor of Operation Smoky. One editor wrote that the poachers' lawyers would doubtless plea for leniency. "They will describe their clients as good ol' boys who, though they slighted the law, didn't really have criminal intent. They were just doing what their daddies and granddaddies always had done. Such pleas should be turned aside. Those men knew exactly what they were doing. They knew it was destructive to mountain bears. They just didn't give a damn. . . . Such people are parasites. . . . They deserve no sympathy at all."

No one thinks that Operation Smoky has put an end to poaching in the southern Appalachians, but it should help reduce it. University of Tennessee

Bear researcher Roger Powell in his office at North Carolina State University. Behind him is an antenna used for locating radio-collared bears and a hide from a road-killed black bear. Powell suspended his collaring operation when he suspected that poachers were using the signals from the collars to locate and kill hibernating bears in their dens.

biologist Mike Pelton, who headed a 1983 study that indicated that poaching was a major cause of black bear mortality in southern Appalachia, said the arrests should help reduce illegal hunting by slowing down poachers. Some, he believes, will give up poaching. The operation also garnered a lot of press coverage and interested local people in anti-poaching activities, which should benefit bears and other wildlife.

Cook believes the help came none too soon, that putting an end to poaching is crucial to survival of black bears in the Smokies. The bears, he says, are under a great deal of pressure from human development and from sheer numbers of people. Almost 10 million people visit the Great Smoky Mountains National Park each year—more than visit Yosemite, Grand Canyon, and Yellowstone combined. Roads are jammed, and towns catering to visitors have

sprung up, pressing into the bears' habitat. "We indeed could lose this population in the southern Appalachians," Cook believes. "The status of the black bear in this area has been truly tested. The combination of illegal killing of bears in this area is the—should be—our major concern as wildlife managers."

Despite the benefits of Operation Smoky, Pelton fears reprisals. He worries that poachers may set forest fires or put out poison for bears. He knows of one case in which a conservation officer's house was burned. In addition, after arrests were made, park rangers arrived at the Great Smoky Mountains National Park one morning to find that severed bear paws had been placed at the door to the park's public information building. They found a bear's head in front of an entrance sign along a heavily used road into the park.

Michael Pelton, a biologist with the University of Tennessee and one of the nation's leading black bear researchers, headed a 1983 study that indicated that poaching was a major cause of black bear mortality in the southern Appalachian Mountains. He thinks a recent federal undercover operation that broke up a poaching ring in Great Smoky Mountains National Park will help cut down on bear deaths, but also fears the poachers will seek revenge by killing more wildlife.

Wildlife Forensics Lab: Finding the Clues to Crime

When conservation officers build cases against poachers, the evidence they use may include organs such as black bear gall bladders, fragments of bone or antler, bits of hair and fur, or even bloodstains on a poacher's clothing. But before that evidence can be submitted in court, the officers have to be able to prove that the organs and blood came from an animal taken illegally. For example, they have to prove that the gall bladders they bought from a suspected poacher are in fact from a bear, not a pig, or that the bloodstains on a poacher's shirt are those of an illegal animal, not from the poacher's cut hand.

Difficulties in identifying evidence to the satisfaction of a court judge have been major obstacles in the prosecution of many cases in the past. But conservation officers received a tremendous boost in September 1988, when the new National Fish and Wildlife Forensics Laboratory opened in Oregon. Located in a rambling, modern building on Southern Oregon State College in Ashland, the lab is the first wildlife crime lab in the United States. Dubbed "the Scotland Yard of wildlife crime," it is equipped to identify the species of origin of various wildlife artifacts and to match the artifacts to suspects and crime scenes, working much the same way that a police crime lab does.

The lab includes a serology section that can determine the source of blood and tissue samples brought in as evidence. Identification is made through chemical analysis and through an examination of tissue DNA, the genetic components found in all plant and animal cells. Specimens that cannot be identified by serology are taken to the Criminalistics Section, which, to identify such substances as sea turtle shells, carved ivory, sea turtle oil, and powdered rhinoceros horn, uses a scanning electron microscope and such techniques as an analysis of the gases given off by a specimen as it is destroyed by heat. The latter technique can be used to determine, for example, whether sea turtle oil is an ingredient in imported suntan lotion.

Electron microscopes are used to identify species by their hair, fur, and leather. Lab personnel can identify poachers by fingerprints left on firearms and other objects and can help investigators by collecting and examining such evidence as footprints, tire tracks, and bullets. Bullets can be test-fired from confiscated rifles to see if marks on the bullets match those on bullets found in illegally killed animals.

The lab includes a decontamination room, where technicians can work safely on material that may pose a health hazard. Also, bald and golden eagles found shot, poisoned, electrocuted on power lines, or dead of natural causes are sent by federal agents to the lab, where the carcasses are entered in the National Eagle Repository. Then the eagles are packaged and sent to Native Americans for use in making ceremonial objects.

The lab is critical in dealing with animal products that enter international trade, especially since the United States is the world's largest wildlife trader, accounting for about a fifth of the estimated $5 billion in trade worldwide. "It is very difficult to look at a handbag, for example, and tell if it was made from an alligator or a crocodile," says Ken Goddard, the lab director. "Alligators are biologically secure and can be sold commercially, but crocodiles are critically endangered. The lab will make identification, and thus prosecution of violators, possible."

Covert Operations: A Real Solution?

Though undercover investigations such as Operation Smoky yield striking results, they are expensive both in dollars and manpower. Also, state legislators are sometimes reluctant to fund covert operations because they believe the investigations give conservation officers an unfair advantage over law violators, an odd attitude that seems to treat wildlife-law enforcement as if it were some kind of game. Covert operations also are designed to work intensively within a small geographic area, getting the worst offenders. They are not effective against the more-common opportunistic poacher. Consequently, the front line of defense against poachers remains the state or federal conservation officer working alone.

To locate poachers, conservation officers routinely patrol their territories, driving and hiking through areas where poaching is likely to occur. In winter, during deer season, they often spend entire nights in rural areas, sitting in chilly pickup trucks, peering into the darkness, looking for the glow of spotlights used by poachers to locate deer. During waterfowl season they work from the darkness before dawn to the darkness of night, checking hunters in the field and looking for illegal baiting. Their task is made especially difficult because most state wildlife-law enforcement agencies are severely understaffed. For example, New York City's police force alone outnumbers the conservation officers of all fifty states combined by more than ten to one. The nation's 17 million hunters outnumber conservation officers about 9,000 to one. Most states are assigned only one or two federal agents and have scarcely one state conservation officer per county, and in some western states a single officer may be responsible for hundreds, even thousands, of square miles of wild country. In areas that lack good roads, rangers can patrol only a small portion of their territory with any regularity.

Conservation officers are further hampered by the many duties assigned to them. In most states, in addition to enforcing wildlife laws, officers are expected to teach hunter-education classes, make public relations appearances at civic functions, and police such activities as recreational boating, snowmobiling, littering, and pollution. It is often a discouraging business, too, because even when arrests are made, judges frequently hand down weak sentences. For example, two men arrested on Long Island, New York, in 1986 for illegal possession of 294 birds, including the largest collection of bald eagles,

hawks, owls, vultures, and falcons ever confiscated in the United States, faced penalties of five years' imprisonment and $104,000 in fines. But a Brooklyn federal court judge sentenced one of the men to only six months in prison, the other to two months. Weak penalties are more often the rule than the exception in wildlife-law violations. Of the four men involved in the killing of yellow-crowned night herons in Louisiana, mentioned at the start of this chapter, only two received jail sentences, each for only two months. One of the poachers was permitted to serve his jail sentence a few days at a time over a period of several years so he would not lose his job. All four received fines of only $500 each, out of a potential penalty running into the thousands of dollars, and each was required to perform 312 hours of community service.

However, most conservation officers believe there are two fundamental solutions to lack of staff and weak sentences. One of these is to educate the public on the need for sound wildlife conservation and for good hunting ethics. Federal special agent

James Bartee believes conservation education should start in the first grade and continue to the end of schooling.

The second solution is the cooperation of the private citizen. Outdoor enthusiasts such as hunters, birders, hikers, and campers spend a great deal of time in the field. Conservation officers urge them to observe what goes on around them. Poaching should be reported to local officers. A license plate number from a vehicle used by a poacher, or even a good description of the vehicle, can lead to an arrest.

To make it easy for citizens to report violations, most states have established special telephone hotlines patterned after the Operation Game Thief program pioneered by the New Mexico Game and Fish Department in 1977. These programs permit people to provide information about poachers anonymously. The call that alerted Louisiana officers to the three men who gunned down nearly 700 yellow-crowned night herons came over Operation Game Thief phone lines. In most cases, rewards are given to callers who provide information that leads to an arrest. In some big-game poaching cases, the reward may be nearly $1,000. New Mexico officials have reported that about 90 percent of the calls they receive reveal crimes that would have remained undetected. About 98 percent of 1,127 violations reported in New Mexico through Operation Game Thief during the program's first eight years resulted in convictions. Private citizens can also help by urging legislators to enact harsher penalties for wildlife-law violations and by expressing their concern to judges who hand down light penalties.

Despite difficulties and obstacles, cause for optimism has never been greater. Says Dave Hall, a special federal agent in Louisiana, "We've made a lot of progress. We're starting to see our prosecutors take it seriously. We're starting to see the people get more involved. I think we're starting to see wildlife crime identified for what it is: It's stealing, no different than taking gold out of Fort Knox."

HUMANITY AND NATURE
TOMORROW'S DILEMMA

PLEASE THINK FOR just a bit about what we have wrought in North America within the past 500 years. We have journeyed from a time in which our forebears stood on the eastern edge of an uncharted Atlantic and pondered its invisible, distant reaches, and come to a time in which the vast ocean has been so humbled that it seems to be rotting from the touch of human industry and waste. Through a combination of advanced technology and precipitously increasing populations, we have become a force capable of shaping the face of the globe. We have altered natural environments so drastically and so often and in so many places that the Earth and the atmosphere that surrounds it are becoming less and less protective and nurturing of living things. Humanity stands in the shadow of global catastrophe.

The signs of that looming catastrophe have been around a long, long time. They were there thousands of years ago, when salts from irrigation water poisoned farmlands in the Fertile Crescent of the Tigris and Euphrates valley. They were there in biblical times when deforestation and overgrazing turned verdant lands in the Middle East into deserts. The signs are with us now, and becoming more urgent. We can see them in Asia, where the cutting of mountain forests in Tibet, Nepal, Bhutan, and northern India since the 1970s has removed the trees and other vegetation that absorbed the monsoon rains. Now the annual floods that once nourished the croplands of Bangladesh with fresh soil and nutrients have turned with increasing frequency into deadly torrents that rush out of the denuded mountains, leaving millions homeless and many dead.

We see other signs in Africa, Asia, and Latin America, where the cutting of forests is leading to erosion of topsoil and creating new deserts, where overgrazing by livestock in arid regions is laying waste to grasslands. Worldwide, desertification is eating up nearly 15 million acres a year, land needed for food production in starving countries.

We see more signs in the United States. Toxic runoff channeled from western agricultural lands into national wildlife refuges, where it kills the birds the refuges were created to protect, is one of the signs. The tumors on the sea turtles of Florida's Indian River and the corroded skins of the dolphins off New Jersey are also signs.

In the past we could ignore the signs and still escape the more tragic effects of our work. We always had more land to move to, new worlds to settle. But as we carry history into the twenty-first century, we are beginning to learn that we have crowded the limits of the Earth.

Challenges and Catastrophes

It is hard to believe that an animal as seemingly frail as a human could challenge the survival of an entire planet, but when there are 5 billion of us at work, and more of us every day—100 million more each year—the cumulative impacts of our actions mount and climb until they overrun land, sea, and air.

In centuries past, when a good day's travel was measured in dozens rather than thousands of miles and people were few in number, the Earth stood out widely on all sides. If the forests were cut in one place, millions of acres more lay just ahead. If we drowned one river valley with a dam, or siphoned off its flow with canals, the impact was local. Seemingly innumerable rivers and streams still ran untouched. Wildlife could be used without limit because, somehow, more would always be there. Even the buffalo hunters of the nineteenth century and the market hunters who wiped out the passenger pigeon did not at first believe that they had killed off the game. They thought the bison and the pigeons had just gone somewhere else, like children in a game of hide-and-seek. It was a while before the hunters realized that they had come to the end of something.

Like the Americans of the nineteenth century we, too, are coming to the end of something. But it is an ending on a mammoth scale. We are coming to the end of things such as fresh air and free-running rivers, the end of vital portions of the global atmosphere, the end of the very climate and weather that have sustained life on our planet. We have gone from the mere slaughter of species to jeopardizing the entire globe. The conservation challenges that face us today, unlike those at the start of the twentieth century, are fights not for the survival of wildlife alone, but for our own survival, and they confront us with an urgency we have never before experienced. Said Thomas Lovejoy, the Smithsonian Institution's assistant secretary for external affairs, when he addressed the American Institute of Biological Sciences in 1988, "I am utterly convinced that most of the great environmental struggles will be either won or lost in the 1990s, and that by the next century it will be too late."

Such a statement is a harbinger of a somber new era for environmentalism. Conservationists traditionally have been concerned with saving resources for future generations. Theodore Roosevelt, the consummate early conservationist, said in an address to Congress in 1907, "To waste, to destroy, our natural resources, to skin and exhaust the land instead of using it so as to increase its usefulness, will result in undermining in the days of our children the very prosperity which we ought by right to hand down to them amplified and developed." The 1916 law that created the National Park Service says that the fundamental purpose of the national parks is "to conserve the scenery and the natural and historic objects therein and the wildlife therein and to provide for the enjoyment of the same in such manner and by such means as will leave them unimpaired for the enjoyment of future generations." This traditional concern with future generations is being overturned because we will not have to wait for succeeding generations to suffer the ruin we cause. We will suffer it ourselves.

We have already seen the first indications of what we will face in the near future. Meteorological data indicate that the Earth is warming, the warmth a byproduct of the greenhouse effect. The greenhouse effect begins when tons and tons of carbon are poured into the atmosphere by the burning of coal, oil, and natural gas and by the burning of tropical rain forests to clear land for agriculture. In 1988 alone, the burning of fossil fuels added 5.5 billion tons of carbon to the atmosphere. From the scorched rain forests came as much as 2.5 billion tons. Within the next twenty years, carbon entering the atmosphere from the burning of fossil fuels could rocket to 10 billion tons yearly.

Over the past thirty years, the amount of carbon dioxide in the air has increased from 315 parts per million to 352, by far the highest concentration of the past 160,000 years. As atmospheric carbon builds up it acts like the glass of a greenhouse, holding in heat from the sun and keeping it from radiating back into space as much of it normally does. The greater the carbon concentration, the greater the amount of heat the atmosphere retains.

opposite: *A stream glows in the morning light of Glacier National Park. In the past, park boundaries protected such scenic areas from human intrusion. But parks are no protection against current problems such as global warming, which threatens to wipe out entire ecosystems, including forests and grasslands.*

This greenhouse effect threatens to raise the average temperature of the globe by as much as eight degrees Fahrenheit by the year 2050, warmer than the Earth has been for some 2 million years.

The damage will be tremendous. A change in average temperature of less than one degree every ten years in northern regions will move the range of some tree species northward 60 to 100 miles. But since trees cannot adapt as quickly as the Earth apparently is warming, whole species are likely to die off. Trees that die ultimately might be replaced by others adapted to warmer weather, but replacement will take centuries. Meanwhile, as the dead trees die and rot, the carbon they contain in their cells will escape into the atmosphere as a gas and speed the warming process.

The problems of global warming will be compounded for wildlife species living in national parks and refuges that are surrounded by developed lands. With no pathway to new habitat, they will be locked within the confines of the withering preserves. Say the authors of *The State of the World 1989*, an excellent handbook on the Earth's environmental status and the source for much of this chapter, "Indeed, various biological reserves created in the past decade to protect species diversity could become virtual death traps as wildlife attempt to survive in conditions for which they are poorly suited. Accelerated species extinction is an inevitable consequence of a rapid warming."

Sea levels will rise, and the salt seas will invade the drinking-water sources of coastal cities such as New York and Miami. Agricultural lands and coastal towns in nations such as Bangladesh and Egypt will flood, forcing more than 25 million people from their homes in just those two nations. Weather will change. Warming is likely to cause severe and unpredictable droughts and heat waves. Vast crop-growing regions of the Earth will fail as rainfall declines. The unusually hot summer of 1988 foreshadowed what in the future may be the norm. In that year, the U.S. grain harvest fell below consumption for the first time in recent history. The reverberations of such a disaster extend beyond U.S. boundaries: The 100 million tons of grain usually available for export each year were lost. If current warming trends continue, the grain and corn-producing regions of the midwestern United States will become semi-arid, cutting crop production in some areas by 50 to 100 percent. In parts of Canada a longer winter growing season will increase the amount of croplands, but

summer corn crops will probably decline. Crop failures in Third World nations, home to some 4 billion people, will bring starvation to millions upon millions.

Despite the relative speed, in geologic terms, with which the temperature increase apparently is occurring—the five hottest years of the past century occurred in the 1980s—it has scarcely been noticed by the average person. Most people may not perceive the change until sometime in the 1990s, when the burning heat waves and prolonged droughts that may soon typify the average summer will begin. But that does not mean that global warming is not already taking place. Scientists who monitor annual average temperatures have found an alarmingly consistent increase in the past two decades.

Global warming is an international problem. It requires an international solution, just as the protection of wide-ranging species such as dolphins, sea turtles, and sharks requires an international solution. As our environmental problems have become global in extent, they have diminished the role that any one nation can hope to play in solving them. This is shown not by global warming alone. We see it in the pollution of our seas, discussed in previous chapters. We see it elsewhere. We see it in acid precipitation.

Acid precipitation is another product of the use of fossil fuels. When coal high in sulfur is burned, the sulfur is released into the atmosphere. When gasoline is burned in automobile engines, nitrogen compounds flow into the atmosphere. The sulfur and the nitrogen compounds each combine with oxygen to form acids. These acids are washed from the atmosphere by rain and snow, and thus enter lakes and streams. In Canada, New York State, New England, and the northern European nations, acid precipitation has killed tens of thousands of lakes by raising their acidity to levels that are deadly to the microscopic animals, insects, and smaller fish that most freshwater wildlife species need to survive. Lakes in which fish once thrived are now barren.

Acid precipitation damages cities, too. It has damaged historic buildings in Europe, slowly dissolving metal and stone sculptures. It is slowly eroding the Lincoln Memorial in Washington, D.C. It is costing billions of dollars yearly in building repairs. And increasing evidence indicates that the pollutants that cause acid precipitation are affecting human health by increasing the intensity and frequency of asthma attacks and by working deep into our lungs

Condominiums loom over a beach on San Padre Island, Texas. Global warming produced by air pollution threatens human coastal development as sea levels rise. Cities such as New York and Miami may be inundated if temperatures continue to climb.

to gnaw at our tissues, perhaps increasing the incidence of certain types of cancer.

Like the greenhouse effect, acid precipitation is a global problem. More than half of Canada's acid precipitation originates in the United States, and acids that originate over the Soviet Union travel into Europe and the arctic. To stop the spread of acid precipitation will cost billions of dollars and require the cooperation of many nations. But throughout the 1980s, prospects for change were slim. For example, the midwestern U.S. power plants that produce most of the acidity that wafts into Canada have refused to accept the burden of moderating Can-

ada's acid-rain problem, and the U.S. government has repeatedly fumbled every offer from Canada for a two-nation effort to limit acid precipitation. In a time when environmental problems have become international in scope, human society has remained heedlessly regional in its commitments.

Another global catastrophe is in the making in the Earth's ozone layer. Ozone gas is relatively rare in the atmosphere—at its highest concentrations some eight to sixteen miles above the Earth's surface it amounts to only a few parts per million. Nevertheless, it is vital to all life because it is the only atmospheric gas that keeps the sun's deadly ultraviolet rays away from us. But human-made chemicals are destroying the ozone layer.

The primary ozone-destroying chemicals are called chlorofluorocarbons, or CFCs. They were invented in the 1930s and marketed for use as coolants in refrigerator and air conditioning systems. One CFC coolant was given the trade name Freon by its manufacturer, E. I. du Pont de Nemours & Company. CFCs also are used to make some types of foam insulation, popularly called Styrofoam, a trade name originated by Dow Chemical Company. Some forms of the chemicals were also widely used to make aerosol cans work.

CFCs released into the atmosphere, for example through leaks in air conditioners or through the use of aerosol sprays, can, through a series of chemical reactions, cause ozone to break down. This was first discovered over Antarctica, where environmental and atmospheric conditions speed ozone destruction, creating huge holes in which ozone concentrations are cut in half. One hole late in the 1980s was twice the size of the United States.

Ozone holes have been discovered over the arctic, too, and ozone concentrations are quite likely declining in areas all over the globe. As the ozone drops off, the amount of ultraviolet light reaching the Earth's surface increases. Ultraviolet light causes drying of human skin and increases the incidence of skin cancers, including melanoma, which kills about a third of its victims. Ultraviolet light has other harmful effects as well. The Environmental Protection Agency estimates that during the next ninety years, increased ultraviolet radiation will cause as many as 2.8 million cases of cataracts, which is a blurring of vision caused by a clouding of the lens of the eye. Some evidence suggests that ultraviolet radiation suppresses the human body's immune responses, making people more susceptible to disease.

Ultraviolet rays will also affect plants and animals. One soybean species important as a food crop declined in productivity when experimentally exposed to the amount of ultraviolet radiation that would occur if the concentration of the ozone layer dropped 25 percent. The microscopic plants, called phytoplankton, that float at the ocean's surface and form the basis of the marine food chain could become more than a third less productive under the same level of ozone depletion. This would affect the fish populations that feed on them, and the animals that feed on the fish. Everything from crustaceans to whales would be jeopardized. Some commercially

opposite: *Effluents roll out of an Oregon lumber mill. Careless discharge of effluents has caused worldwide air and water pollution and now threatens all life.*

important fish species, such as anchovies, would decline significantly at even a 9 percent level of ozone depletion.

The problem underlying such massive threats as ozone depletion and acid precipitation is overpopulation. In 1950 the globe supported 2.5 billion people. By 1987 that number had more than doubled. Within the next four decades it is expected to reach nearly 9 billion.

As populations grow, nations have to draw upon their resources with increasing intensity. As part of the process, they create more wastes and toxic emissions, compounding the environmental problems that face the world today. In some cases, burgeoning populations, and the economic problems they create, force nations to adopt virtually suicidal policies. One example is the destruction of rain forests in Latin America, Southeast Asia, and Africa. In many areas the forests are being cut and burned at unprecedented rates in an effort to create croplands. However, because rain-forest soils generally are not fertile enough to be turned into productive farmland, the populations of these areas are ultimately faced with a crisis in the availability of foods and other needs. Meanwhile, in return for the quick profits made by converting the forests to crops, these nations destroy a valuable resource that could provide income indefinitely if properly husbanded.

Similarly, as populations in major cities grow, air pollution from industry and automobiles increases. Waste disposal becomes a more and more difficult challenge, especially in an era in which the oceans seem no longer able to hold all the garbage that is dumped into them. Even in affluent nations such as the United States, increasing amounts of wildlife habitat are being lost as cities and suburbs sprawl into surrounding countrysides. Moreover, demand for energy and other resources, as outlined in the chapter on the Arctic National Wildlife Refuge, is sending human development into all corners of the globe. Even the Antarctic is threatened by overfishing as nations such as Japan and the Soviet Union send vessels there to harvest massive quantities of krill, the small creatures upon which many other species in the Antarctic ecosystem depend.

Global Problems, Global Solutions

At the start of the twentieth century, most problems in conservation could be corrected at the national level. The exceptions, such as migratory-bird protection, were relatively few. Even today, many problems can be solved within national borders. Wolf protection within the United States is one example. But because many vital environmental problems have become global in their effects, we need global cooperation to solve them.

In some cases this has already been attempted. On September 16, 1987, at a meeting held in Montreal to investigate ways to stop ozone depletion, twenty-four nations signed a protocol calling for a 50 percent cut in CFC production by 1998. Since then, other nations have signed the protocol, bringing the number of signatories close to forty. Similarly, in 1989 representatives of twenty-four nations gathered at an environmental summit conference in The Hague to discuss the need for international cooperation on environmental problems. One suggestion called for establishing a new United Nations organization called Globe that would monitor environmental problems and set various goals, such as air-quality standards. Globe also would be empowered to take sanctions against nations that ignore the antipollution regulations.

Actions such as these have proved only superficially promising. Loopholes built into the CFC protocol are so liberal that if all were taken advantage of, they would prevent the signed nations from achieving their goal of halving CFC use. Also, the limits on CFC production were designed to cut ozone depletion to 2 percent by the year 2075, but recent research has shown that the global ozone layer is *already* 2 percent depleted, with depletion even greater near the poles. Similar weaknesses surfaced at the international environmental conference. Leading nations such as France opposed the idea of a monitoring board on the grounds that the board would interfere with national sovereignty. And four of the world's biggest polluters—the United States, the Soviet Union, China, and Great Britain—did not even participate.

The world's various national governments are playing much the same game that the states played in the early days of wildlife conservation—placing more emphasis on their political and legal rights than on the need for a sound and healthy environment. If the nations continue to function in this way, then the environment is likely to continue its deterioration to a point at which it brings crisis into all lives—human, animal, plant, and planet. Such a crisis undoubtedly would galvanize citizen concern and force governments to initiate programs designed to correct the situation. But by then it probably would be too late to minimize the damage. We can see this happening with global warming. Both our society and our government ignored the warnings of scientists who predicted a rise in global temperatures at least a quarter of a century ago. Now, it is impossible to reverse the warming trend. We can only hope to stop it before it becomes so intense that the Earth as we know it cannot abide.

To avoid letting other environmental problems reach the point of no return, we should insist that our government join or initiate international treaties that set strong guidelines for stemming such problems as ozone depletion, air pollution, waste disposal, and pollution of the seas. Ultimately, we should establish an international agency, or at least an international plan, for protecting the global environment. In the words of the authors of *The State of the World 1989*, "This will require a strengthening of international institutions and a willingness to give up unilateral authority in some areas. . . . But just as national governments themselves first emerged as tentative and weak efforts to unite diverse tribes or city-states, so international institutions may one day become far more robust and central to the issues of our time."

In the 1940s we saw nations unite to fight a merciless common enemy that threatened millions of lives. The environmental enemies we face today are no less merciless. Every year in the United States, particulate pollution alone kills an estimated 100,000 people—about 1.25 times the number of U.S. military personnel killed in battle in each year of World War II. This is just a prelude to what lies ahead if problems such as ozone depletion are not solved or reduced. We are, in effect, fighting an invisible invasion force, and the battle is truly on the level of a world war. Yet the governments of the world have not approached this war with commitment or alacrity. For example, in 1986 the United States spent $273 billion to protect itself from other governments, but less than $20 billion to combat

International cooperation in solving environmental problems is vital if wild creatures and wild places as we know them are not to dissolve into little more than memories.

the pollution threats that surround and permeate the nation at all times. Germany in fiscal 1985 spent as much on military procurement and research and development—nearly $11 billion—as it would have taken to clean up the West German sector of the badly polluted North Sea. A mere two days of global military spending—about $5 billion—could fund for twenty years a United Nations plan to stop Third World desertification. The cost of research into the U.S. Star Wars Strategic Defense Initiative for 1987 alone—$3.7 billion—could have paid for a solar power system for a city of 200,000. Every two months Ethiopia spends on its military enough money—$12 million—to cover the annual cost of the United Nations' anti-desertification plan for that country. The cost of building three B-1B bombers equals the total amount spent by the U.S. government on renewable energy in fiscal years 1983 to 1985.

It is time, don't you think, that we armed ourselves with the wisdom and skills that an international community has at its disposal to fight the most threatening enemy that humankind has ever faced—the deadly byproducts of human technology and overpopulation. It is a fight to preserve all gen-

erations and all living things, from ancient trees to ocean creatures, from migrating cranes to wolves and humans.

What You Can Do

If somehow we could solve all the environmental problems and achieve all the conservation goals outlined in preceding chapters—ocean pollution, destruction of ancient forests, protection of endangered species—we would be on the threshold of a glowing new era in human history. We would have accomplished the unprecedented. And, most importantly, we would have laid the groundwork for solving the ever-bigger and more urgent problems that are rushing down upon us. Our ability to protect sea turtles or ancient trees is a measure of our ability to solve the many immense environmental problems we will meet within the next decade. It also is a measure of the hope we have for our continued survival in a healthy world.

You can play a vital role in conservation by making your views known to the elected officials who set the nation's political agenda. Letters to elected officials from citizens concerned about the state of our environment can help counter the influence of industries that too often place profit before environmental integrity and health. Revealing your beliefs and concerns to your elected officials can help shape the actions of legislative bodies. That is why the importance of contacting your congressional delegation is highlighted again and again in the following suggestions for how you can help create a better national environmental policy.

Here are some specifics.

What You Can Do for Wolves

Indiscriminate persecution of wolves by government programs has ended in the lower forty-eight states. However, as outlined in the chapter on wolves, the animals often still face the ages-old prejudices that led to their destruction on most of the continent in the past. Ranchers in Montana and Wyoming have at times galvanized local and congressional opposition to wolf reintroductions, both natural and artifi-

cial. Powerful elements in the hunting community, too, have entered the anti-wolf club. In 1987, *Outdoor Life* magazine, which caters to those who hunt and fish, ran a cover story telling hunters that they would lose massive quantities of big game if wolves returned to the West, even though no biological evidence supports this idea. In Minnesota, deer hunters have historically opposed wolf protection. In Alaska, the Department of Fish and Game has sought for decades to carry on annual wolf-control programs on the grounds that the wolves deprive human hunters of sporting opportunities by feeding on caribou, moose, and other natural game. The preferred method of control has been the shooting of wolves from airplanes. In some cases, individual wolves have been radio-collared so that the state's professional aerial hunters can use radio telemetry to locate the wolf when it rejoins its pack. That way, entire packs can be shot at once.

Congressional Action: Successful wolf management, including sound protection of wolves in Minnesota and reintroduction of wolves in the West, such as at Yellowstone National Park, depends on the success of wolf advocates in combating the many groundless arguments made against the wolf. You can help by letting your congressional delegation know that you would like to see wolves restored to Yellowstone National Park. There the wolf would once again become a part of the balance of nature, feeding on the park's burgeoning elk and bison herds. Also urge your delegations to resist efforts to allow ranchers in the northern Rocky Mountains to kill wolves indiscriminately. Urge them, too, to support plans to compensate ranchers should any livestock be lost to wolves and to provide sound control programs in the Rockies so that only identified livestock-killing wolves would be trapped.

You might also write to Alaska expressing your concern over plans to reduce wolf numbers in the name of game protection when little or nothing has been done to reduce the killing of caribou and other hoofed game by human hunters. In many cases, the hoofed species are low because of extensive human hunting and because of the impact of a series of severe winters. You might suggest to the Alaska Department of Natural Resources that hunting as a human pastime should not be given precedence over the natural relationship that exists between wolves and their prey. Urge the department to reduce human hunting levels before reducing wolf populations.

What You Can Do to Protect Our Shark Resource

Although sharks attack few people worldwide each year, humans kill millions of sharks. In fact, to even the score, sharks would have to wipe out about 4 million people yearly. As discussed in the shark chapter, scientific data suggest that sharks cannot stand the heavy losses they incur each year to sport and commercial fishing. Every shark biologist interviewed for this book predicted that severe population declines will occur in every shark species that is commercially fished if sound regulations governing take were not soon established and enforced. This would be a terrible loss, because sharks are important sea predators and doubtless fill an important ecological role that biologists have not yet begun to understand.

Sharks provide excellent meat for human consumption. However, if we are to enjoy them as a food resource, we have to manage their take carefully. Unfortunately, this is impossible at present. A panel of shark biologists who studied data on shark kills recently concluded that we do not have the data necessary to make sound decisions about shark management. You can help get these data by writing to the National Oceanic and Atmospheric Administration (NOAA) in the Department of Commerce in Washington, D.C., urging officials to establish a program for the study of shark population dynamics and of commercial and sport taking of sharks. Ask the officials to issue sound regulations to govern the take of sharks, with particular emphasis on tight restrictions on take until data are collected for making scientifically based management decisions.

Remember, too, that commercial fishing is based on consumer demand. As long as a market for

shark meat exists, fishermen will try to supply it. You may help slow the kill by refusing to buy shark meat until the resource is being properly managed.

Sport fishermen should make it a practice to release small sharks unharmed and should never kill sharks just for a picture with a kill. They should also refuse to take part in shark tournaments that lack size and catch limits.

Commercial fishermen should avoid overkill and should not fish in known shark birthing areas or in nearshore areas where shark pups mature.

Both sport and commercial fishermen should support biological researches, including tagging programs, since these help biologists understand shark population dynamics and provide information that helps ensure that no one ruins a resource valuable to both sport and commercial activities.

Congressional Action: Urge your congressional delegates to require NOAA to develop the programs and regulations mentioned here.

What You Can Do to Help Sea Turtles

Loss of nesting beaches to development has reduced many sea turtle nesting areas. Development is often controlled by local officials. If you live in areas where sea turtles nest, urge you local government to ensure that the animals are not jeopardized by development. In Florida, for example, local governments are working to find out what kind of beach lighting does not disrupt the normal behavior of sea turtle hatchlings as they break from their nests and head toward water.

Trade in sea turtle products is another problem. Even if you live inland, or come from a nation without sea turtles, if you travel to other countries you may encounter sea turtle products for sale, including soups, leather goods, and whole mounted turtles. Do not buy them. U.S. citizens will not be allowed to bring them into the country, since trade in sea turtle goods is banned here. If you try to import products from these animals, you can be arrested or fined, and the illegal material will certainly be confiscated. Tell dealers that you oppose the sale of these goods.

Jack Woody, head of the U.S. Fish and Wildlife

Service's sea turtle program, says the Fish and Wild-life Service has offered to give airline companies free brochures about illegal trade in wildlife products so that the brochures can be put into the envelopes in which the airlines distribute tickets. Though the airlines carry similar brochures about car rentals, they refuse to help inform customers about the laws governing international trade in wildlife. Urge the airlines to carry these brochures, which will benefit air travelers by letting them know in advance which wildlife products they cannot import into the United States.

Congressional Action: Sea turtles are international animals. Most species cross national boundaries, complicating the problems of protection and management. "No one nation can save them," says Woody, "but one nation acting alone can wipe them out." For this reason, Woody believes that one of the most important things that you can do is write your congressional delegation urging them to support establishment of international treaties for sea turtle conservation. One problem that an international treaty could address is the killing of thousands of turtles each year in drift nets set on the high seas by the Japanese, Koreans, and Taiwanese. The nets are up to 35 miles long and, says Woody, "catch and kill everything that hits them." It is estimated that some 35,000 miles of drift nets are being used in the Pacific alone.

Because one of the biggest problems facing sea turtles is pollution of the seas, Congress also should be urged to consider a multinational treaty governing the dumping of wastes on the open seas. At present, no law controls the use of the open seas, and tons of waste, including toxic materials, are dumped yearly into the oceans. However, any materials dumped at sea are likely to affect some nation eventually. "It all comes ashore somehow, somewhere," Woody says. You can also encourage the Environmental Protection Agency and the U.S. Army Corps of Engineers to establish and enforce powerful guidelines on coastal waste disposal. Oil companies and other corporations should be encouraged to practice safe transport of toxic materials. You can make your environmental concerns known to oil and chemical companies by telling your congressional delegations that you do not want approval given to drilling in refuges, to transporting toxic materials along coastal corridors, or to offshore oil development until private industries create sound plans for dealing with spills and other problems they generate.

What You Can Do to Protect Dolphins and Porpoises

Dolphin and porpoise populations are being assaulted on several levels. Evidence is mounting that ocean pollution is affecting dolphins and porpoises much as it affects sea turtles. Toxic pollution of the seas could wipe out entire dolphin populations.

The chapter on dolphins and porpoises describes how open-ocean populations of certain species, notably the spinner dolphin and spotted dolphin of the Eastern Tropical Pacific, are being ravaged by tuna fishermen who set huge nets that can trap thousands of dolphins at a time, drowning or crushing them. Common porpoises die in the thousands yearly in nets set off eastern Canada, while thousands of Dall's porpoises drown in salmon nets set by Japanese, Taiwanese, and South Koreans off Canada and Alaska. In Japan, local coastal populations are quite likely being decimated by killing for meat and to eliminate dolphins thought to compete with humans for fish and squid.

You might be able to help control or end the deaths of dolphins and porpoises in fishing nets by refusing to buy any tuna except albacore tuna, which is caught on hook and line, a method that does not harm the cetaceans.

It is difficult to influence the practices of another nation in its own waters, but if you express to the Japanese your disdain for the killing of porpoises for meat, you might be able to shape Japanese policy. Americans buy many Japanese products, and a lot of letters from American consumers may catch the attention of Japanese policy makers.

Your own personal habits can have an effect, too. If each of us can find ways to limit our production of waste products, we can go a long way toward solving the problems of ocean dumping. Also, keep in mind that a new federal ocean-plastics-pollution law says that if you spot a cruise ship or other vessel dumping plastic wastes at sea, you can receive a reward if you report information leading to the conviction of the vessel owners.

To stop or limit the deaths caused by such ocean

pollution, Bob Schoelkopf of the Marine Mammal Stranding Center at Brigantine, New Jersey, suggests that you write to the Environmental Protection Agency urging it to enforce regulations for cleaning up coastal waters and for putting an end to the indiscriminate dumping of wastes in ocean waters. Areas of particular concern include Boston Harbor; the New York Bight off New York and New Jersey, where New York City has for years dumped tons of wastes daily; Chesapeake Bay, where runoff from farm fields laden with fertilizers and pesticides is destroying the bay; the Gulf Coast, particularly along Texas and Louisiana where oil refineries stud the shoreline; and San Francisco Bay, where urban and agricultural runoff is taking a toll of the biological community. In addition to writing to EPA, concerned citizens should also express to city and state officials their interest in environmentally sound waste disposal.

Congressional Action: Let your congressional delegates know that you want the nation's pollution-control laws strictly enforced. Let them know that you are dissatisfied with the mediocre enforcement of the Clear Water Act, which has seen deadlines for cleanups ignored and extended. Urge them to support embargoes of fish products from nations that kill porpoises in fishing nets. Encourage support of legislation that requires that all tuna cans be labeled with the method of catch so consumers will know if dolphins and porpoises died to fill the can.

What You Can Do to Protect Our Untouched Forests

National Audubon Society wildlife specialist James Pissot has suggested that you urge the Forest Service to:

1. Reduce logging on the national forests to levels that can be sustained indefinitely. Eighty to 90 percent of the forests in Washington State and Oregon have been cut, and loggers are now squabbling over the few bones that remain. The ancient forests and the wildlife they sustain, says Pissot, can no longer tolerate political compromise and economic indulgence.

2. Move away from policies driven by logging and to move toward policies that seek to protect wildlife and the last stands of untouched forest.

3. Protect forever any stands of native, untouched forest that cover more than eighty acres.

Congressional Action: Write your congressional delegation asking them to order the Forest Service to initiate the goals outlined here.

What You Can Do to Improve U.S. Oil Development

Oil and natural gas are presently two of the world's most important fuels. Although the development of alternative fuels, such as solar and wind power, could eventually free us from or diminish the need for oil and gas, right now we are locked into those fossil fuels. To help ensure that our reliance on oil and gas does not continue to contribute to such environmental problems as global warming, acid precipitation, and pollution from spills, you can curb your own use of oil and gas by such simple measures as being sure that your house is well insulated—poorly insulated windows waste more oil through heat loss than the Prudhoe Bay oilfield produces each year. Also, avoid buying large, over-powered automobiles that gobble fuel.

Congressional Action: James Pissot, the National Audubon Society's wildlife specialist in Washington, D.C., recommends that you encourage your congressional delegation to:

1. Vote for better fuel efficiency standards for motor vehicles and for general lighting standards.

2. Ban offshore oil development in ecologically significant and sensitive areas unless strong regulations to limit spills, waste discharges, and other problems are imposed on the oil industry and strictly enforced.

3. Support efforts for the development of more efficient energy sources such as solar and wind power.

4. Keep the Arctic National Wildlife Refuge free of oil and gas development until the refuge's oil reserves become genuinely needed for national security *and* can be developed without ecological damage.

What You Can Do to Help the Platte River and Other Threatened Wetlands and Streams

The National Audubon Society's Edward Pembleton, who has worked for years to seek wise management of Platte River development, suggests that you can learn more about the threats facing the Platte River and adjacent wetlands and about Audubon's efforts to protect the Platte by requesting information from Audubon's Water Resources Program at 801 Pennsylvania Avenue SE, Suite 301, Washington, D.C. 20003. If you are interested in seeing the crane's spring migration and learning firsthand about the Platte River, write to Audubon's West-Central Regional Office, 200 South Wind Place, Suite 205, Manhattan, Kansas 66502 and ask the staff to put you on the list of participants in the annual Audubon Rivers Conference. At the conference you will learn more about water-development plans, river wildlife, and what you can do to promote wise use of rivers and wetlands.

Congressional Action: Let your delegates know that you do not want them to fund unneeded water projects, such as Two Forks Dam, that destroy valuable streams and important wildlife habitat. Water projects are vastly expensive. Let your delegates know that you do not want millions of federal dollars invested in water projects that are not based on a real social or human need.

How You Can Help Stop Wildlife-Law Violators

If you hunt or fish, you should be sure that you are familiar with all rules and regulations regarding your sport. Be sure you can recognize correctly the spe-cies you are hunting so that you will not shoot the wrong birds.

Find out about the Operation Game Thief or equivalent program in your state. Write down the toll-free telephone number that gives you access to your Game Thief hotline. This is useful not only to those who hunt and fish, but to anyone who spends time in the outdoors. If you see a game-law violation, report it immediately. You can also report violations to your local conservation officer.

Write your state wildlife officials urging them to seek better funding for law enforcement work. If the agency is funded by the state legislature, contact your legislators and let them know how you feel about better funding for wildlife-law enforcement.

Congressional Action: Federal wildlife agencies also need more support for their law enforcement divisions. These include the Fish and Wildlife Service, National Park Service, Forest Service, and National Marine Fisheries Service. Let your congressional delegation know that you want more funding for the wildlife-law-enforcement work done by these agencies.

It is doubtlessly clear that the issues outlined here overlap. Oil development, for example, influences levels of ocean pollution which affects sea turtles, sharks, dolphins, and porpoises. Ultimately, all environmental issues become interlocked. But if conservation problems tend to be interrelated, so too are the solutions to the problems. That is why your help in solving problems such as pollution of the seas is so critical. A single sound environmental measure can reverberate around the globe.

If you want to be kept up to date on all the issues covered in this book and more, write to National Audubon Society, 801 Pennsylvania Avenue SE, Suite 301, Washington, D.C. 20003 and ask to be put on the activist list. As an activist you will receive newsletters alerting you to a full range of conservation issues and events and providing you with guidelines on what you can do to help.

Appendix I
Common and Scientific Names of Sharks

Angelshark—*Squatina* spp.

Australian School—*Galeorhinus galeus*

Basking—*Cetorhinus maximus*

Big-eye Thresher—*Alopias superciliosus*

Blacktip—*Carcharhinus limbatus*

Blue—*Prionace glauca*

Bull—*Carcharhinus leucas*

Caribbean Reef—*Carcharhinus perezi*

Cigar or Cookiecutter—*Isistius* spp.

Dusky—*Carcharhinus obscurus*

Frilled—*Chlamydoselachus anguineus*

Great White—*Carcharodon carcharias*

Grey Reef—*Carcharhinus amblyrhynchos*

Hammerhead—*Sphyrna* spp.

Lemon—*Negaprion brevirostris*

Mako—*Isurus* spp.

Megamouth—*Megachasma pelagios*

Night—*Carcharhinus signatus*

Porbeagle—*Lamna nasus*

Pygmy Ribbontail Catshark—*Eridacnis radcliffei*

Sandbar—*Carcharhinus plumbeus*

Sand Tiger—*Eugomphodus taurus*

Sawsharks—*Pliotrema warreni* and *Pristiophorus* spp.

Spinner—*Carcharhinus brevipinna*

Spiny Dogfish—*Squalus acanthias*

Swellshark—*Cephaloscyllium*

Tiger—*Galeocerdo cuvier*

Whale—*Rhincodon typus*

Whitetip—*Carcharhinus longimanus*

Appendix II
Common and Scientific Names
of Dolphins and Porpoises

Bottlenose Dolphin—*Tursiops truncatus*

Common Dolphin—*Delphinus delphis*

Common or Harbor Porpoise—*Phocoena phocoena*

Dall's Porpoise—*Phocoenoides dalli*

False Killer Whale—*Pseudorca crassidens*

Orca or Killer Whale—*Orcinus orca*

Spinner Dolphin—*Stenella longirostris*

Spotted Dolphin—*Stenella attenuata*

REFERENCES

Man and Nature: The Ancient Conflict

Bean, Michael J. 1983. *The Evolution of National Wildlife Law*. Praeger Publishers. New York.

Chandler, Alfred D. 1988. "The National Marine Fisheries Service." In *The Audubon Wildlife Report 1988/89*, William J. Chandler, ed. Academic Press. San Diego.

Chandler, William J. 1985. "The U.S. Fish and Wildlife Service." In *The Audubon Wildlife Report 1985*, Roger L. DiSilvestro, ed. National Audubon Society. New York.

DiSilvestro, Roger L. 1989. *The Endangered Kingdom: The Struggle to Save America's Wildlife*. John Wiley & Sons, Inc. New York.

Drabelle, Dennis. 1985. "The National Wildlife Refuge System." In *The Audubon Wildlife Report 1985*, Roger L. DiSilvestro, ed. National Audubon Society. New York.

Du Mont, Philip A., and Henry A. Reeves. 1984. "The Darling–Salyer team." In *Flyways: Pioneering Waterfowl Management in North America*, A. S. Hawkins, R. C. Hanson, H. K. Nelson, and H. M. Reeves, eds. Department of the Interior, Fish and Wildlife Service. Washington, D.C.

Elfring, Chris. 1985. "Wildlife and the National Park Service." In *The Audubon Wildlife Report 1985*, Roger L. DiSilvestro, ed. National Audubon Society. New York.

Fosburgh, Whit. 1985. "Wildlife and the U.S. Forest Service." In *The Audubon Wildlife Report 1985*, Roger L. DiSilvestro, ed. National Audubon Society. New York.

Graham, Frank, Jr. 1971. *Man's Dominion: The Story of Conservation in America*. M. Evans and Company. New York.

Hawkins, Arthur S. 1984. "Aldo Leopold." In *Flyways: Pioneering Waterfowl Management in North America*, A. S. Hawkins, R. C. Hanson, H. K. Nelson, and H. M. Reeves, eds. Department of the Interior, Fish and Wildlife Service. Washington, D.C.

Lauwerys, J. A. 1970. *Man's Impact on Nature*. The Natural History Press. Garden City, New York.

Marsh, George Perkins. 1964. *Man and Nature*. David Lowenthal, ed. The Belknap Press of Harvard University Press. Cambridge, Massachusetts.

Reeves, Henry M. 1984. "FWS operating branches." In *Flyways: Pioneering Waterfowl Management in North America*, A. S. Hawkins, R. C. Hanson, H. K. Nelson, and H. M. Reeves, eds. Department of the Interior, Fish and Wildlife Service. Washington, D.C.

Wolves

Banville, Daniel. 1983. "Status and management of wolves in Quebec." In *Wolves in Canada and Alaska*, Ludwig N. Carbyn, ed. Canadian Wildlife Service. Ottawa.

Benet's Reader's Encyclopedia. 1987. Harper & Row. New York.

Brown, David E. 1983. *The Wolf in the Southwest*. The University of Arizona Press. Tucson.

DiSilvestro, Roger L. 1989. *The Endangered Kingdom: The Struggle to Save America's Wildlife*. John Wiley & Sons, Inc. New York.

Gunson, John R. 1983. "Status and management of wolves in Alberta." In *Wolves in Canada and Alaska*, Ludwig N. Carbyn, ed. Canadian Wildlife Service. Ottawa.

Heard, Douglas C. 1983. "Status and management of wolves in the Northwest Territories." In *Wolves in Canada and Alaska*, Ludwig N. Carbyn, ed. Canadian Wildlife Service. Ottawa.

Kolenosky, George B. 1983. "Status and management of wolves in Ontario." In *Wolves in Canada and Alaska*, Ludwig N. Carbyn, ed. Canadian Wildlife Service. Ottawa.

Lopez, Barry. 1978. *Of Wolves and Men*. Charles Scribner's Sons. New York.

Miller, Thomas. 1988. "Wyoming wolves? Yes!" *Wyoming Wildlife*. March:4.

Peterson, Rolf L. 1986. "The wolf." In *Audubon Wildlife Report 1986*, Roger L. DiSilvestro, ed. National Audubon Society. New York.

Ream, Robert R., Michael W. Fairchild, Diane A. Boyd, and Daniel H. Pletscher. 1987. *Wolf Monitoring and Research in and Adjacent to Glacier National Park*. School of

Forestry and Montana Cooperative Wildlife Research Unit, University of Montana. Missoula.

Seton, Ernest Thompson. 1953. *The Lives of Game Animals*. Charles T. Branford Co. Boston.

Simpson, Alan. 1988. "Wyoming wolves? No!" *Wyoming Wildlife* March:8.

Smith, Bernard L. 1983. "Status and management of wolves in the Yukon Territory." In *Wolves in Canada and Alaska*, Ludwig N. Carbyn, ed. Canadian Wildlife Service. Ottawa.

Tilt, Whitney, Ruth Norris, and Amos S. Eno. 1987. *Wolf Recovery in the Northern Rocky Mountains*. National Audubon Society and National Fish and Wildlife Foundation. Washington, D.C.

Tompa, Frank S. 1983. "Status and management of wolves in British Columbia." In *Wolves in Canada and Alaska*, Ludwig N. Carbyn, ed. Canadian Wildlife Service. Ottawa.

Young, Stanley, and Edward A. Goldman. 1944. *The Wolves of North America*. Dover Books. New York.

Sharks

Brownlee, Shannon. 1985. "On the track of the real shark." *Discover*. July:26.

Elasmobranchs as Living Resources: Recent Advances in Systematics, Physiology and Ecology. 1987. Harold L. Pratt, Jr., ed. American Elasmobranch Society. Narragansett, Rhode Island.

Gilmore, R. Grant, Jon W. Dodrill, and Patricia A. Linley. 1983. "Reproduction and embryonic development of the sand tiger shark, *Odontaspis taurus* (Rafinesque)." *Fishery Bulletin* 81:201.

Gruber, Samuel H. 1986. "Sharks: a fragile resource." *Florida Sportsman*. June:50.

———. 1986. "Studying the savage shark." *1986 Science Year, The World Book Science Annual*. World Book, Inc. Chicago.

———. 1987. "The facts about sharks." *Salt Water Sportsman, California Edition*. March:50.

———. 1988. "Sharks of the shallows." *Natural History*. March:50.

Hoenig, John M., and Samuel H. Gruber. 1988. Unpublished manuscript. "Life-history patterns in the elasmobranchs: Implications for fisheries management."

Lydekker, Richard. 1896. *The New Natural History*. Merrill & Baker. New York.

Soucie, Gary. 1976. "Consider the shark." *Audubon*. Sept:2.

Stafford-Deitsch, Jeremy. 1988. *Shark: A Photographer's Story*. Sierra Club Books. San Francisco.

Stevens, John D. 1987. *Sharks*. Facts on File Publications. New York.

Wilson, E. O. 1985. "In praise of sharks." *Discover*. July:40.

Sea Turtles: Ancient Nomads

Bierce, Rose, Susie Criswell, Jill Perry, and Michael Weber. 1986. *Sea Turtles & Trawlers*. Center for Marine Conservation. Washington, D.C.

Bjorndal, Karen A., Archie Carr, Anne B. Meylan, and Jeanne A. Mortimer. 1985. "Reproductive biology of the hawksbill *Eretmochelys imbricata* at Tortuguero, Costa Rica, with notes on the ecology of the species in the Caribbean." *Biological Conservation* 34:353.

Carr, Archie. 1967. *So Excellent a Fishe*. Natural History Press. Garden City, New York.

———. 1980. "Some problems of sea turtle ecology." *American Zoologist* 20:489.

———. 1982. "Notes on the behavioral ecology of sea turtles." In *Biology and Conservation of Sea Turtles: Proceedings of the World Conference on Sea Turtle Conservation*. Karen A. Bjorndal, ed. Smithsonian Institute Press. Washington, D.C.

Carr, Archie, Harold Hirth, and Larry Ogren. 1966. "The ecology and migrations of sea turtles, 6: The hawksbill turtle in the Caribbean Sea." *American Museum Novitates* No. 2248.

Ehrenfeld, David. 1987. "Archie Carr: In memoriam." *Conservation Biology* 1:169.

Ehrhart, Llewellyn M. 1983. "Marine turtles of the Indian River lagoon system." *Florida Scientist* 46:337.

———. 1987. "Human and natural causes of marine turtle nest and hatchling mortality and their relationship to hatchling production on an important Florida nesting beach." *Florida Game and Fresh Water Fish Commission Nongame Wildlife Program Technical Report No. 1*. Florida Game and Fresh Water Fish Commission. Tallahassee.

Ehrhart, Llewellyn M., and Paul W. Raymond. 1987. "Loggerhead turtle, *Caretta caretta*, and green turtle, *Chelonia mydas*, nesting densities in south Brevard County, Florida, 1981–84." In *Ecology of East Florida Sea Turtles*, W. N. Witzell, ed. U.S. Department of Commerce. Washington, D.C.

———. 1987. "Marine turtle mortality in the vicinity of Port Canaveral, Florida, 1977–84." In *Ecology of East Florida Sea Turtles*. W. N. Witzell, ed. U.S. Department of Commerce. Washington, D.C.

"The legacy of Tortuguero." 1987. *Natural History*. June:2

Lydekker, Richard. 1896. *The New Natural History*. Merrill and Baker. New York.

Ogren, Larry H. 1988. "Biology and ecology of sea turtles." Unpublished manuscript.

———. 1989. "Distribution of juvenile and subadult Kemp's ridley turtles: Preliminary results from 1984–1987 survey." In Proceedings of the First International Symposium on Kemp's Ridley Sea Turtle Biology, Conservation, and Management, Charles W. Caillouet, Jr., and Andre M. Landry, Jr., eds. Texas A&M University Sea Grant Program. Galveston.

Phillips, Pamela. 1989. *The Great Ridley Rescue*. Mountain Press Publishing Co. Missoula, Montana.

Wexler, Mark. 1988. "Modern mission to save an ancient mariner." *Natural History*. June:4.

If Dolphins Could Talk

Aristotle. 1952. *Great Books of the Western World, Vol. 9: Aristotle II*, Robert Maynard Hutchins, ed. Encyclopedia Britannica. Chicago.

Bean, Michael J. 1983. *The Evolution of National Wildlife Law*. Praeger Publishers. New York.

Booth, William. 1988. "The social lives of dolphins." *Science*. 3 June:1,273.

Brower, Kenneth. 1989. "The destruction of dolphins." *Atlantic Monthly*. July:35.

Chandler, Alfred D. 1988. "The National Marine Fisheries Service." In *The Audubon Wildlife Report 1988/89*, William J. Chandler, ed. Academic Press. San Diego.

Ellis, Richard. 1982. *Dolphins and Porpoises*. Alfred A. Knopf. New York.

Harrison, Richard, and M. M. Bryden, eds. 1988. *Whales, Dolphins, and Porpoises*. Facts on File Publications. New York.

Lydekker, Richard. 1896. *The New Natural History*. Merrill & Baker. New York.

Melville, Herman. 1971. *Moby-Dick or The White Whale*. Bantam Books. New York.

Rogers, Linda, and C. Dominique Van De Stadt. 1988. "Early warning." *World Press Review*. December:6.

Weber, Michael. 1985. "Marine mammal protection." In *The Audubon Wildlife Report 1985*, Roger L. DiSilvestro, ed. National Audubon Society. New York.

Ancient Forests: Rage Over Trees

America's Vanishing Rain Forest: A Report on Federal Timber Management in Southeast Alaska. 1986. The Wilderness Society. Washington, D.C.

Bakeless, John. 1950. *The Eyes of Discovery*. J. B. Lippincott Co. Philadelphia.

Bean, Michael J. 1983. *The Evolution of National Wildlife Law*. Praeger. New York.

Daniel, John. 1988. "The long dance of the trees." *Wilderness*. Spring:18.

Day, David. 1981. *The Doomsday Book of Animals*. The Viking Press. New York.

DiSilvestro, Roger L. 1989. *The Endangered Kingdom: The Struggle to Save America's Wildlife*. John Wiley & Sons. New York.

End of the Ancient Forests: Special Report on National Forest Plans in the Pacific Northwest. 1988. The Wilderness Society. Washington, D.C.

Feeney, Andy. 1989. "The Pacific Northwest's Ancient Forests: Ecosystems under Siege." In *The Audubon Wildlife Report 1989/90*, William J. Chandler, ed. Academic Press. San Diego.

Kelly, David. 1988. *Secrets of the Old Growth Forest*. Gibbs M. Smith Inc. Layton, Utah.

Kessler, Winifred. 1982. *Wildlife and Second-Growth Forests of Southeast Alaska: Problems and Potential for Management*. U.S. Department of Agriculture, Forest Service. Juneau, Alaska.

Laycock, George. 1987. "Trashing the Tongass." *Audubon*: November:110.

Longhurst, William M., and W. Leslie Robinette. 1981. *Wildlife and Fisheries Habitat Management Notes: Effects of Clearcutting and Timber Management on Sitka Black-Tailed Deer*. U.S. Department of Agriculture, Forest Service. Juneau, Alaska.

McKee, Russell. 1988. "Tombstones of a lost forest." *Audubon*. March:62.

Morrison, Peter H. 1988. *Old Growth in the Pacific Northwest: A Status Report*. The Wilderness Society. Washington, D.C.

Sanders, Scott Russell, ed. 1986. *Audubon Reader: The Best Writings of John James Audubon*. Indiana University Press. Bloomington.

Schoen, John W., Olof C. Wallmo, and Matthew D. Kirchhoff. 1981. "Wildlife–Forest Relationships: Is a Reevaluation of Old Growth Necessary?" *Proceedings of the Forty-Sixth North American Wildlife Conference*:531.

Sitka Black-Tailed Deer: Proceedings of a Conference in Juneau, Alaska. 1979. U.S. Department of Agriculture, Forest Service. Juneau, Alaska.

The South's Fourth Forest: Alternatives for the Future. 1988. U.S. Department of Agriculture, Forest Service. Washington, D.C.

The South's Fourth Forest: Opportunities to Increase the Resource Wealth of the South. 1988. U.S. Department of Agriculture, Forest Service. Washington, D.C.

Swain, Roger R. 1988. "Notes from the radical underground." *World Monitor*. November:16.

Wallmo, Olof C., and John W. Schoen. 1980. "Response of deer to secondary forest succession in southeast Alaska." *Forest Science* 26:448.

Arctic Refuge: A Vanishing Wilderness?

Bruemmer, Fred. 1985. *The Arctic World*. Sierra Club Books. San Francisco.

Drabelle, Dennis. 1985. "The National Wildlife Refuge System." In *Audubon Wildlife Report 1985*, Roger L. DiSilvestro, ed. National Audubon Society. New York.

Hall, Sam. 1987. *The Fourth World: The Heritage of the Arctic and Its Destruction*. Alfred A. Knopf. New York.

Hubbard, H. M. 1989. "Photovoltaics today and tomorrow." *Science* 244:297.

Kizzia, Tom. 1987. "Confrontation in the north." *Defenders*. September:10.

Laycock, George. 1987. "Wilderness by the barrel." *Audubon*. May:100.

Lee, Wendy Smith. 1986. "The National Wildlife Refuge System." In *Audubon Wildlife Report 1986*, Roger L. DiSilvestro, ed. National Audubon Society. New York.

Lopez, Barry. 1987. *Arctic Dreams: Imagination and Desire in a Northern Landscape*. Bantam Books. Toronto.

Management of Wastes from Crude Oil and Natural Gas Exploration, Development, and Production on Alaska's North Slope (Draft). 1989. Environmental Protection Agency. Washington, D.C.

Miller, G. Tyler, Jr. 1988. *Living in the Environment: An Introduction to Environmental Science*. Wadsworth Publishing Company. Belmont, California.

Mountfield, David. 1974. *A History of Polar Exploration*. The Dial Press. New York.

Norris, Ruth, and Cynthia Lenhart. 1987. "The National Wildlife Refuge System." In *Audubon Wildlife Report 1987*, Roger L. DiSilvestro, ed. National Audubon Society. New York.

Sage, Bryan. 1987. "What price arctic oil?" *Defenders*. September:7.

Wille, Chris. 1988. "Briefings." *Audubon*. September:130.

Crane River

Bakeless, John. 1950. *The Eyes of Discovery*. J. B. Lippincott Co. Philadelphia.

Barton, Katherine. 1986. "Federal wetlands protection programs." In *Audubon Wildlife Report 1986*, Roger L. DiSilvestro, ed. National Audubon Society. New York.

Becker, James. 1980. "The lesser sandhill crane." *Outdoor Oklahoma*. November/December:45.

DeVoto, Bernard. 1947. *Across the Wide Missouri*. Houghton Mifflin Co. Boston.

Drago, Harry Sinclair. 1968. *Roads to Empire: The Dramatic Conquest of the American West*. Dodd, Mead & Company. New York.

Krapu, Gary L. 1987. "Sandhill recovery." *Birder's World*. January/February:4.

Krapu, Gary L., and Jan Eldridge. 1984. "Crane river." *Natural History*. January:69.

Lewis, James C. 1986. "The whooping crane." In *Audubon Wildlife Report 1986*, Roger L. DiSilvestro, ed. National Audubon Society. New York.

Marcy, Randolph B. 1981. (Originally published in 1859.) *The Prairie Traveler: A Hand-Book for Overland Expeditions*. Time-Life Books. New York.

Mitchell, John G. 1989. "On the seacoast of Nebraska." *Audubon*. May:56.

Norris, Ruth. 1987. "Water projects and wildlife." In *Audubon Wildlife Report 1987*, Roger L. DiSilvestro, ed. Academic Press. San Diego.

Schlissel, Lillian. 1982. *Women's Diaries of the Westward Journey*. Schocken Books. New York.

Shoemaker, Thomas G. 1988. "Wildlife and water projects on the Platte River." In *Audubon Wildlife Report*

1988/89, William J. Chandler, ed. Academic Press. San Diego.

Strom, Kenneth J. 1985. "Protecting critical whooping crane habitat on the Platte River, Nebraska." *Natural Areas Journal* 5:8.

U.S. Army Corps of Engineers. 1988. *Final EIS, Metropolitan Denver Water Supply EIS, Vol. II, Appendix 1-A Mitigation*. U.S. Government Printing Office. Washington, D.C.

———. 1988. *Final EIS, Metropolitan Denver Water Supply EIS, Vol. III, Appendix 1*. U.S. Government Printing Office. Washington, D.C.

U.S. Fish and Wildlife Service. 1981. *The Platte River Ecology Study: Special Research Report*. U.S. Fish and Wildlife Service, Northern Prairie Wildlife Research Center. Jamestown, North Dakota.

———. 1987. *Two Forks Reservoir and William's Fork Gravity Collection System Projects, Colorado: Fish and Wildlife Coordination Act Report*. U.S. Fish and Wildlife Service, Region 6. Denver.

Winckler, Suzanne. 1989. "The Platte pretzel." *Audubon*. May:86.

Greed and Wildlife: Poaching in America

Carlock, David M., Richard H. Conley, John M. Collins, Philip E. Hale, Ken G. Johnson, A. Sydney Johnson, and Michael R. Pelton. 1983. *Tri-State Black Bear Study*. Tennessee Wildlife Resources Agency. Nashville.

Chandler, William J. 1986. "State wildlife law enforcement." In *Audubon Wildlife Report 1986*, Roger L. DiSilvestro, ed. National Audubon Society. New York.

Hurt, Henry. 1988. "Slaughter at Albemarle Farms." *Reader's Digest*. November:82.

Linden, Eugene. 1989. "Wildlife cops on a bust." *Time*. 20 February:18.

Pelton, Michael. 1987. "The black bear." In *Audubon Wildlife Report 1987*, Roger L. DiSilvestro, ed. Academic Press. San Diego.

Trout, John, Jr. 1988. "Poachers are stealing your deer!" *Petersen's Hunting*. March:38.

Wilkinson, Todd. 1988. "Yellowstone's poaching war." *Defenders*. May/June:30.

Newspaper Articles

"Officials Nab 43 on Bear Poaching Counts." *The Knoxville Journal*. August 24, 1988.

"43 Charged with Bear Poaching." *The Asheville Citizen*. August 24, 1988.

"Poaching Arrests Will Discourage Illegal Hunters, Officials Say." *The Mountaineer*. August 24, 1988.

"Send a Message to the Poachers." *The Asheville Citizen*. August 25, 1988.

"Urine Test Has Bearing on Smoky." *The Asheville Citizen*. August 25, 1988.

"Bear Poaching Suspect Remains in Jail." *The Asheville Citizen*. September 1, 1988.

"Korean Faces Charges Related to Buying Bear Parts in Park." *The Mountain Press*. September 30, 1988.

Humanity and Nature: Tomorrow's Dilemma

Brown, Lester R., Christopher Flavin, Lori Heise, Jodi Jacobson, Sandra Postel, Michael Renner, Cynthia Pollock Shea, and Linda Starke. 1989. *State of the World 1989*. W. W. Norton & Company. New York.

Comp, T Allen, ed. 1989. *Blueprint for the Environment: A Plan for Federal Action*. Howe Brothers. Salt Lake City.

Roan, Sharon L. 1989. *Ozone Crisis: The 15-Year Evolution of a Sudden Global Emergency*. John Wiley & Sons. New York.

ILLUSTRATION CREDITS

Humanity and Nature: The Ancient Conflict

Page Chichester xvii top, 2, 8, 9, 11
Courtesy of the National Audubon Society 6

Wolves

Scott Ian Barry 21, 22, 26
Page Chichester xvii bottom, 16, 20, 32, 33, 34, 35, 36 top, bottom, 37, 39 top, bottom, 40, 41
Mary Maule 29
Courtesy of the National Audubon Society 19, 24
U.S. Fish and Wildlife Service 30, 31

Sharks

J. Castro 59
Page Chichester 55, 57, 70 bottom, 71
Chip Clark/ Smithsonian Institution 49
Howard Hall 52, 56, 58, 61 top, bottom, 63, 64, 65, 67, 68, 70 top
Paul Humman/Jeff Rotman Photography xviii top, 46
The Collections of the Library of Congress 48
Drawings by Ayn Svoboda 50–51, 53

Sea Turtles: Ancient Nomads

Mark Boulton/Photo Researchers 79
Page Chichester 81, 84, 88, 90, 92, 93, 94 top, bottom
Gregory G. Dimijian 97
Tom McHugh/Photo Researchers 89
J. A. Mortimer 82
Michael Murphy/Photo Researchers 95
Jeff Rotman xviii middle, 74
Janey Sauvanet/Photo Researchers 76
U.S. Fish and Wildlife Service 78 top, bottom, 80, 85, 91, 96

If Dolphins Could Talk

Bill Curtisinger/Photo Researchers 117
Howard Hall xviii bottom, 102, 113
Tom McHugh/Photo Researchers 109
Lawrence Migdale/Photo Researchers 110, 112
Drawings by Ayn Svoboda 105, 114, 120
Julia Whitty 106
Mel and Bernd Wuersig 108 top, bottom

Ancient Forests: Rage Over Trees

Ken Bevis 150
Page Chichester xix top, 128, 134, 147, 148 top, inset, 149, 152, 153, 155, 156, 157 top, bottom, 158, 159 top, bottom, 160, 162
Forest Service Collection, National Agricultural Library 130
The Collections of the Library of Congress 131, 146
Courtesy of the National Audubon Society 133, 136, 137
U.S. Forest Service 141, 144, 145
Susan Warner 143

Arctic Refuge: A Vanishing Wilderness?

Macgill Adams 183 top, bottom
Courtesy of Defenders of Wildlife/Bob Pratt 179
David C. Douglas 170, 173, 181 top, 186 top
Ted Kerasote/Photo Researchers xix middle, 169, 182, 185
Wilbur Mills 180
Jon R. Nickles 186 bottom
Thomas C. Rothe 175
Una G. Swain 184, 190
U.S. Fish and Wildlife Service 171, 176, 177, 181 bottom
Lori Ward 188

Crane River

Page Chichester 202 top, bottom, 203, 206, 207, 208, 209, 210, 211, 219, 221
Stephen J. Krasemann/Photo Researchers xix bottom, 194, 200, 201
Tom McHugh/Photo Researchers 212
Courtesy of the National Audubon Society 199, 215
Courtesy of the National Audubon Society/Joe LeMonnier 196, 205
Courtesy of the Thomas Gilcrease Institute of American History and Art, Tulsa, Oklahoma 196 bottom
Joseph Van Wormer/Photo Researchers 198

Greed and Wildlife: Poaching in America

Page Chichester xx top, 224, 227, 229, 231, 232, 233, 234, 241, 242 top, inset, bottom, 243, 244, 245, 246, 247, 248
Sharon Duchene 236
The Collections of the Library of Congress 226, 228

Humanity and Nature: Tomorrow's Dilemma

Page Chichester xx bottom, 254, 257, 259, 261, 263

INDEX

Numerals in italics indicate an illustration of or relating to the subject mentioned.